"A remarkable saga of heroism under fire. DeFelice's account of the American Rangers' baptism of fire two years before D-Day is as compelling as it is provocative. This is military history at its best."

—Colonel Cole C. Kingseed,
coauthor of *Beyond Band of Brothers*

"From El Guettar in Tunisia to Pointe du Hoc in Normandy and beyond, Rangers led the way in World War II. They established a reputation second to none, and *Rangers at Dieppe* is a fitting commemoration of those Rangers who were first to fight. The fifty men who landed alongside the British and Canadians were novices to combat: its chaos, its fear, its unending noise. But Rangers were never supermen—just men who did extraordinary things extraordinarily well. Their legend began on the beaches of Dieppe, and DeFelice is its fitting chronicler."

—Dennis Showalter,
author of *Patton and Rommel:
Men of War in the Twentieth Century*

"A carefully researched and brilliantly executed narrative of the modern Rangers' baptism in blood. DeFelice's skillful account of this almost unknown story sheds bright light onto the origins of a great American military tradition."

—*America in WWII* magazine

RANGERS AT DIEPPE

THE FIRST COMBAT ACTION
OF U.S. ARMY RANGERS IN WORLD WAR II

Jim DeFelice

BERKLEY CALIBER
NEW YORK

THE BERKLEY PUBLISHING GROUP
Published by the Penguin Group
Penguin Group (USA) Inc.
375 Hudson Street, New York, New York 10014, USA
Penguin Group (Canada), 90 Eglinton Avenue East, Suite 700, Toronto, Ontario M4P 2Y3, Canada
(a division of Pearson Penguin Canada Inc.)
Penguin Books Ltd., 80 Strand, London WC2R 0RL, England
Penguin Group Ireland, 25 St. Stephen's Green, Dublin 2, Ireland (a division of Penguin Books Ltd.)
Penguin Group (Australia), 250 Camberwell Road, Camberwell, Victoria 3124, Australia
(a division of Pearson Australia Group Pty. Ltd.)
Penguin Books India Pvt. Ltd., 11 Community Centre, Panchsheel Park, New Delhi—110 017, India
Penguin Group (NZ), 68 Apollo Drive, Rosedale, North Shore 0632, New Zealand
(a division of Pearson New Zealand Ltd.)
Penguin Books (South Africa) (Pty.) Ltd., 24 Sturdee Avenue, Rosebank, Johannesburg 2196,
South Africa

Penguin Books Ltd., Registered Offices: 80 Strand, London WC2R 0RL, England

The publisher does not have any control over and does not assume any responsibility for author or third-party websites or their content.

Copyright © 2008 by Jim DeFelice
Cover design by Steven Ferlauto
Cover photographs courtesy of the National Archives
Book design by Kristin del Rosario

PRINTING HISTORY
Berkley Caliber hardcover edition / January 2008
Berkley Caliber trade paperback edition / January 2009

The Library of Congress has catalogued the Berkley Caliber hardcover edition as follows:

DeFelice, James.
    Rangers at Dieppe / James DeFelice.
        p. cm.
    Includes bibliographical references and index.
    ISBN 978-0-425-21921-8
    1. United States. Army. Ranger Battalion, 1st. 2. World War, 1939–1945—Regimental histories—United States. 3. Dieppe Raid, 1942. I. Title.
    D769.311st.D44 2007
    940.54'21425—dc22   2007014539

PRINTED IN THE UNITED STATES OF AMERICA

10 9 8 7 6 5 4 3 2 1

For the grandchildren and great-grandchildren of the veterans of World War II: May we be inspired by our grandparents' courage, and instructed by their mistakes.

Contents

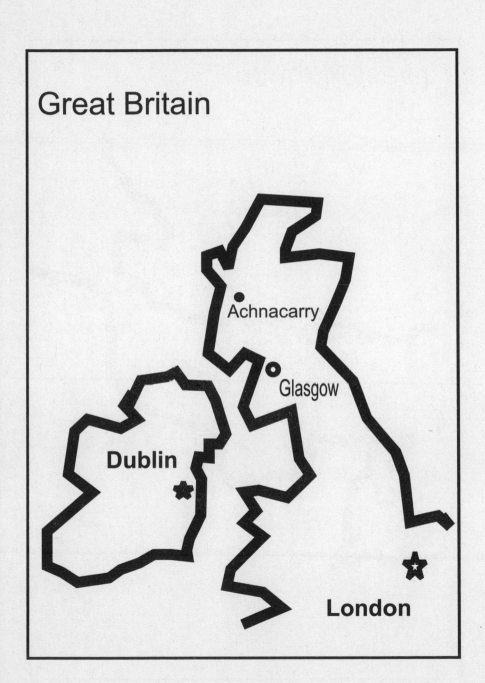

Great Britain

Achnacarry

Glasgow

Dublin

London

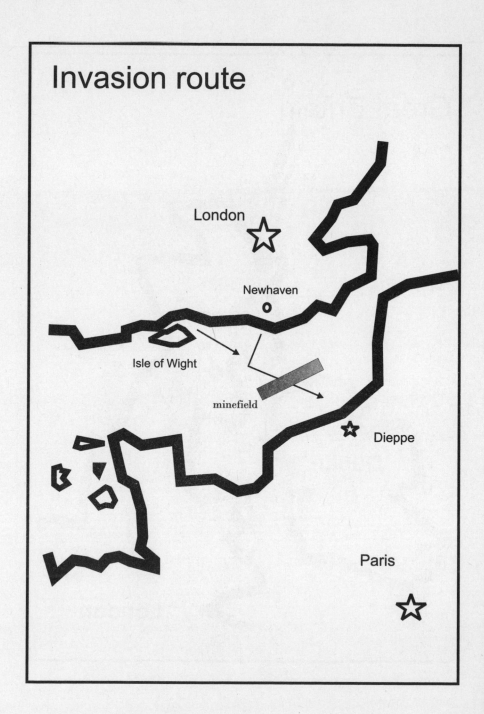

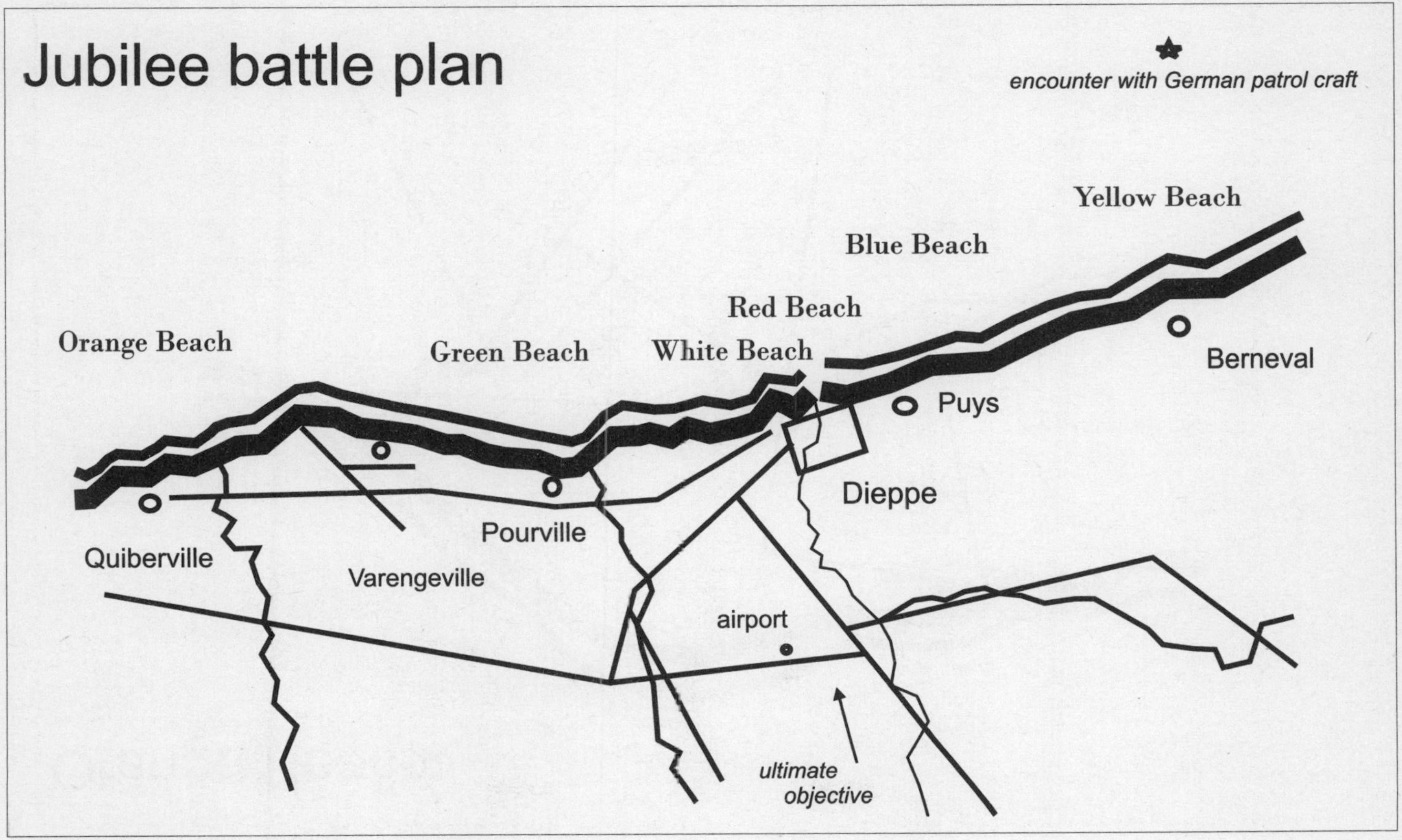

Jubilee battle plan

Orange Beach

Green Beach

Red Beach

White Beach

Blue Beach

Yellow Beach

Quiberville

Varengeville

Pourville

Dieppe

Puys

Berneval

airport

ultimate objective

encounter with German patrol craft.

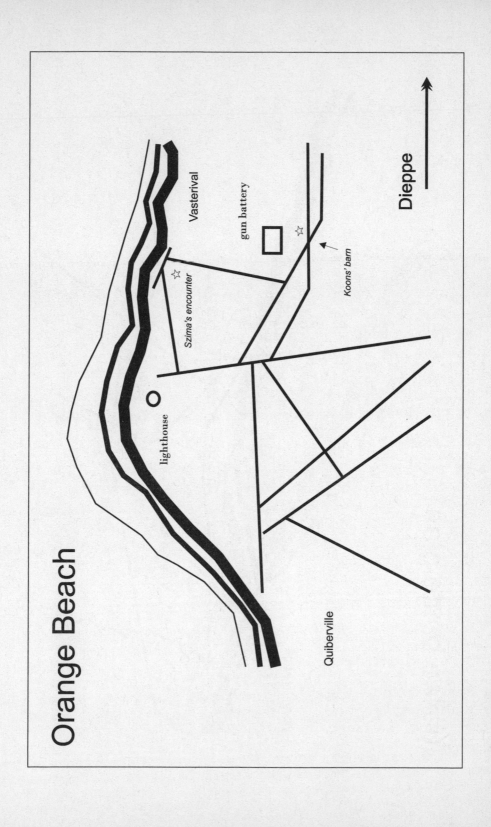

Orange Beach

Dieppe

Vasterival

gun battery

Szima's encounter

Koons' barn

lighthouse

Quiberville

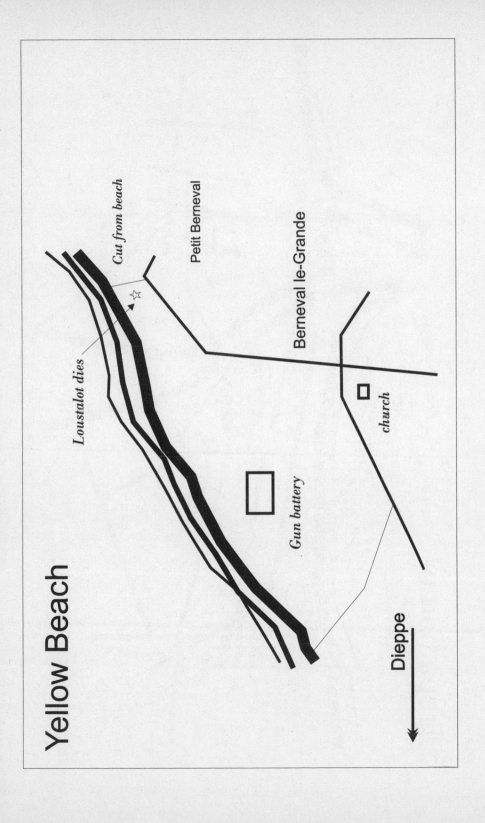

Yellow Beach

Loustalot dies

Cut from beach

Petit Berneval

Berneval le-Grande

church

Gun battery

Dieppe

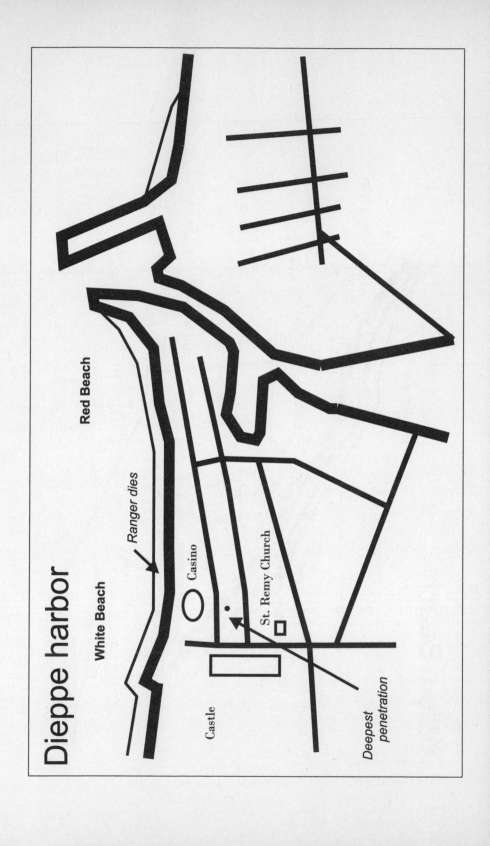

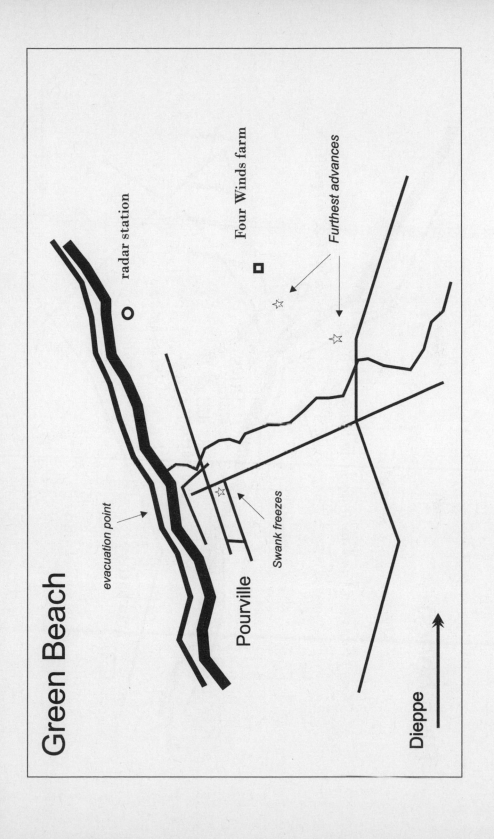

Green Beach

evacuation point

radar station

Four Winds farm

Furthest advances

Pourville

Swank freezes

Dieppe

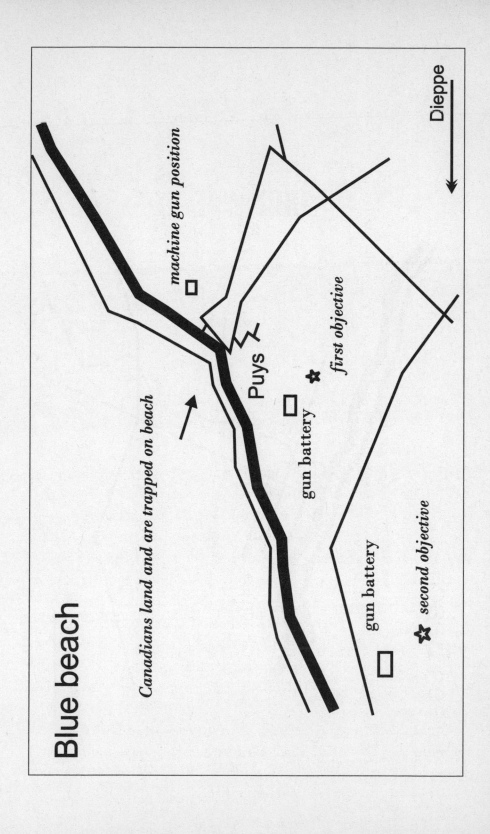

Blue beach

Canadians land and are trapped on beach

machine gun position

Puys

gun battery

first objective

gun battery

second objective

Dieppe

PROLOGUE

■ ■ ■

It's rained on and off all day, and a curtain of clouds hangs just off-shore when I reach Berneval-le-Grand, a few miles east of Dieppe on the French side of the English Channel. Though it's midafternoon, the place is deserted, and as I thread my way around the narrow one-way streets directly above the coastline, my thoughts wander back some sixty years, rearranging a wall here, repainting a house there, until I see the place as it was on August 19, 1942. I park near what would have been a farmer's field back then, and within a few minutes I'm walking across the rocks on the shore. The water laps gently at my feet as I stare up at the chalky cliffs, assessing the natural cuts in the rock and trying to determine how much the landscape has changed in six decades.

Some of the changes are easy to determine—the paths between the water and tiny village were filled with barbed wire, and the cliff was studded with machine-gun positions. The large six-inch guns, capable of blowing a boat and even a small ship out of the water, were set much farther back, not visible from the beach, but they're gone as well. Knocking those weapons out was the goal of the U.S. Army Rangers who came to Berneval that morning. The Rangers did not succeed; one of them, Lieutenant Edwin V. Loustalot, died trying.

Time has worn the blood from the rocks and path up to the village. The steps seem to be made of relatively new concrete. But other things have not changed. The port city of Dieppe lies quietly to the west, just out of view around a jutting cliff. The surf seems too violent for sand; the sea pounds the shore relentlessly, washing backward and forward, smoothing the rocks into round stones, some so large they barely fit in my hand.

Armed with accounts of the battle, I walk along the shoreline, plotting out where in 1942 the shallow-draft boats landed. I walk up the cut in the cliff, turning at the spot where the guns would have been. I gaze toward the hamlet and the tidy yards, fields, and orchards that were here during the war. I see the spot where a hail of German bullets took Loustalot down. I walk to the spot where he died and pause, staring at the ground, transported.

But the act of imagination is not entirely complete. I can picture the battle scene in my mind, but it's based on one account of the fight. There are at least two other versions of what happened, each putting him in a slightly different spot, each subtly changing why he died: leading a charge up the hill toward the objective, leading a charge down the hill to get his men safely home, blundering accidentally into a cross fire.

Which was it?

I walk back and forth across the cliff above the beach, trying to figure out which story is right. Having spent several years reading accounts of the battle, studying reports, talking and corresponding with witnesses, I came finally to Dieppe to see the place for myself. I thought doing so would settle the last questions I had about what

happened here sixty-five years before. But as the sun slowly sets, cast-
ing the beach in shadows, I realize I know much less than I thought.
The facts I armed myself with turn out to be flimsy and subject to
interpretation, even guesses. Not even looking at the beach itself helps
me sort them out. Lieutenant Loustalot died here—or here, or here,
or there.

If I can't master the simple fact of where he died, how can I
understand and communicate what it meant to fight here?

I walk back to my car as the darkness gathers. A road sign offers
one last glimmer of hope; its name commemorates the Commando
brigade that made the assault. The bolts holding the sign to the post
are rusted and some of the colors faded, but the lettering is easily vis-
ible, even at dusk. Oblivion has not yet claimed all that happened on
these beaches.

In most accounts of World War II, the Allied landing at Dieppe in
August 1942 is barely mentioned. When it is, it is generally called a
precursor to D-Day, a noble raid conducted to show the Allies how
to use landing tanks, or what the Germans were likely to do during
an invasion, or even a necessary but bloody experiment that proved
the difficulties of attacking fortified harbors.

None of those descriptions is entirely accurate. They flow not
from historical hindsight but political justifications made by British
military leaders and politicians immediately after the operation and
following the war. In truth, Dieppe was an unnecessary and foresee-
able fiasco, an avoidable bloodbath. It was launched not because of
military necessity, but for reasons that included hubris, service politics,
and "morale"—the 1940s term for public relations, or propaganda,
depending on your perspective. It is an object lesson in what can happen when such things override sound tactical and strategic planning.
Not to mention common sense.

The justifications of the men involved have cast a shadow on the actions of the roughly ten thousand men who had a part in the invasion and the air war above the beaches. The soldiers' bravery and sacrifice have been largely forgotten. Even in Canada, which tallied several thousand killed, wounded, or captured in the operation, veterans of Dieppe had to struggle for recognition.

But if the Canadians were forgotten, the Americans involved in the operation have been almost completely ignored. That's a great injustice, not simply to the men who were here but to the U.S. Army and Rangers in general.

The lessons of Dieppe—not those of tactics or strategies, but of what physically happens to a man when he is thrown into the hellfire of combat—entered the Army's soul here. The battle is part of the Rangers' DNA; every assault owes part of its success to the men who fell here.

Until now, America's Dieppe story has been relegated mostly to footnotes and passing comments. Even in the books that are considered the most definitive studies of the battle—Terence Robertson's encyclopedic *Dieppe: The Shame and the Glory,* Robin Neillands's *The Dieppe Raid,* to name just two examples—the American story is scattered about, a few sentences here, a mention there. In many instances, the few facts recorded are wrong—a product not of historians' errors but of the thin material they had to rely on.

What was the American experience at Dieppe? In some ways, it was as scattered as the historical references. To sum up: fifty soldiers were drawn from the 1st Ranger Battalion and inserted into various units involved in the operation. Most went with British Commandos who attacked the gun batteries on Dieppe's flanks; a handful were assigned to Canadian units that attacked Dieppe and the closer shore guns essentially head-on. The Rangers shared the experiences and the sacrifices of the larger units. Where the bigger units succeeded, the

Rangers succeeded. Where they failed, the Rangers mostly died or were taken prisoner.

In sheer numbers, the Canadian losses are so large they're almost incomprehensible: of the five thousand or so men on the raid, over eight hundred were killed outright, with over thirteen hundred taken prisoner and nearly six hundred others returning wounded. A substantial number of the men who escaped injury did so only because they weren't able to land on the beach. The battle shattered the Canadian 2nd Division, and remains the greatest loss in Canadian military history.

The Rangers' contribution was smaller, but on a proportional level its losses were just as significant. Of the fifty men who set out from England for the raid, three were killed, three were taken prisoner, and five were wounded by the end of the day—a 22 percent casualty rate. Since most of the Americans who took part in the raid never made it to shore because of problems with their landing craft, the casualty ratio was actually considerably higher: only four men who made the beaches got back to England without being wounded, killed, or captured—a 73 percent casualty rate.

Remarkably, the 1st Ranger Battalion had been formed less than two months before the raid on Dieppe. The battalion had not completed its training when it was tapped for inclusion in the battle. If ever a unit can be said to have had a fiery birth, it was the Rangers— appropriately so, given the subsequent history of the elite fighters. The Rangers went on to play important roles in Torch, the assault on Africa; in the Italian campaigns in 1943; and perhaps most famously, during D-Day at Pointe du Hoc and the surrounding area. Disbanded then reorganized, Rangers played important roles as individuals and as a coherent unit during the Cold War conflicts; they were involved in the first Gulf War, and served in Afghanistan and Iraq during the war on terror. Today, Rangers form an important part of the United

States Special Operations Command. While there are still debates on how to best use them, there is no question that the soldiers are one of the most potent fighting forces in the world.

It all started in 1942, at Dieppe. This book is about that start. It is the story of many men: of Major William Darby, the Rangers' first commander, who was ordered not to take part in the invasion. Of Sergeant Alex Szima, who laughed when his Commando commander accused him of being on the Army rifle team and said he was just a Dayton, Ohio, bartender. Of Corporal Franklin "Zip" Koons, who probably killed twenty Germans but simply shrugged after the battle and said he'd done his bit and couldn't be sure of anything. Of Owen Sweazey, a future Silver Star winner who never made it to shore at Dieppe but was as scared as he would ever be again. Of Marcel Swank, who had to choose whether to save himself or stay with his wounded Ranger companion. Of Edwin Loustalot, Joseph Randall, and Howard Henry, all of them killed on French soil during the battle.

Their story is one of courage and bravery in the face of great odds. It is a story of lessons learned, and lessons forgotten.

ONE

THE COMING OF WAR

Pine Island, N.Y.
Summer 2006

* * *

The voice on the other end of the line sounded youthful, but if I hadn't known better, I might have mistaken him for his father.

"Is this Ron Sweazey?"

"Yes. Jim?"

"Thanks for answering the letter," I tell him. "Like I said, I've been trying to track down the original Rangers from the Dieppe Raid. I'm interested in telling their story."

Ron's father, Owen Sweazey, had passed away several years before. Fortunately, he'd given a long account of his days in the Rangers to a state historian before he died. He'd also started a small memoir about his service. Between those two things, some old newspaper clippings, and the few stories he told of the war, the Sweazey family has a good picture of his service.

But I can fully understand what Ron means when he says that he wishes he had more. There's so much about the war, and the men who served, that seems impossible to recover—little details, seemingly insignificant: Did they wear helmets or hats into combat? (The answer varied at Dieppe depending on the unit they were attached to.) And huge ones: What did it take for them to get out of the boats and brave the murderous fire they faced? We can find answers to the little questions, but the big ones remain unanswered, even by them.

Owen Sweazey won Silver and Bronze Stars during World War II; the medals were awarded for bravery under fire, and weren't handed out easily. Yet his son tells me that he never really talked about the war that much. He certainly never bragged about what he had done, much less called himself a hero.

Heroes were other guys, his son often heard him say. It's a comment I hear over and over again.

Fort Knox, 1940

■ ■ ■

ALEX SZIMA

If Alex Szima hadn't had bad luck, he might not have had any luck at all.

Then again, Szima was the kind of man who made a habit of turning bad luck into an opportunity. He'd managed to get a waiver to join the Army—necessary because a six-inch scar ran down his cheek from his left eye. But as he went through basic training, it became clear from the comments of his instructors that the scar was going to disqualify him from military service. Not that it was a physical problem for him—he'd had it since an accident when he was younger—but the doctors and officers and just about everyone who looked at it thought it was going to get infected and maybe, just maybe, make his eye fall out. Plus it was hell to look at. Szima had busted his buns doing everything he could to win a place, but it was pretty clear that as soon his ninety-day training period was over, he was getting bounced.

And then, three days before his trial period was over, he was shot. Some boob of a new trainee mishandled a Thompson submachine gun, and Szima landed in the base hospital with a slug in his thigh.

Of all the dumb luck.

But lo and behold, the slug proved a blessing. Szima couldn't be bounced from the Army, not while an investigation was being conducted into the shooting. And then, somehow, the idea of bouncing him got lost, either in the paper shuffle or the growing concern about the need to increase the Army's size. Szima came out of the hospital a private first class—not because of anything he did, but because everyone else who'd gotten through basic by that time had been promoted to PFC.

The investigation into the firing-range accident continued. Szima found a way to testify that the accident was truly an accident—the range officer had not been derelict in his duty. The testimony helped the officer, a West Pointer whose career could have been ruined by the black mark. It was not something the officer would forget.

Hobbling with a cane, Szima managed to get into the first class of the Armored Force school at Fort Knox. Finally an officer gave him a choice: either work as a clerk, or be discharged on a disability. Szima, though hardly the clerkish type, chose the desk job. Sooner or later, he figured, he'd be walking again. And he wanted to do it in the Army. America wasn't in the war yet, but like a lot of other men, he could sense it coming.

He worked on his typing, and soon made corporal.

THE WORLD WAR IN 1941

The war in Europe—already called World War II in most newspapers and magazines—had been going on for at least a year and half, depending on whether one uses the German invasion of Poland in

September 1939 or the earlier takeovers of Austria or Czechoslovakia as the start. While President Franklin Roosevelt had declared America neutral in a *Fireside Chat* immediately after the invasion of Poland, American sentiment and government policy clearly favored the Allies. The tilt only increased as Germany invaded Norway, Denmark, Luxembourg, Belgium, the Netherlands, and then France in the summer of 1940. In September of that year, the United States gave Britain fifty destroyers in exchange for leases on bases in Newfoundland and the West Indies. The leases themselves were a thinly disguised plan to help Great Britain, since they meant British troops could be redeployed home for defense. That same month, Congress passed a law authorizing the first peacetime draft in U.S. history. The law called for 900,000 men to be inducted per year; the population of the country at the time was roughly 131 million.

Meanwhile, the National Guard was mobilized for training under a phased-in plan that aimed at bringing the units up to regular Army standards. Unlike today, when Guard units are well integrated into the standing military structure, the Guard units in the 1940s were disorganized and in many cases amateurish. The soldiers tended to be short of equipment and training; their officers were generally little better, with fewer than half having attended any sort of Army training or school. In the late 1930s, Guard units typically met for one-hour drills once a week, and spent two weeks every summer on maneuvers. Men as young as sixteen joined, many in hopes of making a little extra money during the hard times.

The regular Army was willing to take the National Guard units because in many ways it was not much better off itself. When Szima joined up in 1940, the Army had only 280,000 men, and it had recently increased to that size following a recruitment campaign energetic enough—if that's the right phrase—to overlook deficiencies such as Szima's, considered relatively serious at the time. The size was a sharp contrast to that of the German Army, which had between five and six million men under arms.

Despite the fact that Germany's integrated armor and mobilized infantry Panzer divisions had revolutionized warfare, the U.S. had only one armored division: Szima's unit, the 1st Armored Division. With its roots in the cavalry, a good number of the officers knew more about horses than they did about tanks.

Among the first National Guard units to be organized into a division was the 34th Infantry Division, which, in February 1941, was formed from the National Guard in North and South Dakota, Iowa, and Minnesota. As soon as it was activated, its members were sent to a new camp in Louisiana called Camp Claiborne for basic training.

GOING SOUTH

Lester Kness looked at the fields and pine trees as the train traveled south, studying them with a curious eye. For Kness and most of the men in the train car, it was hard to believe they were in Louisiana. When most northerners thought of the state, they pictured New Orleans or perhaps the nearby swamps, damp wet places with shallow boats and snapping crocodiles. The place they were passing through was a forest filled with pine trees; the smoke and steam from the train's locomotive mixed with the fresh scent of needles and pine tar.

Not yet twenty-two, Kness had spent his youth on a farm in Iowa and loved to hunt; he was curious about what might live in the woods. Mechanically inclined, he came from an inventive family— his dad had invented a foolproof mousetrap, and as a young man Les had helped manufacture it. But that was all behind him now; his future, or at least his immediate future, was with the Army. The Iowa National Guard had been called to active duty, and Lester E. Kness was determined to become a good solider.

He and the other men on the train welcomed the warm weather, a change from the chilly northern states where they lived. The flies and dampness were a different story. As the train wheels clicked rhythmically over the tracks, a few thought about their recent past, years spent at the tail end of the Depression, when it was still hard to make a living. But for most, it was the future that troubled them. The United States was not at war, yet a deep foreboding hung over the country, as thick as the black smoke curling from the engine's stack as the train fought its way up a sharp hill.

While the Army's expansion and the National Guard mobilization were criticized, Americans as a whole were not as isolationist as popular histories sometimes make us think. In June 1941, the *New York Times* reported that a survey showed 62 percent of the public would support a war rather than allow Great Britain to be overrun by Germany. While the *Times* was pro–Great Britain and pro-interventionist, the same sentiment had helped Roosevelt win an unprecedented third term in 1940, when Hitler's armies had conquered most of western Europe and Great Britain appeared to be next. The public was well informed about the war, or at least was supplied with plenty of newspaper and radio stories about it. Local newspapers carried front-page stories about battles in Europe, Africa, and the Atlantic nearly every day as the war progressed. Americans responded to various pleas to help civilians caught in the war, including one headed by former president Herbert Hoover, to send food and humanitarian supplies to war-stricken areas under Nazi control.

CAMP CLAIBORNE

The training camp Kness and the other National Guard soldiers found in February 1941 had been established nearly ten years before as a state facility. Carved from the Kisatchie National Forest in central Louisiana, Camp Claiborne's twenty-three thousand acres had been taken over by the Army and expanded just before the 34th arrived. Rolling hills and forests surrounded a lake and vast fields of recently cut pine trees. Building was under way at a furious pace. Besides basic training, the post was used for artillery school and instruction in combat engineering; a variety of specialized units, including one that could construct train cars and railroads, also trained there. Eventually half a million Americans would pass through its gates; the camp would also hold German POWs before the end of the war. At its peak, concrete roads covered seventy-nine miles, and there would be eighty-three hospital buildings in addition to the acres of tents and barracks. While most later soldiers would live in "squad barracks"—tar-paper shacks—the soldiers who arrived in February 1941 made do with square-shaped tents. Five men bunked in each tent, with a small gas heater to keep warm at night. Even for men who had grown up during the Depression, the surroundings were austere.

"The camp was all mud and junk," remembered Bob Koloski, a 34th Division soldier who was still a teenager when he arrived at the camp in February 1940. "We got there before they were completely ready for us."

The men from the 34th carried their gear in steamer trunks and duffel bags, settling in for a training regime that would last several months. A good number had been issued uniforms that were far too big, and had to roll their trousers at the bottom.

Most Guard members were part-timers who had drilled one night a week at most. While there were exceptions, the enlisted men were treated essentially as new recruits. Besides close-order drill, soldiers received rifle and pistol training, and learned how to use mortars and other weapons. Lessons often took place in the fields, where soldiers sat in knee-high grass, listening as their instructors reviewed the basics of rifle maintenance or other military arts. They wore cloth caps, dark denim pants, and light-colored shirts, with many-pocketed cartridge belts at their waist; their rifles were bolt-action Springfields, officially known as the M1903. Two-man teams were trained to operate Browning automatic rifles, a light, squad-level machine gun that would play an important role in the war.

In August and September of 1941, members of the 1st Armored Division and the 34th Infantry Division took part in the largest Army maneuvers held in the United States. Known as the Great Louisiana Maneuvers and nicknamed "The Big One," the war games involved nineteen Army divisions and covered 3,400 square miles of Louisiana and Texas. Among the officers who took part were George Marshall, then Army Chief of Staff, Dwight Eisenhower, George Patton, and Omar Bradley.

While impressive for their size, in retrospect the maneuvers showed just how dire America's military situation was. Two years after German mechanized divisions had proven once and for all that the days of cavalry were over, the U.S. Army was still fielding horse troops and artillery pulled by mules in large numbers. Tanks and field guns were so scarce that the Army used stand-ins at the exercises: dilapidated trucks and tree trunks.

Hitler's invasion of the Soviet Union that summer had taken the war crisis to a new level. German armies advanced rapidly through the lands of their supposed ally. While longtime Roosevelt critics like Congressman Hamilton Fish of New York continued to oppose the war—"I do not believe that American mothers want to send their sons to Soviet Russia and die for communism," declared Fish—other prominent critics gradually toned down their opposition or came over to the President's side completely. The more insatiable Hitler's appetite for territory became, the more likely it seemed that war would come to America. As summer turned to fall and winter loomed, the question for many Americans wasn't if the U.S. would get involved in World War II, but when.

And yet, when the war did finally come, it was a shock.

REVENGE

"Yesterday, December 7, 1941—a date which will live in infamy—the United States of America was suddenly and deliberately attacked by naval and air forces of the Empire of Japan. The United States was at peace with that nation, and at the solicitation of Japan, was still in conversation with its government and its Emperor looking toward the maintenance of peace in the Pacific . . ."

By the time Roosevelt delivered his famous war speech on December 8, 1941, Szima had thrown away his cane. He'd also managed to lose something else: the papers in his file that showed he'd needed an enlistment waiver because of his scar. Those papers, he figured, would keep him from joining the 1st Armored when it went overseas and got in the war. More than anything, Szima wanted to get in the war. He wanted to exact some revenge for the men who'd been killed at Pearl Harbor. Whether it was in Japan or Europe didn't much matter, as long as he went.

Szima was in a good position to tear up the papers: not only was he a sergeant by then, but he was assistant personnel sergeant major for the 13th Armored Regiment, the top kick's sidekick. And it just so happened that one of the important officers of the unit was the same man his testimony had helped clear after the firing-range accident. If Szima wanted to go overseas, no one was going to stop him.

For Kness and the other members of the 34th Infantry Division listening by radio in their barracks, Roosevelt's speech seemed to mark the passage from a time of waiting to a time of action. To a man, they were anxious to get to the front and take on the enemy. Within weeks, they had an assignment: they were to ship to Ireland, becoming the first American infantry unit to be stationed in Europe since the end of World War I.

First, though, they were shipped to Fort Dix in New Jersey. There they waited. And waited. And waited—the infantryman's lot.

"We had a little training . . . but it was just killing time, I think," recalled Owen Sweazey many years later. Like many of his comrades in the division, Private Sweazey found it, and the barracks life he was subjected to, boring at best. Pearl Harbor, and the German declaration of war a few days later, had filled them with anger and adrenaline, and they were in a rush to use it.

OWEN SWEAZEY

Though he came from the midwest, Sweazey was not a Guardsman but a draftee added to the 34th as it was brought up to full strength for the war. Born on June 6, 1920, Sweazey was drafted in October 1941. He joined the division in February 1942 while it was waiting for its transfer to Europe.

The son of a coal miner turned carpenter, Sweazey had spent two years in high school before leaving in 1935 at the age of fifteen to join the Civilian Conservation Corps so he could help support his family. The New Deal program taught him to operate heavy equipment such as bulldozers; it was a skill he would use for much of his life—but not in the Army, which saw him more valuable as a rifleman.

Sweazey had actually tried to join the Navy about a year before he was drafted, only to be rejected for "bad teeth." The Army wasn't quite so picky.

IRELAND

Traveling by ship, the 34th Division started shipping out soon after Sweazey arrived. It went to Northern Ireland in three waves, with the last arriving in May 1942. Together with the 1st Armored Division, it formed V Corps, the vanguard of the U.S. Army's European ground force.

The Irish landscape was a sharp change from Fort Dix. Dirt roads bounded by tall hedges crisscrossed rugged hills and wet moors or bogs. The two divisions began training immediately, but the training was hardly ideal and would later be lambasted by Private Frank B. Sargent, whose written report was circulated throughout the Army in 1943.

"In Ireland I have seen patrols go out in the following manner," wrote Sargent, referring the 34th Division. "The patrol leader had a vague idea about his mission, while the rest knew nothing at all. The leader did not check his men before they left for equipment that would reflect light or rattle. The patrol followed a road without even considering investigating bushes or hedges on the sides of the roads. The patrol marched in a helter-skelter formation, in columns of twos, no scouts, no point, no organization whatsoever."

Whether it was the lackadaisical training or the routine of barracks life, a large number of men grew bored. The German offensive in Russia meant that the immediate threat of an invasion in Great Britain had passed. It seemed obvious to the infantrymen that they weren't going to be called into action anytime soon. Many of the young men *wanted* to fight; even those like Sweazey who'd been drafted thought they would rot away before they saw action.

And then one day in camp, Sweazey noticed a sign tacked on the bulletin board announcing that a new outfit was forming. There wasn't much information about it, but one thing got his attention right away—the unit was going to be modeled after the British Commandos.

He signed up immediately. So did Kness, now a staff sergeant in the 34th Infantry. So did more than eight hundred other members of the division.

Over in the 1st Armored Division, Szima saw the same notice and knew it was finally his chance to leave the desks behind and get into action. He volunteered—as did several hundred others from the unit.

Within days, the men were en route to a small town named Carrickfergus, about twenty miles north of Belfast, Ireland. The unit they had signed up to join was so new it didn't even have a name.

TWO

DARBY'S RANGERS

Washington, D.C.
April 1942

· · ·

LUCIAN TRUSCOTT

Lucian Truscott hadn't been in Washington, D.C., in quite some time, but the city seemed little changed as the colonel headed toward the former War College building, now pressed into service as the Headquarters of Army Ground Forces. More men in uniforms, maybe. Otherwise, the city, with its trees and plants in bloom and its traffic as yet unaffected by gas rationing, looked exactly as it had during peacetime.

Appearances were deceiving, however. Like the rest of the country, Washington was mobilizing for a war it had long seen coming yet had not fully been prepared to enter. Truscott, like many veteran regular Army officers, was still adjusting to the demands of changing times. Now forty-seven, he'd spent the bulk of his Army career in the cavalry. Recognizing that combat had been revolutionized by armor and aircraft, Truscott had joined the 13th Armored Regiment at Fort Knox in June 1940, spending time as a battalion and regimental S-3— the staff officer generally in charge of operations, including battle plans and training. A staff job as assistant S-3 at the IX Army Corps at Fort Lewis Washington led him to rub elbows with other up-and-coming officers, most especially Dwight D. Eisenhower, at the time a colonel and IX's Chief of Staff. But Truscott had returned to cavalry in November 1941, leading the 5th Cavalry Regiment of the 1st Cavalry Division at Fort Bliss, Texas. It was a dream job, even if the days of horse soldiers were long gone.

Then in April 1942, Truscott was summoned to Washington. He was told he was getting a new assignment somewhere where the weather was cold, but nothing else. With a mixture of reluctance—he truly loved the cavalry—and excitement, he walked into the head-quarters building and reported to General Mark. W. Clark, the Chief of Staff for Army Ground Forces.

"How would you like to join the Commandos?" said Clark.

Truscott could not have been more surprised had he been asked to flap his arms and fly.

Eisenhower, now the Pentagon's Chief of Operations, had picked Truscott to head a small group of U.S. officers assigned to the staff of Britain's Combined Operations Command, the somewhat prosaic name of the war group in charge of the British Commandos. Truscott—and millions of Americans—had already heard of the Commandos, thanks to well-publicized reports of raids they'd conducted in Northern Europe. No soldiers, no airmen, no sailors were more celebrated than the British Commandos. If fighting men were rock stars, the Commandos would have been the Beatles.

Army head George Marshall, traveling with key Roosevelt aide Harry Hopkins, had just returned from England. Besides discussing overall war strategy, Marshall had also discussed the possibility of having Americans take part in Commando raids. There were two reasons: first, he wanted Americans to get experience in amphibious operations, knowing that they would be necessary during the war. And second, the President had recognized that the positive public relations for the war effort—"morale," as it was referred to then—was something the Commando units had in spades. Roosevelt would turn out to be a major proponent of special operations during the war, both for their military and morale value.

Marshall told Eisenhower to follow up; Ike turned to Truscott, assigning him to figure out how such a unit could be formed and trained.

At least on its face, the assignment was an odd one. Truscott had very limited experience with ground troops, let alone amphibious assaults or working with the Navy. In fact, he'd only been in a small boat on the ocean twice in his life. When Truscott pointed out his lack of experience, Eisenhower downplayed it, and in fact the selection may have had as much to do with Truscott's ability with horses as with his military credentials. The head of Combined Operations was Admiral Lord Louis Mountbatten, who had written a book on polo—a sport that Truscott had played in earlier years. When pressed on the military issues involved, Eisenhower sent Truscott off with the comment, "You can learn, can't you?"

MOUNTBATTEN

If Truscott arrived in London thinking of Mountbatten as the embodiment of slightly eccentric British aristocracy, he would not have been the only American to have that impression. Mountbatten had toured the United States in the late summer and early fall of 1941. Arriving ostensibly to take command of the British aircraft carrier *Illustrious,* which was being repaired in the American naval yards at Norfolk, Virginia, the photogenic British lord and his wife were a public-relations tag team, drumming up support for the British war effort. They spent weeks talking to the American media and meeting with everyone from radio personality Walter Winchell to President Roosevelt. Charming, gracious, and perpetually smiling, Lord Louis thanked Americans for their support in one breath and in the next told of his recent stint as a destroyer commander in the Mediterranean, where his destroyer had been sunk by German bombers. The fact that Mountbatten had remained on his bridge until the rest of his crew escaped was added quite matter-of-factly, as if it were the expected thing to do. The fact that he had nearly died in the battle—well, jolly good that he didn't, wasn't it?

But Mountbatten was not just any British hero; he was related to the King. Queen Victoria, his great-grandmother, had asked that her name be incorporated into his when he was born, and so he was christened Louis Francis Albert Victor Nicholas—and called "Dickie" by all who knew him, a somewhat arbitrary nickname applied during his childhood. His speech was dotted with adjectives— *marvelous, lovely, extraordinary*—commonplace in England but unexpected in America, where they seemed to add to Mountbatten's wit and charm.

Mountbatten's tour of America ended abruptly that October 1941 when British prime minister Winston Churchill decided to name him to head Combined Operations, replacing seventy-year-old Admiral of the Fleet Lord Keyes. Mountbatten's official biographer, Philip Ziegler, says that the captain would have preferred taking command of the aircraft carrier *Illustrious,* but the assignment was to a higher office and could not be gracefully turned aside. Even after a promotion to commodore, Mountbatten found himself outranked by many of the people he was in theory dealing with as equals. His relatively young age—he was forty-one when he took over—was also a handicap, though one he was generally able to overcome with energy and tact.

More difficult to deal with were the service rivalries and conflicting priorities within the main branches of the British military services. Combined Operations relied largely on cooperation from the other services, the Navy in particular, for resources, and it wasn't easy at times to get them.

Combined Operations had several missions; it was tasked with training both the Navy and Army for amphibious landings and planning for the large-scale invasion of France. But its most famous mission, even at the time, was directing small raids in occupied Europe. To do this, it developed its own strike force of special operations soldiers: the British Commandos.

THE COMMANDOS

If Americans might have regarded Mountbatten as jolly and slightly eccentric, they saw the Commandos as serious war fighters, just short of superheroes. The Germans, too, knew them and, while their raids were probably of greater psychological than strategic value, expended considerable manpower trying to corral them. Hitler even issued orders directing that they be killed rather than taken prisoner.

Supposedly inspired by accounts of irregular action in the South African or Boer War (1899–1902), the British began experimenting with Commando-style warfare almost from the beginning of the war in 1940. Four small special operations units known as the Independent Companies were formed in 1940. Trained in what we now call guerrilla warfare, the companies landed in Norway on May 13, 1940, at two small fishing villages, Mo i Rana and Bodö. Ranging through the mountainous terrain, they diverted the attention of German units that were marching north. Now almost entirely forgotten, the Independent Companies withdrew through Bodö after about a month's worth of fighting.

These early commandos were under the direction of the Military Intelligence Research section, which was later associated with the Special Operations Executive—the organization responsible for encouraging and supporting partisans throughout occupied Europe. The formal Commando organization was born in June 1940, immediately after the British evacuation of Dunkirk ended, with the creation of a special command in the War Office known as Section MO 9.

The Commando force began with two units, 1 Commando and 2 Commando, which were formed from the Independent Company. Seven more units—3 through 9 Commando—were formed at roughly the same time; with two other units joining around the end of the year. These were 11 Commando—made up primarily of Scottish soldiers—and 12 Commando, a unit with Irish and Welsh men. Norwegian, French, and Dutch troops were incorporated into 10 Commando at the beginning of 1942. The units were originally organized as fifty-man troops, ten to a Commando. In 1941, a reorganization settled on sixty-five-member troops, with six to a Commando.

When British prime minister Winston Churchill had pushed for the creation of the force early in the war, he originally envisioned them as carrying out small invasions with from five to ten thousand men. Incursions that large were out of the question in 1940 and 1941, however; among other reasons, the British lacked landing vessels and support craft, and there was a severe manpower shortage as a German invasion appeared imminent. Small raids with anywhere from a handful to a few hundred men were possible, however, and teams of Commandos conducted reconnaissance and sabotage missions throughout 1941. There were at least ten larger-scale operations in France, the Channel Islands, and Norway that year; they would make roughly twice as many in 1942.

Combined Operations has generally been credited as being particularly media savvy. There's no doubt that the unit knew how to get good public relations; Mountbatten's staff had extensive media contacts with foreign as well as British journalists. Not only were his officers accomplished at what today we call "spin," they controlled the flow of information to the media and had the added advantage of wartime censorship—stories concerning Combined Operations had to be approved by in-house censors before they could be filed.

But at the same time, Combined Operations had something the media, and its audience, dearly wanted—stories of heroes braving incredible odds to strike a blow for the good guys. The Commandos allowed Britains, after years of retreat, to finally feel as if they were on the offensive. Shrouded in mystery, their operations were presented and received as David and Goliath stories, eagerly awaited by a public that knew very well it was the real underdog in the battle.

One raid in particular summed up the Commando mystique: Saint-Nazaire.

OPERATION CHARIOT

If there was such a thing as a typical Commando raid, the attack on Saint-Nazaire on March 22, 1942, wasn't it. The port city was among the most highly defended in France and the attack was made directly in the teeth of the German defenses. But in terms of sheer audacity, no other successful raid launched by the Commandos comes close. Well publicized following its completion, Saint-Nazaire helped make the word *Commando* a byword for derring-do forever more.

One of the busiest ports in Europe during the 1930s, Saint-Nazaire was the home of the large ocean liner the SS *Normandie*. Partly to accommodate it, the French had constructed massive drydock and other shipyard facilities, making Saint-Nazaire among the most modern and capable ports in the world. When the war came, it was the only port on the French coast big enough to handle the German battleships *Bismarck* and *Tirpitz*.

The *Bismarck* was sunk in 1941, leaving her sister ship *Tirpitz* as the German's main capital ship. Even so, the *Tirpitz*'s eight fifteen-inch guns, twelve six-inch guns, and sixteen four-inchers, made her more than a match for any individual British warship, and if the *Tirpitz* were to travel to the Atlantic, she would wreak havoc with British convoys there.

After a number of direct attacks on the *Tirpitz* failed, the British Navy decided that the best way of dealing with the battleship was to attack Saint-Nazaire. The harbor was necessary for the ship if she operated in the Atlantic; without it, the *Tirpitz* would have to sail either through the Channel or all the way around Great Britain to reach a port big enough for repairs. In that case, she could be sunk by a war of attrition, pummeled continually until her defenses gave way.

Assuming, of course, she left port at all.

But the harbor was heavily defended; British warships could not hope to get close enough to bombard it. And the dry dock seemed impervious not just to the shells from naval guns but to bombs as well, especially the poorly aimed ones of World War II.

And so the job of striking Saint-Nazaire was given to the Commandos. Mountbatten's planners came up with an ingenious suggestion: ram the dry dock's lock gate with a ship crammed with explosives, rendering it useless. And since they were going there anyway, an additional attack would then be launched at the heavily reinforced submarine pen and buildings and docks nearby.

The ship chosen as the suicide bomber was the HMS *Campbeltown*. Originally launched in 1919, the destroyer was the former USS *Buchanan,* an American destroyer "leased" to Great Britain under the Lend Lease program. Modified so that its silhouette made it look like a German destroyer, the vessel was stocked with explosives.

These were sealed off and a timer set so that the explosion would occur after the force had safely retreated.

A force of 246 commandos accompanied the ship, most in small wooden motor launches. These boats were small craft, roughly the equivalent of American PT boats. Barely eighteen feet at the beam, they measured 112 feet from stem to stern. A 20mm cannon stood on their foredecks; in most cases there were mounts for machine guns on the bridge wings and aft of the superstructure.

The members of Number 2 Commando made up the primary raiding force, but men from 1, 3, 4, 5, 9, and 12 Commando were also on the raid. A total of 241 Commandos were involved, and with sailors and everyone else, the force had just over 600 men.

Though challenged, the *Campbeltown* made it to the dock intact, striking the gate at just after one-thirty in the morning on March 27, 1942. Her crew opened the scuttling valves, flooding her compartments and leaving her embedded in the dock as her bombs began ticking away.

The Commandos, meanwhile, fanned out across the harbor, wrecking whatever targets they could find before retreating to the boats. It was a costly venture, with nearly 50 percent casualties: 169— 59 of them Commandos—were killed; an additional 129 were captured, 109 of them Commandos.

The *Campbeltown* exploded the next day. The blast wrecked the outer gate of the dock, and the destruction was enough to make Saint-Nazaire unusable by the *Tirpitz* for the rest of the war.

Reports of the raid appeared in America within days. While some stories were wildly inaccurate—a report in the *New York Times* on May 4 claimed that British Commandos, "aided by enthusiastic Bretons" or local citizens, captured the German headquarters there and held it for two days. They also neglected to mention the casualty rate, which was relatively large compared to earlier raids, and which would have been considered disastrous in most conventional operations.

But considering the wartime limits imposed by British military censorship, overall the newspapers gave a fairly accurate account of the operation. An editorial March 30, 1940, in the *New York Times* began, "For sheer daring the British commando descent on St. Nazaire surpasses any similar raid of the war." The Commandos had caught the imagination of the world.

IN LONDON

Colonel Truscott arrived in London on May 17, 1942, a few days before the British government announced that three Saint-Nazaire raiders would receive the Victoria Cross. The British capital seemed deserted. Besides ravaging large parts of the city, the attacks by German bombers had sent many natives to the countryside. Those remaining faced serious shortages of nearly everything. Many of the civilians Truscott saw were on lines, waiting for a turn to buy something they needed.

Truscott met with the American general staff in England, headed by Brigadier General Charles L. Bolte. Bolte and some of his aides resented the fact that Truscott had been sent by Marshall; they viewed the mission as interference. They chafed at the fact that Truscott was essentially being assigned to work under Mountbatten, believing Americans and British should retain separate commands. And they didn't seem particularly sold on the idea of an American Commando force either.

Truscott's meeting with Mountbatten at Combined Headquarters, a yellow-brick building overshadowed by the War Department and the other government buildings across the street, went more smoothly. Truscott's Texas accent was the cause of some humor, but he had just as much trouble understanding the English officers as they did him.

The truly unique aspect of Combined Operations was not its targets or even the methods its soldiers used, but the fact that it coordinated naval and Air Forces as well as Army units in its operations. Mountbatten told Truscott that the Americans' participation in Combined Operations would lay the groundwork for the eventual combined and cooperative command that would be needed to oversee any full-scale invasion of Europe; it was a prophetic prediction at a time when most officers, British and American, believed each should be in complete command of all the units in an operation, theirs as well as others.

Truscott was a quick study and an energetic officer. Barely a week after arriving in London, he prepared a report for Marshall outlining the formation of an American unit to work alongside the Commandos. The report was submitted May 26; by May 28, a cable had arrived telling him to go ahead.

A DOUBLE PURPOSE

The orders for the creation of the Ranger battalion contained an inherent contradiction. On the one hand, they stated that the unit was being formed to give the U.S. Army firsthand experience with amphibious missions; their expertise would be shared among the rest of the Army. "It is expected that after such training and experience," read one of the formation orders, "as many men as practicable will be returned to their organization." On the other hand, the unit was supposed to enter combat. Like all combat units, its effectiveness would depend a great deal on the coherence that comes only from experience and working together over a long period.

The contradiction reflected a difference in opinion among Army leaders about how the commando-like battalion should be used. Was it a specially trained group of soldiers to be kept together and used for specific objectives? Or were the individuals "merely" extremely well trained and fit infantrymen, supersoldiers if you wish, who could be returned to their units, where they would lead by example?

Another debate would develop as the unit progressed: How should the battalion be used? The Commandos were small infantry units designed to be self-supporting—but only for very short missions, generally lasting no more than thirty-six hours. That was the perfect setup for a raid, which by definition was a hit-and-run affair taking place over the course of a day or even less. But a highly trained asset like the Commandos could be extremely valuable in a traditional military campaign. If it made sense to use it to take a difficult position at the start of the campaign, wouldn't it make sense to keep on using it in the fight? To use more modern terms than were popular at the time, shouldn't the steep investment in training pay higher dividends than a small raid every few months?

The Army never answered those questions—or rather, it answered them differently throughout the war, and afterward. Americans trained in the Commando style would be used as a coherent, special operations unit. More often, though, they were used as a spearhead in relatively conventional infantry campaigns. And before the end of the war—and immediately afterward—some men were spark plugs, sprinkled in as members of regular combat groups.

With the approval in hand, Truscott began the arduous task of turning it from an outlined flowchart to a flesh-and-blood force. Needing soldiers, he turned to the only available U.S. force then in the British Isles—V Corps, the 34th Infantry, and the newly arrived 1st Armored Division. The units were in Northern Ireland, under the command of Major General Russell P. Hartle, the commanding general, United States Army Forces Ireland. Truscott asked Hartle if he knew of anyone who might take command of the unit; Hartle recommended one of his aides, William O. Darby. After interviewing several candidates, Truscott agreed.

It was to be a momentous choice.

WILLIAM O. DARBY

Darby was born in 1911 in Fort Smith, Arkansas, where his father was a printer and amateur musician. Well liked and a bit of a practical joker, Darby was elected class president in his freshman year in high school. He played football and ran track, where he favored the high and broad jumps. The young man was also a member of a Boy Scout–like group called the Boy Rangers, which spent time hiking and camping in the nearby woods. He was an average student, graduating 177 in a class of 346. He seems to have liked to joke around and kid more than studying; when he returned to the school to speak during the war, he called himself the class fool.

But he had a serious side as well, and he had hopes of pursuing it in the Army. Named by his local congressman as an alternate candidate for West Point, Darby won an appointment to the academy in 1929 when the congressman's top two choices turned the appointment down.

After West Point, the young second lieutenant joined the 82nd Artillery, part of the 1st Cavalry Division. He spent the next eight years in artillery-related posts. Promoted to captain in the fall of 1940, he took part in the Louisiana exercises and an amphibious assault exercise the following winter, and received additional training in shore landings, making him one of a handful of Army officers with *any* firsthand experience, however slight, in amphibious operations when the war began.

After Pearl Harbor, Captain Darby was assigned to General Hartle's staff. Chosen by the general as his aide, Darby arrived as part of the advance team in Belfast on January 26, 1942. By spring, he'd grown tired of his role as the general's aide. It's not clear whether he volunteered for the position as commander of the battalion when he heard it was to be formed, or whether the idea originated with Hartle—accounts differ, and Darby was characteristically laconic about his appointment in his memoir, handling it in a single sentence and saying only that he received orders to head the unit. Whatever the specifics, Darby jumped at the opportunity. Truscott interviewed several candidates over a few days, then chose the one Hartle had recommended.

On June 1, 1942, General Hartle received formal orders directing him to seek volunteers for the new fighting unit Truscott had sketched out. By June 8, Darby had been appointed, promoted to major, and had gone to work finding officers for the new unit. He took only a few days to find the officers he wanted; as soon as they were picked, he had them help him cull the records and interview the enlisted men who'd volunteered to join.

Darby's officers were drawn primarily from the units the enlisted men came from. Perhaps his most significant selection was that of Captain Herman Dammer, at the time an adjutant in an antiaircraft unit. Not only was Dammer not a West Point graduate, he had been a member of the National Guard rather than the regular Army. This made a great deal of sense, given the fact that most of the men in the selection pool had themselves been in the Guard, but at the time the division and prejudice between regular Army and Guard—to say nothing of West Pointers, another clique within the leadership corps—were so strong that it was unusual. Four other captains, thirteen first lieutenants, and eleven second lieutenants filled out Darby's roster of officers.

The initial order describing the force indicated that specialists were needed in different areas, including scouting (or "woodcraft" as one order called it), mountain climbing, demolition, and the use of small boats. The screeners were also told to give "special consideration" to men who had experience in rough carpentry and "pioneer"-style rigging. Candidates needed twenty-twenty uncorrected vision, good hearing, and "normal" blood pressure.

V Corps was not a perfect cross section of the United States, but it did represent something of a cross section of the Army at the time.

The 1st Armored Division was a "regular" unit; most of its enlisted men were either volunteers or recent draftees, primarily from the eastern seaboard. The 34th, though it had been filled out with draftees and recent enlistees, was still largely a National Guard unit, with strong roots in the midwest. The two thousand volunteers were eventually whittled down through selection and then washouts to roughly five hundred men.

Two hundred and fifteen were drawn from the 133rd, 135th, and 168th Infantry Regiments, the main units making up the 34th Division. The next biggest group—thirty-one men—came from the 1st Armored Regiment, part of the 1st Armored Division, with another thirty from the 6th Armored Infantry. The rest were selected from across the two divisions, with men coming from antiaircraft, engineering, quartermaster, and even hospital units. The majority were privates or privates first class; there were eighty-two sergeants and another seventy-eight corporals or T-5s, the equivalent of a corporal in rank. Most of the noncommissioned officers—eighty-six—were drawn from the 34th's three infantry regiments.

Looking at the men who would eventually end up in the Dieppe Raid, less than a handful were nineteen or twenty years old; the rest ranged up to forty-two, clustered around twenty-two to twenty-five. All were white; blacks would not be integrated into the Army until after the war. Most of their ancestors had come from Europe. There were no Japanese-Americans in the unit, and German and Italian surnames earned extra scrutiny though did not necessarily bar anyone from being picked. Even a man like Szima, whose family came from Hungary, felt he was watched at times because of his heritage.

The volunteers were overwhelmingly single; available military records of the Dieppe veterans show only one who had any dependents, and he was divorced. While a few had attended college and one or two had a degree, the bulk of the enlisted men were about evenly split between high school graduates and men who'd gone through only two or three years of secondary education. Their jobs before the war were a real smorgasbord: sign painters, carpenters, millwrights, and auto mechanics rubbed shoulders with actors and an aeronautical engineer. All of the men had one thing in common: they wanted to fight.

THE BUSINESS OF WAR

James Altieri, whose book *The Spearheaders* describes his experiences as one of the first Rangers, remembered that the connection with the Commandos was an important reason he and many other men signed up. Altieri, at the time a technician fifth grade (essentially a corporal) with the 1st Armored Division, had heard all about the raid at Saint-Nazaire as well as others in France and Norway. After his unit's top sergeant announced that volunteers were wanted, Altieri and a friend eagerly discussed the possibilities. They saw volunteering as a way to do some real fighting—and to avoid some of the more tedious aspects of Army life, like picking up cigarette butts around the barracks.

As gung ho for battle as Altieri seemed, inside he had some doubts. Did he really want to see combat? he wondered. Or was he just "bluffing"?

The next day, he put himself to the test, appearing with his friend and fourteen other men from their battery before his captain. The captain eliminated two of the sixteen volunteers; doctors crossed off the names of three more after an extensive physical the next day.

The process was repeated throughout the 1st Armored and the 34th Infantry. Darby had made it clear that he wasn't forming an imperial guard type of unit filled only with bruisers; a man could be chosen regardless of his stature or physical prowess. The initial orders asking for volunteers stressed common sense and initiative, not strength, as qualifications.

The volunteers who made it past the initial screening were then interviewed by Darby's officers, who generally worked in pairs. The questions they asked made it clear that they were trying to gauge men's character and makeup. Altieri—an Italian-American—was asked if he would object to killing Italians in battle. He admitted he'd prefer to fight Germans or the Japanese, but said he'd have no qualms about doing his duty. He was asked if he could swim—a requirement for all soldiers in the new unit.

"Two miles was the longest I ever tried," said the corporal. It was a lie, but he'd heard the unit wanted strong swimmers and didn't want to get disqualified.

"Have you ever been in any brawls," asked the captain, "barroom fights, gang fights where people have been hurt bad?"

"Yes, sir. I grew up in a tough neighborhood," answered Altieri, who came from Philadelphia. "You either fought or you didn't live."

"Did you ever kill a man?"

"No, sir," said Altieri, surprised by the question. "I never went quite that far."

"Do you think you would have guts enough to stick a knife in a man's back and twist it?"

"I guess a fellow can do anything in the heat of battle," said Altieri. "Sure, if it had to be done, I think I could do it."

The truth was, Altieri didn't even like to see chickens killed, let alone people. Like most of the other volunteers in the unit, he had no experience with killing, much less the business of war. But like the others, he was willing to learn, if that's what it took.

SERGEANT MAJOR BY COMMAND

Alex Szima was another man bored by the drudgery of the routine; in his case, he was held back—at least in his mind—by his abilities as a clerk and low-level bureaucrat. Szima saw the call for volunteers as his ticket to the real fighting, and he volunteered the moment he saw the call. He made it past the first screening, and then was pleased to find himself summoned before Major Darby himself.

Before going overseas, Szima had bragged to his friends in the poolroom that he was going to be the first guy over the top taking on the Germans. Now those words rang in his ears. Major Darby had called him into the hut serving as a temporary command post and sorting station not to welcome him as the sort of blood-and-guts fighter Szima longed to be, but as a behind-the-scenes noncom. The new unit needed a sergeant major, and Darby had decided Szima was it.

For most enlisted men, the offer to become the top sergeant of a battalion, especially a new one, would be regarded as an honor. The unit's highest noncommissioned officer, the battalion sergeant major, had a wide range of responsibilities and a good-size staff to help him carry them out. While the officers gave the orders, it was not an exaggeration to say that the sergeant major was really the man responsible for the unit's functioning. There was no more powerful position for a noncom.

On the other hand, as important as the position was, it generally did not involve combat.

Szima had two qualifications that set him apart from the rest of the unit: one, he had served as assistant to several sergeant majors before coming to Ireland, and two, he was regular Army. But becoming the first sergeant of the headquarters company was the last thing he wanted.

No thanks, Szima told his commander.

Darby, not pleased, nodded when the sergeant asked if he could explain why he didn't want the job.

Szima began in classic noncom fashion: talking about the good of the unit rather than his own preferences. He told Darby that most of the volunteers—80 percent, by his calculation, though this was exaggerated—were from the National Guard. It would be better to have someone from the Guard in the position, easing the friction between the Army's two halves.

And besides, admitted Szima, there was no way he was going to last. He wanted to be a fighter, not a paper pusher. If he had to be a paper pusher, he'd push himself out of the job inside a few months. He just wasn't the right person for the job.

"I'll be the judge of that," snapped Darby. Then he ordered Szima to take the job temporarily. A sergeant major would be transferred in as soon as possible; in the meantime, Szima should get to work. Latrines and the mess hall were to be in order; calisthenics were to kick off at reveille in the morning.

Darby gave him a watch and a whistle—tools of the office—congratulated him, and told him to get to work.

THE FIRST CUT

Altieri, Szima, Sweazey, Kness, and roughly eight hundred other men were chosen for the new unit. After the selection was complete, they were driven by truck to a camp outside of Carrickfergus, Northern Ireland. After getting settled in, they began training with the most basic of Army exercises: marching. Altieri remembered the nearby hills echoing with song, including this one, an old infantry ditty that he had never heard before:

> *The Infantry, the Infantry,*
> *With dirt behind their ears,*
> *They can lick their weight in wildcats*
> *And drink their weight in beers.*
> *The Cavalry, the Artillery,*
> *The lousy Engineers,*
> *They couldn't lick the Infantry*
> *In a hundred thousand years.*

The marches if not the songs increased in length and speed until after about two weeks they were covering twelve miles in two hours. Men began dropping from exhaustion; quietly they were removed from the unit. The fear of being sent back—of "washing out"—propelled many of the others.

Each morning, Altieri thought he'd be gone by the end of the day. But the idea of returning to his unit as a failure pushed him on. He didn't want to be branded as a gutless, all-talk wonder. So he pushed on. Finally, after roughly three weeks, the troop was organized into a battalion with companies that themselves were subdivided into platoons and a headquarters section. Altieri was still there.

Truscott's plans for the 1st Battalion called for six companies with three officers and 63 men, with a headquarters company of eight officers and 69 men. With a margin of roughly 10 percent to allow for accidents and injuries during training, the battalion's strength was set at 520 men—or a little more than half the size of a typical American infantry battalion, which called for 886 enlisted and officers.

Exactly how many men were culled during the three weeks of marches isn't clear. Altieri says he was told the unit started with 2,000 volunteers; others estimate that no more than 200 were sent back to their units from Carrickfergus. The official diary compiled by the battalion during its first two weeks of training states that only 104 men were rejected, while the entry for June 22 indicates that 488 enlisted men were selected. In any event, the physical demands were just beginning; before they were considered trained, the soldiers would look back somewhat longingly on those early marches.

Getting into good physical condition was certainly important for the future Rangers, but Altieri noticed that physical prowess wasn't necessarily the last word on a man's qualifications. In fact, some of the best soldiers were proving to be thin, frail-looking clerk types who would pass unnoticed in a crowd, but who turned out to have a large store of stamina, intelligence, and what for want of a better word might be called "heart." The men who stuck with the unit weren't all exceptionally gung ho in the Hollywood sense—Szima's vocal desires to kill Germans stood out—but they did have a determined character, a will to succeed despite the odds, and an ability to accept challenges without wilting.

A VISIT FROM THE QUEEN

Toward the end of their stay at Carrickfergus, the Rangers were reviewed by four special visitors—the British royal family. Szima, for one, was surprised not just that the royals were there, but that they appeared so *normal.* Raised on Hollywood movies, he expected flowing robes and bejeweled crowns, and of course cups of tea poured at every opportunity. But the King and Queen and their daughters seemed nothing like the movie images. The Queen approached one of the men and asked him about his rifle, the newly issued M1.

Szima watched in awe as the Queen took the gun and examined it like an expert. She expressed admiration for the same qualities that endeared it to the soldiers—its lightness and ample, easily loaded clip.

Until now, the former bartender had tended to view women, especially English women, chauvinistically, placing most of them on a pedestal. Now, in England, he had a completely different view. Women were manning barrage balloons, driving vehicles, handling dozens of Army and civilian tasks that in America had only been performed by men. As he'd say much later, they were "taking their chances with the rest." The stereotypes he'd grown up with no longer seemed to apply—one of the few positive effects of the war, though he wouldn't have a chance to evaluate it for quite some time.

But the royals weren't the only important visitor the Americans received. On June 19, 1942, Darby introduced them to Brigadier General R. E. (Bob) Laycock. Laycock, whose exploits included an unsuccessful mission to kill the German general Erwin Rommel, was in charge of Commando training in northern Scotland; Darby was in effect turning his unit over to Laycock for their formal training.

"Men have come and men have gone," Darby added, "until now the chosen few remain. You few are now officially known as the First American Ranger Battalion, a name honored in American military-history annals, since it first was used by Rogers' Rangers of Indian war fame."

It was the first time the name of the unit had been used.

ALL IN A NAME

Many people took credit for suggesting the name Rangers, including Lord Mountbatten. It is likely, however, that the credit belongs to Truscott, who takes it in his memoirs.

Eisenhower had already told Truscott that the Americans shouldn't be called Commandos, since the word would inevitably be associated with the British. In his memoir, Truscott noted that *ranger* had been used during colonial days and the Revolution, but he neglected to mention who suggested the word to him in the first place.

Few modern histories of the Rangers neglect to mention Rogers' Rangers or the rules for irregular warfare that the colonial fighting unit is supposed to have lived by. The general term *ranger* was in common use in America during the eighteenth and nineteenth centuries, generally to refer to small units that patrolled the frontier or battled with Indians. But the word had fallen out of favor in the twentieth century, and no American Army unit had ever used it as a formal title. Author Robert W. Black, in his book *Rangers in World War II,* points out that Rogers' Rangers were featured prominently in Kenneth Roberts's popular prewar novel *Northwest Passage,* and hypothesizes that the interest in the term may have been sparked by the book. Another likely source of inspiration was the movie of the same name, which starred Spencer Tracy and was released in 1940.

The men on the parade ground had barely enough time to digest the new name before General Laycock took the podium and began telling them about the training they would undergo under the direction of the British Special Services Brigade.

"You are pioneering in a daring field of warfare at a critical time when our fighting forces, reeling from early defeats, must rebound and assume the offensive," concluded Laycock, a short, slight man who carried a riding crop in his hand. "In the British Army, the Commandos have provided the spark for that offensive spirit; you men are destined to provide that offensive spark for the American forces in Europe."

Within a few days, the Rangers were packed on board a British ship and transported to Fort William on the Scottish west coast. As eager as they might be to do battle, and as heralded as their future seemed, they had a long way to go before they measured up to the Commandos they were seeking to emulate.

Fort William, Scotland
November 2006

After spending the day exploring the Rangers' first training camp at Achnacarry, I return to my hotel in Fort William and an unexpected bonus: members of the Royal Commando Association have gathered at Fort William for a Remembrance Day celebration over the weekend. Within a few minutes, I'm listening to a World War II Commando describe the training at the site I've just come from. A bucolic heaven now, sixty-some years before the facility was a hell-on-earth, as close to the reality of war as its instructors could make it.

One Commando introduces me to another, and then another, and so on. The group includes men from more recent conflicts as well as World War II and the Cold War era. They're hospitable, friendly, and above all humble—there's no bragging here. When they are pressed for accounts of the war, there is always a slight hesitation before they begin to speak. Perhaps it comes from the pain of remembering fallen comrades, or a measure of the difficulty of remembering things that now are far in the past. Maybe their experiences are difficult to share with an outsider. But it is hard to escape the impression that these men— heroes by nearly any definition of the word—are at heart humble men, on some level still in awe of what they have done and witnessed.

As for myself, I'm simply humbled. After a few hours, I meet a man who knew Lieutenant Loustalot. Unlike some of the others, who are in wheelchairs, he is extremely energetic. Well into his eighties, he still radiates the seasoned calm of a noncommissioned officer, the sort of sergeant you'd follow just because you heard his voice in the distance.

We talk for a long while in a quiet corner of the nearby banquet room. I apologize for monopolizing his time.

"Not at all," he says graciously. Then he looks around the room. "There used to be more of us. Others with better stories. But gradually . . ."

His voice fades. We get up from our seats; there's nothing else to say.

I'd spent the morning thinking of the Rangers as they were— young men in their twenties, slugging through forced marches and ducking live ammunition. But now I see that there was considerably more to them, both before the war and long after. Their lives weren't frozen in the photographs I've seen, much less the stories they've told or I've read. No matter how momentous World War II was in their lives, it was only one point in the progression.

For most of them, the progression has come to an end. Their passing has dimmed our memory not only of Dieppe but of all that had happened during the World War.

I'd experienced this myself already, trying to track down the few survivors of the original Ranger raid. Modern databases had made it possible to find two men, now well into their eighties. Ten years before, I would have found a dozen or more.

There are plenty of other sources of information, a wealth of memoirs and personal papers that ultimately allowed me to reconstruct the battle. Still, there is a difference between reading a piece of paper and asking a live person a question.

And it wasn't simply information I was after—data about how many people were selected for the raid or what caliber the guns were. The real questions were more difficult: What did it feel like to be shot at, to run through a hail of bullets, to know you were going to die, to be a hero? While I might have some inkling of what to expect, the exact answer differed from man to man, and the difference mattered.

And there were many questions that wouldn't occur to me at all: Who would know to use the word humble to describe a Ranger or a Commando without having met him and observed it firsthand?

World War II seems unlikely to slip from the public consciousness anytime soon. But losing the connection to the men who had really been there, who could say what happened in ways that go beyond the numbers or words on a printed page, will inevitably dim our image of the war. When memory ceases to be a living thing, it becomes something much less important. The ceremonies at the memorials will go on, but gradually drain of meaning. Being unanswerable, the questions will no longer be asked.

Fort William, Scotland
July 1942

■ ■ ■

TRAINING

The train ride from Fort William to Spean Bridge took perhaps ten minutes, certainly no more than twenty. When the men arrived, it was raining—a very common occurrence in Scotland, especially in the West Highlands. It was also 9 p.m., though the depot was far enough north that it was still light.

The Rangers had left their camp at 0500—5 a.m. Most were tired and maybe stiff from the long ride.

Tough.

Whistles sounded. The men assembled on the platform to the bellows of their first sergeant, who urged them to fall in smartly. Barracks bags and packs were manhandled as the Rangers, tired and a little rumpled from the twenty-six-hour boat ride from Ireland, found their places.

A young lieutenant watched the proceedings with a critical eye. A native of Louisiana, Lieutenant Edwin Loustalot was short and wiry, but in his few weeks at Carrickfergus he had earned a reputation for spit and polish among the men. As one Ranger put it later, he seemed to have eyes in the back of his head, always on the lookout. He snapped off a salute to the sergeant when the men were squared away, then turned to present them to Major Darby and the Commando officer who'd come to meet them.

And then they started to march to Achnacarry, seven miles away.

Though only about eighty miles as the crow flies from Glasgow, Achnacarry was isolated, distant not only from the war but from most of Britain. Loch Ness—the famous home of the bashful sea creature "Nessie"—was nearby, but few people cared to hunt for fabled monsters when the ocean held dangers all too real. Aluminum plants helped the war effort, and West Highlands natives had opened their homes to relatives and other refugees from the bomb-ravaged areas of southern England, yet the area remained thinly settled.

Achnacarry is the ancestral home of Clan Cameron, used by the chiefs of the clan since the mid-seventeenth century. The Camerons are a famous Scottish clan; their support was important to Prince Charles Edward Stewart—Bonnie Prince Charlie—and his ill-fated 1745 Jacobite Uprising. Burned after the rebellion failed, the clan house at Achnacarry was rebuilt in 1802 in the Scottish baronial style to look like a castle, with large stones and pseudo ramparts. Lord Lochei—the head of the clan—volunteered the property to the government for the duration of World War II. Surrounded by rugged hills and near both the ocean and lochs, it was perfect for Commando training. Part of the grounds was cleared fields used for farming and raising sheep, but most of the surrounding countryside remained wild and untamed in 1942—just as it does today. Narrow paths ran by waterfalls, skirted moors, paralleled streams. The few roads were narrow, bounded by moss-crusted rocks. Mountains rose all around them; most days they were shrouded in mist.

To the arriving Rangers, the main building did, indeed, look like a castle. The fields before it were filled with tents and Quonset huts—the latter called Nissen huts by the Rangers. Altieri likened the eight-man tents to wigwams; the men arranged themselves like the spokes of a wheel around the center post when they bedded down each night.

THE BEST?

A Commando lieutenant took charge of each Ranger company's training. The British officers and the sergeants who worked with them, two to a company, were well practiced in the twin arts of intimidation and motivation.

"You're the *best* the Americans can offer?" the instructors thundered. The words were a challenge, of course, but the instructors weren't bluffing when they told the Yanks they'd make them into "men" or kill them in the process.

Speed marches were the backbone of the training at Achnacarry. More than sixty years later, the Commandos who were there remembered the marching better than anything else. Altieri wrote of instructors pitting company against company, claiming that one Ranger unit marched seven miles in an hour—and that therefore the next had to do it in fifty-five minutes. The marches were done with rifles and full backpacks, and even for men who had spent the last two or three weeks marching the pace was torrid. The idea wasn't just to build endurance; the men were being pushed to their physical limits so that their instructors and officers could see who might not be able to stand the stress of combat.

Darby often participated in the marches. Sweazey would see him at front, talking to some of the men at the head of the column. Then the major would drift back, encouraging someone else. A few minutes later, he would be back at the head of the line, his short legs pumping. Darby seemed to already know every man—officer, sergeant, private—in the unit by name.

While they ran the Americans ragged, the Commandos actually looked on the newcomers with some affection, and the sergeants tended to take a softer approach than the officers. "Look here, laddie, sure you can do better than that," one "sarn't" would tell members of Altieri's company when they failed. "And what would the bloody Hun be doing if you did that way in battle?"

BUSTED OARS

Owen Sweazey strained at the oar of the small boat, pushing as hard as he could in the early morning light. He and the rest of his company were assaulting a beach at the Achnacarry training grounds; so far the exercise had gone off like clockwork. The night was quiet, the Rangers taking as much care as possible as they worked their oars. They were in a Goathly Folding Boat; with wooden bottoms and canvas sides, the boat looked like an oversize rowboat and was the World War II equivalent of today's rigid-hull inflatable assault craft.

Suddenly a shot rang out from shore. A Bren machine gun

opened up to their left. Someone in the boat cursed in a low voice. Everyone else ducked and began paddling harder.

A few moments later, the shoreline flashed as dynamite charges were ignited.

"Almost there!" yelled someone from the front of the vessel. As the Rangers pushed harder, Sweazey heard a loud *kerplunk* to his right. Instinctively, he ducked.

It was a good thing. Grenades exploded all around the boat, one so close that his oar snapped.

Utterly surprised, Sweazey glanced ahead at his first sergeant, Les Kness. Kness calmly jumped from the boat and led the men ashore toward their objective. They splashed in, aiming their Springfield rifles at a series of metal plates set up on the rocks as targets.

It was only a drill, but Sweazey and his companions remained wary nonetheless. The bullets flying around them were real, and during the course of training they would lose several men to injuries.

Using live ammunition was an important part of Commando training, designed to familiarize the men with the sound and sight of bullets flying nearby. The Commandos doing the shooting were generally among the best shots in their units, and were instructed to aim their bullets away from actual bodies. But there were plenty of stories of bullets striking Rangers who didn't move quite fast enough for their Commando instructors. While many may be apocryphal, at least one Ranger, Sergeant Donald Torbett, was shot during training. The bullet creased his backside; Sergeant Torbett rejoined the unit but was called "Butt" ever afterward.

TOUGH STANDARDS

If the Commandos were tough on the enlisted men, they were even more critical of the officers, all of whom took part in the training regardless of other duties. A fitness report issued only a few days after the Americans arrived singled out five officers for improvement. Captain William Martin was said to be "a very nice fellow" who had to "improve his power of leadership if he is going to be a successful commander." First Lieutenant Leonard Dirks was lambasted for thinking "he has nothing to learn . . . The sooner he tries to teach and instill into the men under his command all that he knows the better for him and his company."

The training was constant. An itinerary for a visit by the general in charge of the Scottish command shows a succession of demonstrations, beginning with a "death ride"—a journey across a ravine on an overhead toggle rope line—followed by an assault on a pillbox and an assault in folding boats under ball ammunition. In between were visits to the assault course, a reconnaissance demonstration, and a cliff-climbing exercise. All featured Rangers who were actually undergoing training.

Not that British amenities were completely forgotten; the general's visit ended with tea on the rifle range.

A complicated grid was used to track the different assignments on each range and at each area, with companies moving through drills in forty-minute segments from 8:30 a.m. to 5:40 p.m. To the surprise of many Rangers, the Commando exercises included close-order drills, parade-ground stuff they hadn't expected at a combat school. Like everything else, the spit-and-polish marches and presentations were designed to encourage teamwork and discipline.

The Rangers copied the Commandos' buddy or "me and my pal" system, working in pairs on obstacle and live-fire courses. They scaled cliffs together, and used ropes to climb and descend Achnacarry walls.

The Ranger weapons ranged from the .45-caliber Colt pistol to Thompson submachine guns (better known as tommy guns) and mortars. But their most important weapon was the M1 rifle, apparently introduced to the men at Achnacarry. The M1 Garand held a number of advantages over the Springfield, especially for a light infantry group such as the Rangers. A semiautomatic, it fired from an easily reloadable clip, giving an infantryman fifteen or thirty shots before having to reload; the Springfield held five. Unlike the Springfield and most other infantry rifles at the time, the bolt was operated by the gas expended by the cartridge rather than by hand, making it easier to operate in combat. Just as important, the weapon was shorter and lighter than the Springfield. An empty M1 weighed about five and a half pounds compared to just over eight and a half for the Springfield. Measuring thirty-five and a half inches from butt to barrel point, the M1 was about eight inches shorter as well. These two characteristics made it easier to carry both in assault craft and on marches, and the shorter length made it easier to wield.

Many of the Commandos who saw the M1 became jealous, immediately recognizing its utility. The Americans were also, as a group, good shots, especially compared to the Commandos. A good number had been familiar with rifles as young men, and simply came to the task with more experience.

To Altieri's dismay, the Rangers also learned to use knives—the Commando Sykes knife, now closely associated with the Rangers. They were also issued brass knuckles and learned a rough kind of judo for self-defense. "Each man had to learn the easiest and fastest way to take a man out," recalled Sweazey later. "It wasn't the best way or the nicest way, but you took him out as fast as you could."

While they had helmets—the tin-plate type common among Americans at this point in the war, replaced a few weeks later by the familiar bucket helmet—many of the exercises called for them to wear watch caps rather than helmets to keep noise at a minimum. Combat boots had not yet been issued; the men's Army-standard leggings were modified to make them easier to march in. The leggings became something of symbol; two later battalions, the 3rd and 4th, wore them, though by that time boots were common.

FOOD

Since time immemorial, there has been one way to start a conversation in the Army—ask about the food.

Such conversations at Achnacarry were likely to be short and laced with expletives. The Americans did not like the Scottish food, and were not exactly shy about saying so.

Most of the complaints were about the fish, uniformly described as oily and hardly edible. The plain Scottish oats weren't much better, and the Americans had little use for the tea, which Altieri called "rotten tea," almost as if it were one word.

There was so much grumbling, in fact, that cooks were eventually called in from the 34th Division to supplement the British rations. After Achnacarry, things got considerably better, as the Rangers were allowed to shoot game for food, and the Army cooks proved adept at preparing venison and other game. But the Scottish meals remained burned in their palates for all time.

Some sixty years later, surviving Commandos confessed that they didn't care much for the food either.

INFANTS AND WHISKEY

Despite the heavy training schedule, there was some room not just for humor but other diversions as well.

Because of his position as first sergeant in the headquarters company, Szima was entitled to eat in the sergeant majors' mess at Achnacarry—a privilege not to be taken lightly, not only because the other sergeants were the instructors, but also because the mess was in the Achnacarry castle. But the first night Szima showed up, he and the other Americans were met with a loud guffaw.

"Gad," said one of the Brits. "They're sending bloody infants!"

Szima took the slam good-naturedly, sitting across from the man who said it. The Brits began talking to the "Yanks," and Szima was soon commenting he'd been in the Army for only two years.

"Two years!" exploded one sergeant major, who happened to be one of the men responsible for training the guards at Buckingham Palace. "It took me seven to make corporal."

"Some people are naturally slow," countered Szima.

The table exploded with laughter. Szima was able to win over the sergeant major not just with his efforts during training, but with the purchase of whiskey three nights running.

TAKING SPEAN BRIDGE

As the Rangers' training progressed, they were presented with what Darby called "problems." These were open-ended combat simulations that saw them ranging over the local terrain, sometimes even in the populated areas. Narratives were added to give the exercise a realistic feel.

In a typical exercise, the Rangers were divided into two groups. One was sent to Spean Bridge and told to hold the small inn there. The other was then told that the first group had ravaged the hotel and taken one of the proprietresses hostage. It was their job to rescue her. The women played along, even serving tea when the mock battle was complete.

Creativity and surprise were valued in equal measures. A Ranger unit solved one problem by slipping into shepherd's clothes and bringing "their" flocks into town unchecked; at a signal they revealed their weapons and won without even a mock fight. And a lieutenant—his name wasn't recorded—donned a nurse's uniform so that he could get into his rivals' headquarters and take the commander without a fight after pulling a tommy gun from under his dress.

REDUCTION

Darby estimated that the unit lost 20 percent of its men during the first few days of training. While a few had been injured and one drowned, most of dropouts simply couldn't keep up with the demanding pace.

The worst thing about washing out was having to go back to your unit and explain what had happened. The men, said Altieri, had nothing to be ashamed of; they'd given it their all. But many if not most Rangers and Commandos feared having to go back and explain what had happened. In their eyes, they would have felt like failures.

Several times Altieri himself came close to quitting, and in fact he credited another Ranger he called Junior Fronk with keeping him in. Thinking he was exhausted one day during a march, Altieri noticed Fronk stumbling a few paces ahead. Obviously drained and yet refusing to give in, Fronk stubbornly did his best to march on. Ashamed that he'd been ready to quit, Altieri found new energy. He leaped forward, grabbed one side of Fronk, and together they marched the final three miles.

By the end of July, the Rangers had completed their training at Achnacarry and were ready for more advanced lessons. As their stay wound down, the individual Rangers were called in to meet with their British trainers for a quasi–exit interview. Altieri found himself in front of Lieutenant Cowerson—he never used the officer's first name—a man he'd come to both hate and respect. He recorded the exchange in his book:

"How did you like the training, Corporal?" asked the Commando lieutenant.

"I think I am twice the man I was before I came here."

"Do you wish to continue with the Rangers?"

"Yes, sir. I wouldn't think of quitting now."

"Bloody good. Bloody good. Always remember this—it is all in the mind and the heart."

It was Cowerson's signature line, and one the Rangers had come to believe.

GRADUATION

The sun dawned on a clear sky on August 1. The Rangers were gathered on the meadow that served as a parade ground. Marching to the strains of bagpipes, they were reviewed and congratulated by Colonel Vaughn, who'd met them at Spean Bridge a month earlier.

"You Yanks bloody well surprised us," said Vaughn. "We expected to grind you to bits."

Justifiably proud, the Rangers took their leave of their trainers, returning to their tents to pack. They knew they were in for more training, though they hadn't been told yet where it would take place.

They also hadn't been told that, contrary to usual custom, they weren't going to be given a few days off before the new assignment. There was more than a bit of grumbling when they heard the news.

Company F commander captain Roy Murray had his men fall out and then told them that the battalion was being split up for more training. Forty-four Rangers, including himself, were going to advanced training in demolitions. Six enlisted men from Company F had been chosen, as had Lieutenant Loustalot. The list included Sweazey and Kness—but not Altieri or Szima, who was still assisting the unit's new sergeant major and feared he was going to end up getting stuck with the job himself despite everything he'd done.

Demolitions?

Altieri hadn't heard that there was a chance to sign up for that. But with the unit moving out, he gave it little thought.

It wasn't until much later that the exact nature of the "demolition" training would be shared with the rest of the battalion. For the Rangers were on their way not to learn how to blow things up efficiently, but how to do it while on the shores of France. And this time, the bullets they faced wouldn't be fired by men aiming to miss.

THREE

SECOND FRONT

London
Early July 1942

. . .

RUTTER

Nineteen Rangers had actually already been assigned to see combat in France; they just never got a chance to get there.

While their comrades had been speed-marching around Achnacarry, the Rangers had been boarding ships at the Isle of Wight in southern England. Slightly bewildered and feeling somewhat out of place, they'd been told little if anything about their assignment. Singled out by Colonel Darby, the men hadn't even been told why they were chosen, but it is obvious now from the roster that they included some of the older and most promising Rangers, especially among the noncoms. The list:

1st Lieutenant Frederic F. Ahlgren

1st Lieutenant Walter F. Nye

1st Lieutenant William B. Lanning

1st Lieutenant James B. Lyle

1st Lieutenant Leilyn M. Young

2nd Lieutenant Robert L. Johnson

Staff Sergeant Clyde A. Dahlquist

Staff Sergeant William M. Musegades

Sergeant Joseph Dye

Sergeant William J. Huckle

Sergeant Ernest R. Jensen

Sergeant Walter Klebanski

Sergeant Edwin Mahoney

Sergeant Gerrit J. Rensink

Sergeant Clyde C. Thompson

Sergeant John R. Van Skoy

Corporal William E. Arimond

Corporal James R. Baines

The five thousand or so Canadian strangers whom they were with knew only a little more than they did. Members of the 2nd Canadian Division, the Canadians had twice practiced large-scale assault landings at West Bay, Bridport, Bradpole, and the nearby areas on the southern shore of England in Dorset. Some of the men the Rangers met assured them that this was to be another replay of those practices, neither of which had gone off all that well. Others, though, sensed a difference.

The men with the premonitions were right. On the afternoon of July 3, clouds gathering above them, 2nd Division commander Major General John Hamilton "Ham" Roberts boarded each ship and gave a short speech urging them to the task.

"This is not an exercise," the general informed them. "At last you are going to meet the enemy. Shortly after midnight you sail for France. The target is the port of Dieppe."

Rangers Gerrit "Ted" Rensink and Clyde Thompson found the Canadians aboard their ship rather easygoing and friendly. Sergeants Rensink and Thompson had just found a small cabin in their assault ship when they were told that they had a visitor. They went above to what looked like a large suite, where they found an officer with his feet on the desk. A bit taken aback when they realized the man was none other than General Dwight D. Eisenhower, they snapped to attention.

"At ease, Sergeants, at ease," said the American commander. He straightened in the chair as the men tried to relax. "You know, this could be your last trip," said the general. "If you have anyone to write to, it might be a good idea to do that."

The general then gave them a second piece of advice that Rensink never forgot: if you get into any hand-to-hand combat, he told them, don't get mad.

Rensink, at the time twenty-three years old, took both pieces of advice to heart. Back in his quarters, he wrote out letters to his mother and to his sweetheart. Then he waited for the operation to begin.

General Eisenhower, who had been appointed to head the American Army in Europe only a few weeks before, visited the rest of the American troops as well. He promised the Rangers that they were the "first of thousands who will eventually go to Europe." Their target was Dieppe, some sixty-five miles across the Channel.

Code-named Rutter, the operation the Rangers had joined as observers—they had no formal combat role—called for the city to be seized and held for the better part of a day before withdrawing. Though the initiative for the attack had come from Combined Operations, the vast majority of the men in the two-hundred-odd ships taking part in the raid were members of the Canadian 2nd Division. The Canadians had been in Britain for nearly two years, and were happy to finally face the prospect of action. They greeted the announcement of their target with applause and loud cheers.

Speeches done, cheers faded, the men waited for their ships to pull up their anchors and set sail. The clouds thickened and the wind kicked up; still they waited.

They were still waiting at dawn. The high winds had made it impossible for gliders and paratroopers to carry out a planned assault on guns guarding the city's flanks. Since the airborne attack was to be a critical part of the operation, the raid was put off for a day.

While the Rangers and Canadian foot soldiers grumbled and traded smokes on the deck, the top commanders huddled. The meteorologists predicted that the weather would clear by July 8. Fresh intelligence reports added a new wrinkle: a Nazi tank unit, the 10th Panzer Division, had been spotted in Amiens, a city about seventy miles by road from Dieppe. The highway from Amiens to Dieppe would allow the tanks and other motorized vehicles to sweep into the city before the planned withdrawal. While Rutter's plans called for Churchill tanks and some lighter vehicles to hit the beach with the infantry, they'd be no match for the German reinforcements. The solution was to lop the planned occupation in half; the assault would begin in the predawn hours and end at 11 a.m. with the changing of the tide.

Besides being the first day when the weather looked promising, July 8 was also the last day that the moon and tides would be sufficient for the planned landing that month. The Canadian officers in charge of the troops remained optimistic. They—and their men—also remained on the ships.

On the morning of July 7, at 6:15, a flight of four German aircraft spotted the armada at anchor. They attacked two of the largest ships, the infantry landing ships *Princess Astrid* and *Princess Josephine Charlotte,* striking both vessels. Though they did relatively little damage, the attack was the final straw for Mountbatten. He pulled the plug on the operation. Roberts, disappointed, disbanded his invasion force. The Rangers, still somewhat mystified about the whole business, were shipped back to Achnacarry to start the training they had missed.

A "REAL" INVASION

The plan for Rutter turned out to be a rough draft of the August 19, 1942, raid on Dieppe; the August raid was basically Rutter with a few tweaks. Recriminations, blame shifting, and propaganda after the failure of the August raid have led to confusion about its genesis and the reasons it was launched. Many commentators have treated the plan to attack Dieppe as a sop thrown to the Americans and Soviets by Churchill, in lieu of a "real" invasion. It's also occasionally been confused with plans—never more than vaguely outlined—for what would have been an "emergency" assault on the continent in the fall of 1942.

Neither the aborted Rutter raid nor the August 19 raid was intended to substitute for a larger invasion. The attack on the city was never anything but a large raid, part of a continuing series of raids designed to harry the Germans and boost morale. Documents from the time, including communications between the principals, clearly show this. As does common sense. Neither Roosevelt nor Soviet premier Joseph Stalin would confuse a force about a quarter the size of a division with the full Army Corps of six divisions that even a "sacrificial" invasion of the continent would require. Nor would the Germans, who even if Rutter had been successful would have been unlikely to shift large amounts of troops from the Eastern front because of it. There were ample forces near the Channel cities to deal with raids, even by much larger forces than the one gathered for Rutter.

GENESIS

Even before the Saint-Nazaire raid, Mountbatten and his staff had worked up plans for large raids, assaults that were clearly beyond what one or two Commando brigades could mount. One incredible plan—apparently real—called for a tank landing on the coast, followed by a race to Paris. More seriously, Combined Operations suggested an attack on Cherbourg, a prominent port in northern France that would one day figure into the D-Day plans.

Unlike Commando raids aimed at blowing up docks and seizing equipment at radar stations, seizing cities and ports seems like a tall order for a small force, even one as well trained as the Commandos. But the Commandos had already done so in Norway, taking the port of Vaagsö for a few hours in late December 1941.

The Norwegian government-in-exile hadn't been terribly impressed—the attack made things tougher for the civilians there—but there were several reasons for undertaking relatively large-scale raids on the French coast. The Royal Air Force believed that a large raid on the French coast would draw the Luftwaffe into a decisive battle, and proposed that Combined Operations plan one in the Calais or Boulogne area, where large numbers of RAF fighters could be scrambled. The Royal Navy, somewhat less enthusiastically, listed ports whose destruction would harm the Nazis. Last but not least,

Combined Operations believed the raids would provide experience in amphibious assaults, especially in operations that used landing craft and tanks.

Above all there was the morale factor; there was a certain "wow" factor involved in seizing and holding a city, even for a short period. News of a big enough attack would spread to the citizens of occupied Europe as well, reminding them that the war was not entirely over and that resistance, even in spirit, was not futile.

Today we're rather cynical about civilian morale and the propaganda that attempted to stoke it. But the power and appeal of these positive stories—which were based on real actions, however limited— can be clearly seen in the story of the Rangers' beginning. Alex Szima, Owen Sweazey, James Altieri, and all the others who signed up to be Rangers did so because the unit was going to emulate the Commandos. They knew the job would be dangerous and demanding, but they volunteered anyway. The men weren't masochists, and as Altieri's story among others makes clear, they weren't born killers either. The emotional appeal of fighting back, of doing something positive when the world seemed filled with negatives, was as powerful a motivator as the need to help one's friends turned out to be under fire.

Nor was that emotion limited to soldiers.

News of the American air raid on Tokyo in April was cheered by countless Americans when they heard or read about it. The point of that bombing raid, championed by Roosevelt, was not the minimal damage it inflicted but the fact that it had been launched. It gave the public a sense not just that America was fighting back but that the tide had been turned, a phrase used by the media that year in connection with several different operations.

The emotions of the public were important because World War II was a conflict that involved civilian populations to an immense degree. This was clear in Europe, where strategic bombing made people targets even when they were located well behind the front lines, and in the Pacific, where practically any island could be turned into a battlefield overnight. But it was just as true in America, even though no bomber reached the shores. American production was as vital to the war as the men who made use of it. So was the support of the families of the men who were on the front lines. An army of millions whose members felt alienated from their loved ones back home would have been impotent, especially against a well-motivated professional force like the German and Japanese Armies.

But if Commandos and their parent organization were playing a critical role in the psychological aspects of the war, their successes presented them with a problem. How does one "top" a raid like Saint-Nazaire, and continue to garner headlines and positive news? A march toward an enemy capital implies progress by its very nature; more territory is gained with each step, and the operation feels positive even if only a few miles are gained.

Raids on coastal radar stations and dry docks do not. There is a natural prejudice to think "bigger" as time goes on. A plan to land tanks on a Normandy beach and race them into Paris may seem fanciful now, but it was born from the same logic that made the incredible risks taken at Saint-Nazaire acceptable.

In the spring of 1942, that logic pushed Combined Operations and the British Command toward larger raids of more important targets on the coast. When the Chiefs of Staff rejected Cherbourg as a target, Mountbatten rethought the raid from the RAF and Navy's perspectives. Seven ports were nominated for attack, all within what the RAF considered its air umbrella south of Sussex. By the beginning of April, just before Marshall visited London, Mountbatten selected Dieppe as the target for a large raid to be launched in midsummer.

DIEPPE

While by some accounts Dieppe was the most important port on the French coast in the seventeenth century, by the nineteenth century deeper ports with more extensive infrastructure had left it behind. It became known primarily as seaside resort from the nineteenth century onward. The beaches nearby were painted by Impressionists and other painters, and Paris could be reached easily by train. A casino overlooked the beach, and for a while the city was considered a "poor man's Monte Carlo," a good spot for honeymoons and trysts.

The ferry from Newhaven made it popular with English as well as French tourists; snapshots taken by some of these tourists were later used to plan the 1942 assault.

Tourists could stroll along an esplanade that formed a broad boardwalk between the beach and the city; a sprawling casino sat at the western end of the esplanade, its tower jutting several stories above the seawall. Dieppe had a rocky beach, made up primarily of stones from one to six inches across, a kaleidoscope of white, gray, brown, and black stones rounded smooth by the action of the waves. The British called this "chert"; it was comparable to some of their Channel beaches, including Newhaven, which had a ferry link to Dieppe before the war.

A pair of long jetties on the east side of the city led ships into the city's inner harbor, sheltering them from the harsh winds. A rail line ran up the western jetty, closest to the main part of the city. A sheltered harbor with large mooring basins sat behind the seafront, separating the main part of the city from the highlands on the east.

Actual wartime populations are difficult to determine with certainty, but Dieppe's population just before the war was estimated at twenty-five thousand. The figure may have included some of the residents in the rural areas nearby.

In 1942, Dieppe was not an important military post. A handful of coastal patrol vessels seem to have either been based there or called regularly. A number of landing ships were either being stored or repaired in the harbor as well. But nothing larger than an armed trawler would be in the port when the raid was conducted later that August.

The British believed that the 110th Division defended the city; the division was known to have suffered heavy losses on the Eastern front and thought to be far short of its normal complement. In actual fact, Dieppe and the surrounding area were held by the 302nd Division; about four thousand men in two battalions of the division's 571st Regiment were spread out in the town and nearby Pourville. Some six thousand men and a tank company were held in reserve behind the coastline. The 10th Panzer Division—not discovered by the British until the troops were waiting to launch Rutter—was located at Amiens, a few hours away.

While Dieppe did not house a major German naval base, it had a series of coordinated defenses designed to prevent an enemy from getting an easy foothold on the beach. The defenses started on the beach, where two long rows of concertina barbed wire—long loops stretched to form a kind of wall—would slow down an invader. On at least part of the beach, a wide trench had been started as a tank trap. There were no buildings for about three-fourths of the mile-long beachfront, starting from the breakwater at the harbor entrance on the west and running to the Casino, a large complex that sat on the esplanade and extended most of its length back to the seaside's main street, Boulevard de Verdun. (The Casino, no longer being used, was scheduled for destruction to make defense of the city easier.) To the west of the Casino—its right, when looking at it from the sea—there was a very small number of buildings close to the beachfront. There were gun posts or sniper positions in the Casino and these buildings. A pillbox sat on the beach in front of the Casino. Above on the esplanade was the turret of a French tank, turned into another defensive position. There were a number of other dug-out positions on the beach and on the esplanade for machine gunners and snipers.

A castle built in the fifteenth century sat on the cliff at the immediate west side of the city. Gun positions studded the grounds of the castle and the area to the west; similar defenses were sited on the highlands to the east, across the harbor. Scattered in the various defensive positions were weapons ranging from machine guns— either the MG34 "Spandau" or the recently introduced MG42—to dual-purpose 37mm cannons, at least some of which had come from Czechoslovakia earlier in the war. Three-man crews manned medium mortars—the 8cm *schwere Granaatwerfer*—that had been preregistered (set for targets ahead of time) on the beaches and other defensive perimeters. Larger guns, including captured French 75mm field weapons and 155mm coastal defense weapons, were trained on the seafront and the waters nearby.

As impressive as the list of weapons may seem, Dieppe appears to have been chosen as a target at least partly because the defenders and the defenses were considered relatively weak. The choice was not reevaluated as additional intelligence became available, and even if there had been an opportunity to do so, the intelligence continued to be wrong. The error regarding the division manning the defenses wouldn't be corrected until after the August raid. The troops manning the defenses were not just undercounted; they were considered inferior because a large number were Poles who had volunteered to join the German Army after their country was overrun.

The British did have good aerial reconnaissance of the city, and were able to map all of the defenses. They seem, however, to have missed the fact that the caves in the cliff to the west of Dieppe were outfitted as strongpoints.

As conceived by Combined Operations, the plan called for assaults at four spots on Dieppe's flanks: Berneval, Puys on the east, and Pourville and Varengeville on the west. Paratroopers would land behind the city as the assault troops landed; all of the forces would then meet at Dieppe. The Navy would bombard the defenses while the RAF would hold a shoot-out with the Luftwaffe. The troops would then leave through the pacified city.

Berneval lies about seven miles east of Dieppe; Pourville is roughly five miles west of the city, so the entire beachhead would be spread over twelve miles. The area is among the closest to England, no more than sixty-five miles away at the nearest points.

Once the target was chosen and a skeleton plan drawn up, the operation was given a code name and presented to the Combined Command. The code name, "Rutter," came from a preapproved list, and was selected arbitrarily so it could not give away its objective if leaked. *Rutter* was an archaic word used for German horse soldiers in the fifteenth and sixteenth centuries. According to the *Oxford English Dictionary,* it was once used to refer to swindlers as well.

THE CANADIANS

While Combined Operations had advanced the plan, the size of the raid and one of its aims—to give regular forces amphibious training—meant that the bulk of the assault would have to be made by regular troops. The assignment was handed to the British Army Corps in southern England, the South-Eastern Command headed by Sir Bernard Law, First Viscount Montgomery of Alamein, better known as Lieutenant General Montgomery.

By the end of the war, Montgomery would be a towering figure, the most famous English general in the European theater. He was not quite a titan in 1942, but he was still a formidable figure. He had proven himself in combat during World War I, personally taking a German prisoner in hand-to-hand combat and surviving a bullet wound. Awarded the Distinguished Service Order, he rose from a platoon commander to the divisional Chief of Staff. General Montgomery started the Second World War commanding the British 3rd Division; during the withdrawal to Dunkirk he was appointed head of the 2nd Corps, and oversaw its evacuation to England. Montgomery was a forceful personality, oriented toward offense rather than defense. He was also what might be called a positive thinker, upbeat and confident in a crisis.

In 1942, he was heading the South-Eastern Army, which included forces in Kent, Surrey, and Sussex. Among the units under his command was the Canadian 2nd Division. The Canadians had been in England since December 1940. After the initial excitement of their deployment and the direct threat of a German invasion wore off, the unit had developed a variety of discipline problems. A large number of the division's soldiers were involved in disturbances and petty crimes. From the Canadian point of view, the problem was that there was nothing for the men to do. The government considered withdrawing them from Great Britain and putting them elsewhere; it might have done so had there been a realistic place for them to fight.

During the winter of 1941–42, Hamilton Roberts took over command and shook up the division, replacing older officers with others deemed more aggressive. He stepped up training and increased maneuvers. Even so, the standards were hardly those observed by the Commandos; units were expected to march twenty miles in a week, about what the Commandos expected in a single outing.

Roberts's boss, meanwhile, 1st Canadian Army Corps commander Lieutenant General H.D.G. Crerar, and Crerar's boss, Canadian Army general A.G.L. McNaughton, had been lobbying Montgomery and other British leaders for a real role in the war. Given the Rutter plan and asked to find men, Montgomery went to Crerar and asked if the Canadians wanted to be involved in Rutter. The general immediately accepted.

BIG MISTAKES

Entire books have been written about the political and military conflicts during the planning for the raid. The Rangers were involved in
neither, and dissecting the convoluted process that resulted in the
plan of attack is beyond the scope of this book. Nonetheless, two
very large flaws in the planning were so critical that it's impossible to
talk about Dieppe without mentioning them.

The first was the failure to provide heavy bombardment of the
shore defenses, which included powerful guns on the seafront and the
town's flanks, along with concrete pillboxes, reinforced machine-gun
nests, and mobile artillery. This was not because Combined Operations underestimated the defenses. On the contrary, one of the lessons
that had been drawn from the raid on Saint-Nazaire was that heavy
bombardment of shore defenses was necessary. When Rutter was still
being sketched, Combined Operations called for raids by 150 high-
level bombers, four squadrons of low-level bombers, and heavy naval
bombardment by capital ships.

As the plan evolved, Mountbatten asked for bombardment by at
least one battleship. The Navy refused. Battleships and cruisers were
considered too precious to risk in the English Channel, where they
were easy targets for Nazi bombers. The Japanese had destroyed the
battleship *Prince of Wales* and the battle cruiser *Repulse* by air attack
only a short time before, and Admiral of the Fleet Dudley Pound is said
to have turned down Mountbatten's request with the remark, "Battleships by daylight off the French coast? You must be mad, Dickie."

In the end, the Navy assigned a total of eight *Hunt*-class destroyers
(one was Polish) to escort the invasion fleet and handle bombardment duties. Though called destroyers, the ships were more accurately described as light destroyer escorts; they were slightly bigger
than corvettes but smaller than frigates used by Great Britain during
the war. Each ship had either four or six four-inch guns, capable of

firing a thirty-five-pound high-explosive shell about 19,850 yards or a bit over eleven miles. Not considered particularly accurate, the guns were smaller than the two main shore batteries flanking Dieppe. Devastating against the thin metal hulls of small ships and boats they'd been designed to fight, the guns were next to useless against concrete pillboxes.

After the refusal of the Navy to supply capital ships, Combined Operations sought to fill the gap with bombardment from Royal Air Force heavy bombers. Large-scale bombing of the town would have caused civilian casualties and was against official British policy, but the Chiefs of Staff recommended it be done in this case. Churchill granted permission on June 1—but permission was quickly withdrawn. Why the prime minister changed his mind has never been satisfactorily explained. Assuming he changed his mind—one theory is that he never gave permission in the first place—it may have had to do with Bomber Command priorities, since the RAF was mounting large raids against strategic targets at the time. In any event, the removal of the heavy bombers from Rutter took away any possibility that the worst of the defenses would be neutralized before the troops came ashore.

The RAF did offer a much smaller attack to take place shortly before the assault. But when the plans were reviewed by the Canadian commanders at a meeting June 5, General Roberts worried that the bombing would be too light to be effective, would warn the defenders, and end up clogging the streets of Dieppe, making it impossible for his tanks to advance. His decision effectively settled the matter.

Given the nature of high-level bombing at the time, Roberts's view was not controversial. Air attacks in World War II were far from accurate. Striking a field-gun-size target was difficult if not impossible, especially at night, which was when RAF heavy bombers operated at this point in the war. The bombing that preceded the Saint-Nazaire attack had complicated the assault, and some military planners believed it had done more harm than good there.

Bomber Command also turned down a request to dedicate fifty and then twelve Sterling bombers to be called in for support during the raid itself. The excuse: the planes could not be spared from other bombing missions and would be easy targets for the Luftwaffe while waiting to be assigned targets during the attack.

The RAF did agree to supply close-air support with fighters and light bombers. Such attacks were generally more accurate than high-level bombing, but the weapons used were relatively small. The Sub-marine Spitfire carried two 20mm cannons and four lighter machine guns—excellent weapons against the fuselage of another aircraft, but unable to penetrate the thick concrete surrounding a pillbox. The Spitfire could also carry as much as a thousand pounds of bombs—a single 500-pound bomb under the centerline and a pair of 250-pounders under the wings. Depending on the model, the Hawker Hurricane could carry two 250-pound bombs or 500-pound bombs. The bombs could be devastating if they landed precisely on a target, but without a direct hit most hardened targets would not be damaged.

The Boston Bomber—the American-built Douglas A-20—which also flew over Dieppe, was a twin-engined light bomber that could carry two thousand pounds of bombs in its belly and had four .303-caliber machine guns in its nose. The Boston's weapons had the same limitations as those carried by the fighters.

The RAF did plan to put a lot of planes into the air—close to a thousand, in fact. But most were intended to be used against Luft-waffe bombers and fighters when they arrived to repulse the invasion.

HEAD-ON

The decision not to soften up the defenses before the invasion would have been bad enough had the original pincer plan been adopted, but at least in that case the worst of the defenses would be attacked from the flanks, where presumably they would be most vulnerable. Instead, the plan adopted for Rutter called for a head-on attack on the Dieppe seafront, into the very teeth of the defenses.

According to historians, the decision to attack Dieppe head-on was made by Montgomery when he was first presented with the Rutter plan. One of the plan's most important facets was the landing of tanks, which in the plan would have come in at Pourville and encircled the city. Montgomery argued that there was not enough time to make a flank attack on the town before withdrawal, and by some accounts also contended that intelligence showed it wouldn't be necessary. Once Montgomery had decreed that the attack should be made head-on, no one—most especially Ham Roberts, who was the ground-force commander—seriously opposed the idea.

Launching an amphibious assault onto a heavily defended beach whose defenses had not been softened up was insane. It's easy to make that statement in hindsight, of course, but there is little question that the Combined Operations and Canadian planners responsible for Rutter's details should have made it as well. Historians often cite the only major amphibious operation of World War I, the protracted campaign to take Gallipoli from the Turks in 1915, as an operation the planners should have studied, but the Canadian Army commanders in charge of the land forces didn't have to look that far back. They had just spent the past two years defending an area in southern England with very similar beaches, cliffs, and towns. Their plans for defense had taken advantage of the geography, well-protected positions, and a superior network of supplies and reinforcement. Yet the plans the Canadians prepared for the assault assumed the Germans wouldn't be able to do the same thing.

Canadian forces held two large-scale rehearsals for Rutter, landing on beaches in southern England. Neither went very well, though the second went well enough for Mountbatten to approve the operation.

On July 3, "Simmerforce"—with its small contingent of American Ranger observers—gathered off the shores of the Isle of Wight and nearby England. While the long hours of waiting for the boats and ships to get under way gradually drained their enthusiasm, there was still a great deal of disappointment when the operation was finally canceled July 8. The men were sent back to their bases in Sussex, and the invasion plans were permanently shelved.

Except that permanent turned out to mean a week.

DISAPPOINTMENT

Lucian Truscott had been invited to observe the Rutter operation, and spent several days waiting with the troops on the Isle of Wight before it was called off. Now a brigadier general, Truscott had not been involved in the Rutter planning but did witness some of the bitterness at Combined Operations that followed the raid's cancellation. There was an overall feeling of tension at headquarters when he got back to London.

Part of this was just the normal letdown that comes in the wake of a canceled plan. But there was also a feeling that Combined Operations wasn't up to the torrid pace it had hoped to set just a few months earlier when Mountbatten projected a major raid every two weeks. Fourteen raids reached serious planning stages in the time Truscott was at Combined Operations Headquarters; nine were dropped either because of shortages in landing craft or they were deemed too dangerous to undertake. Ten other plans had been "discussed" but then shelved for similar reasons. Except for Rutter, all of the workable plans were small affairs. The last raid of any size had been Abercrombie, launched against the French village of Hardelot in late April. A force of a hundred and fifty men—including fifty Canadians, who never landed—had landed, intending to knock out a searchlight and conduct a reconnaissance. Even these modest aims weren't met: the force had just reached the searchlight perimeter when a premature signal sent them back to their landing craft.

General Marshall had told Truscott to expect a gradual increase in raids, with the assaults getting larger and larger. The cancellation of Rutter put the momentum in the opposite direction. Even the highest-ranking members of Combined Operations questioned whether the organization was doing something wrong. Captain Hughes-Hallett, the naval adviser and one of the key planners, declared that Rutter's cancellation meant either that the force commanders were weak, or that Combined Operations simply couldn't come up with a workable plan. Outside the organization, criticism was even worse. The naval commander of the British Expeditionary Forces suggested that Commando attacks and similar raids be suspended entirely. While they might be giving the British experience in mounting amphibious assaults, he argued, they were also showing Germans where their weaknesses were. In both the long and short run, suspending the raids would save more lives.

The disappointment and disillusionment were magnified by bad news on other battlefronts. The Germans were continuing to advance in Africa and Russia; the Japanese were moving through Burma. Disgusted with the progress in the war, the British Parliament roundly criticized Prime Minister Churchill. Reverses in Egypt led to debate and then a parliamentary crisis; in early July, Churchill survived a vote of censure. The tally was far in his favor—475 to 25—but the political scene remained difficult.

ROOSEVELT'S ORDERS

It was against this background that President Roosevelt sent Marshall, Hopkins, and head of the Navy Admiral Ernest J. King back to England for a last-ditch attempt to win support for a landing in Europe in 1942. For a while Churchill had thought the matter decided, neither the U.S. President nor his advisers had entirely given up hope.

Both Mountbatten and Churchill had been to America in June adamantly making the case that no invasion could be held in 1942—and, preferably, not even in 1943. The Americans, however, saw a return to the continent as imperative. Roosevelt felt that without massive relief, the Soviet Union was going to lose the war and bow out soon, which would allow the Germans to concentrate once again on Great Britain. Dated July 16, 1942, the President's orders to Hopkins, Marshall, and King said that a 1942 invasion—at the time code-named Sledgehammer—would "sustain Russia this year" and "might be the turning point which would save Russia."

But even as he signed the orders, Roosevelt realized that it was unlikely that the British would support the invasion plan. What he seems to have really wanted was a fight, somewhere, someplace, that would commit U.S. troops to action and change the momentum of the war. Earlier in the year, he had agreed with Churchill that American troops would fight in northern Africa, and these orders implied a follow-up to that earlier commitment.

"If Sledgehammer is finally and definitely out of the picture, I want you to consider the world situation as it exists at that time," he told his advisers, "and determine upon another place for U.S. troops to fight in 1942."

How much of this came from Roosevelt, and how much from his advisers is difficult to determine, but the order did reflect his earlier decisions and his desire to make America focus on defeating Germany before Japan; even after Pearl Harbor, he saw the Nazis as far more dangerous. Roosevelt also wanted to make sure that the American public's support for its troops and the war in Europe was not eroded by a long period of inactivity.

Truscott met with Marshall immediately after he arrived in London July 18, spending the afternoon and evening briefing him on the British attitudes toward a large-scale invasion as well as the planning that was taking place. Truscott detailed the debates on the Combined

Operations staff about assaults on France, focusing on the conflicts between younger staff members who believed it would be possible to take and hold the Cherbourg peninsula that November, and the more senior staff members who dismissed the plan.

Though Marshall, King, and Hopkins pressed Churchill and the British Chiefs of Staff, it was quickly evident that the Allies would not willingly go along with a France invasion in 1942, and that plan was put politely and finally on the back burner. All that remained was a thirty-five-page feasibility study dubbed by the British "Wet Bob" for an attack that would be launched essentially as a desperation move if the Soviet Union teetered on collapse. Intentional or not, the code name amply indicates what the British military commanders thought of it.

Instead of France, the Americans were to join with the British in a large seaborne attack on northern Africa in the fall. The operation would eventually be dubbed Torch; launched November 8 and coming on the heels of a British push against Rommel, the invasion would help clear Africa of German troops and set the stage for the invasion of Italy.

But in the summer of 1942, success was far from guaranteed, and the decision had serious implications for the Soviet Union, for it was unlikely to draw many German troops from the Eastern front. Churchill planned a journey to meet with Stalin at the beginning of August, essentially to break the news that an invasion of France would not take place. In its place, Churchill would emphasize not only the African assault but the large bombing campaign against Germany already promised.

The push for a "second front"—generally taken as shorthand for a land invasion of France—did not simply come from Stalin. A steady stream of stories in the newspapers and on the radio throughout 1942 proclaimed its need, predicted it was coming, and theorized when it would begin. An uptick in the stories and rumors had been partly fueled that spring by Roosevelt and other American leaders who, responding to Stalin's pleas, had promised that a second front would be opened soon. But the idea itself dated to 1941, when Germany invaded the Soviet Union. The "buzz" was strong enough that German forces initially believed that Saint-Nazaire was a "real" invasion, and there were countless false alarms that year.

If news stories can be read as an indication of public sentiment, expressing the spirit of the times, then there was a real hunger for a second front, or at least some major shift in momentum. An invasion of France was simply not feasible militarily, but this was not mentioned to the public. Doing so would have, in effect, told Germany that it didn't have to worry about its coastal defenses and would have only increased the pressure on the Soviet Union. But it would have been a psychological failure as well, and quite likely would have led to political turmoil at an already difficult time. The politicians judged that the public could not face the absolute truth about the war: victory was not in sight, and it would be a long slog before it was.

JUBILEE

It was in this highly charged political atmosphere that the decision to relaunch the raid on Dieppe was made.

Only a few days after the Canadian soldiers had left their boats, Mountbatten, members of his staff, and Ham Roberts, the 2nd Division Canadian leader, were talking about ways of reviving the mission. The need for a large-scale raid was not questioned, nor was the basic premise of using the Canadian force, which had after all spent several weeks rehearsing. The logic ran like this:

- A large-scale raid was necessary and desirable.

- It should be mounted soon, so that if an "emergency" invasion of France later that year (Sledgehammer or Wet Bob, depending on when the argument was made) became necessary, experience would be gained in time.

- The Canadians were already trained and thus "deserved" the chance to execute the raid.

- Detailed plans for striking Dieppe had already been drawn up, saving considerable preparation time.

- Dieppe was still a good target to hit; nothing had changed there to make it less desirable.

The commanders were aware that their decision to strike at the same target represented a security risk. Not only had many of the men in the 2nd Division spent several days on leave, but a news story had been authorized stating that the Canadians had been training on the Isle of Wight for a large-scale raid. Canadian general Ham Roberts nonetheless told the Combined Operations staff that he thought the problem wasn't severe and was ready "to get cracking as soon as possible."

Others—including the brigadier generals who commanded his infantry regiments and the tanks that would be involved in the attack—thought otherwise. Generals William Southam, Sherwood Lett, and Johnny Andres wouldn't learn of the decision until August 1, but when they did they were flabbergasted. Roberts assured them that tactical surprise could still be achieved. General Lett had apparently reassessed the operation following its cancellation and decided that, without heavy bombardment of the defenses, the operation would fail. He and the others protested the lack of bombing strongly. But Roberts insisted that surprise would neutralize the defenses as effectively as bombing.

Montgomery told his boss, Home Forces commander General Sir Bernard Paget, that Rutter "should be off for all time." In his memoirs, Montgomery isn't explicit about why he thought this; from the context he makes it seem as if his concerns were with security, though when he reviews the actual operation a few paragraphs later, he criticizes both the lack of bombing and the fact that too many people were involved in the planning. Ironically or not, he had presided over the meeting when the lack of bombing before Rutter was acceded to; if he protested, it was never noted in the description or record of the meeting. The problem of having too many people responsible for the planning and execution—a critique that historians echo—could be made of many operations, successful as well as disastrous. Montgomery never mentions the decision to stage a frontal assault, and his comments look quite a bit like an attempt to duck any responsibility for the raid.

But the decision wasn't Montgomery's; he had already been tapped to command the 8th Army in Africa. The responsibility for the operation fell jointly to Combined Operations and the Canadians, both of whom were eager to launch it.

For all of Roberts's talk about the value of tactical surprise, he, too, appears to have been concerned with softening the defenses, since he kept pressing for it in the high-level planning sessions that followed. Security became the main focus of criticism; these concerns about security were dealt with by deciding not to concentrate the invading force until the very last minute. The Germans, the commanders believed, might know the Allies were up to something but wouldn't know what it was. And though the words never appear in an official report, it's possible the planners thought the Germans would never believe the Allies would be so audacious as to launch an operation that had already been scratched.

Or so stupid, depending on the point of view.

CONTROVERSY

The decision to remount the Dieppe raid as Jubilee has been a source of controversy ever since the afternoon of August 19, 1942, when word first filtered back to England that the raid had been a disaster.

Questions remain over who precisely was responsible for restarting the operation, and historians have failed to untangle the knot to unanimous satisfaction. The official Canadian military histories quote from Ham Roberts's notes that make it seem as if much higher authorities—he calls them "the Government"—decided that a raid had to be launched very soon and that Dieppe was the only possibility, since it had already been planned for. At the same time, the histories do not indicate that Roberts objected or felt he was going against his own better judgment.

Historian Terence Robertson, whose *The Shame and Glory* has been seen as the definitive work on the raid by a Canadian historian since its publication in 1962, sees the decision as the work of several people, including Ham Roberts and Leigh-Mallory, the naval adviser on the Combined Operations staff. At the same time, the Canadian force commanders over Roberts had pushed to take responsibility for the mission earlier, in effect removing Montgomery and his successors from the picture. This is the majority view, though it begs further explanation, such as what role, if any, Churchill actually played, and why Montgomery's objections—assuming he made them—did not carry greater weight. It also leaves unanswered the question of how much public opinion, and especially the desire for a second front, may have played in the decision.

Some historians, including Robertson, have emphasized the behind-the-scenes clamor for a second front by Roosevelt and Stalin, to a greater or lesser degree claiming that Dieppe was either a substitute, a consolation prize, or a feint that had to be launched because of the decision not to invade France. Denis Whitaker, a Canadian general turned historian who had been a captain and landed at Dieppe, essentially blames American public opinion and political pressure for the decision in *Dieppe: Tragedy to Triumph*. He believes Montgomery tried to stop the revived assault because of the German panzer division, and was eased out of the chain of command over it before his appointment to head the Eighth Army because of his objections. By this theory, Churchill was ultimately behind the decision because he needed the raid to take place to pacify the Americans and Soviets. Author Brian Loring Villa lays out a case in *Unauthorized Action* that Mountbatten was the real driving force for the revival, claiming that he circumvented the Chiefs of Staff to do so. To some extent, all of these arguments simultaneously touch on some truths while wrestling others out of context. Now, some sixty-five years after the decision was made, it's impossible to plot precisely the steps that led to the plan's revival. Whatever the machinations were, however, by the end of July, a new plan had been adopted for a raid on Dieppe.

Renamed "Jubilee," the plan was largely based on Rutter, though there was one notable change: the paratroopers, whose need for near perfect weather had helped scuttle the mission, were deleted. In their place, two groups of Commandos were assigned to make assaults on the shore guns.

That change would make all the difference for the Rangers.

Pine Island, New York
Spring 2006

■ ■ ■

After months trying different methods of tracking down American survivors of the Dieppe Raid, my wife and I have finally managed to locate two men. Both are well into their eighties. I've known this would be the case, of course, yet it still comes almost as a shock when I read a letter from Lester Kness detailing his part in the battle. Though chosen for the raid, Mr. Kness spent his time aboard one of the support vessels and never got a chance to go ashore.

"Not much," he sums up. "But I got credit for being there. I have shook with fright many times but that was the worst.

"Now I am old and really don't want to write these stories," he added. "I have told them many times but now I am too tired."

For the first time, I realize that there's another perspective to the questions I've been asking. Idealistically, I've assumed that because I want to know about the past, others will be glad to talk about it. But the past isn't some objective reality far removed for the survivors of Dieppe—or for anyone who has lived with the past. It's not simply a thing to study for what it might say about the present or future; it's a real thing, painful perhaps, stressful, in any event personal.

Do I really have the right to stir up old memories—to bother people in the name of history?

I ponder the question; months later, walking the beach at Dieppe, I still haven't found an answer.

FOUR

ANTICIPATION

Scotland
August 1942

* * *

ESCAPE

As the first phase of Ranger training wound down, Szima found himself worrying that Darby had forgotten all about his promise that the job as first sergeant of the headquarters company—and acting sergeant major—would only be temporary. A replacement had turned up, and Szima had done everything he could to help the man. But Darby hadn't given him another assignment, and the onetime Dayton bartender feared there was a typewriter in his future.

The special assignment of Rangers for demolition training didn't strike Szima as particularly odd; everyone, after all, was going on for extra training. But when he realized that one of the men chosen had the flu, he saw it as an opportunity to escape. Szima made his pitch to the new sergeant major and then to Darby, arguing yet again that the life of a first sergeant was not for him. Darby at first dismissed him, but in the morning, when the others were getting ready to leave, asked Szima how long it would take to pack his bags. The sergeant said that they'd been packed ever since he arrived, and soon found himself on his way to southern England.

Led by Staff Sergeant Kenneth D. Stempson, Szima, Corporal William Brady, and Corporal Franklin "Zip" Koons were told to report to a Lieutenant Colonel Lord Lovat. Their orders included a provision for food-and-board money—$2.50 a man per day for food, and $1.50 for board—but no hint of what they were going to be doing. The orders didn't even mention the name of Lovat's military unit: Number 4 Commando.

LORD LOVAT

By the time Szima and the others joined Number 4 Commando, the unit had a string of missions under its belt. Established in July 1940, the Commando included a number of men who had volunteered for action in the Spanish Civil War. The brigade had participated in the 1941 raid on the Lofoton Islands in Norway, dubbed Claymore. During those raids, a Royal Navy boarding party captured a German Enigma encryption machine, along with the current encryption settings. More recently, a hundred men from Number 4 Commando had landed at Boulogne on April 22, 1942, in Abercrombie.

Leading Number 4 Commando was a thirtysomething Scottish lord, chief of Clan Fraser of Lovat, Simon Fraser. Known as Lord Lovat—or more popularly to his men and acquaintances, Shimi—Lovat was a tall, athletic officer with Hollywood looks and a friendly nature—except when it came to battle. His nickname came from his title in Gaelic, *Mac Shimdh,* or Son of Simon, meaning Simon Fraser, the founder of the clan. He wore a cropped brush of a mustache and cocked his green Commando beret at a slight angle. Sporting rifle slung over his right shoulder and his pistol holster prominent on his hip, he cut a jaunty figure in the field.

Besides his aristocratic title, Lovat had inherited his ancestors' flair for leadership. Though demanding, he was well liked by his men, with a knack for encouraging his men to speak freely and doing the same. Like the other Commando leaders, he believed in leading from the front; photos taken during the war show him outstriding columns of his men. Lovat impressed the Americans as a larger-than-life character, an upper-class British semi-eccentric filled with the sort of derring-do that would make James Bond blush. Szima, who tended to view even his close friends with a discerning and critical eye, practically gushed when recalling Lovat years later. Lovat was a *true* Commando, a "hard-muscle filled-actioned Commando leader."

While he took his orders from them, Lovat held a somewhat jaundiced view of Mountbatten and Combined Operations in general. He viewed many of the staff as refugees from their original services and thought of others as "powder puffs" who would "look good in silk stockings."

When Lovat was briefed on the mission at the end of July, he was not told the name of the city that was to be attacked. After figuring it out from the description and a postcard he saw during the briefing, he told the Combined Operations Chief of Staff General Charles Hayden that he thought a daylight attack on Dieppe was foolish. The general thanked him for his opinion and dismissed him.

COMMANDO 4'S OBJECTIVE

Dubbed "Operation Cauldron," Number 4 Commando was handed a mission intended to be undertaken by paratroopers in Rutter. The Commando would attack and destroy a battery of six large guns about four nautical miles west of Dieppe near Varengeville-sur-Mer. Dubbed "Hess"—it was code-named by the British after the German deputy führer Rudolf Hess, who'd flown to Scotland and been interned the year before—the battery sat about three-quarters of a mile from the edge of chalky cliffs that overlooked the rocky beach.

The Germans used a number of guns as shore defenses during the war. In this case, the guns—variously described in the plans and official histories as 5.9 and 6 inches—were French 15.5 Kanone 418 (f), 155mm (or 15.5cm) weapons with a range of roughly 24,000 yards. They were trained on the sea in front of Dieppe, 8,600 yards away. Topped with camouflage netting, the heavy guns and their crews sat behind a concrete-and-sandbag berm but were otherwise open to the air. An antiaircraft gun and an observation tower were immediately behind the battery; the barbed-wire defensive perimeter included machine-gun emplacements.

The battery area was to the southeast of a lighthouse, which sat above the cliffs of Cap d'Ailly. This was a rural, wooded area of apple orchards and private yards. Varengeville was a small village, with even smaller hamlets scattered nearby. To the west, or right when looking from the water, sat the village of Sainte-Marguerite-sur-Mer near the mouth of the Saâne River.

Running from east to west, the cliffs ranged from two hundred feet to barely forty or fifty near Sainte-Marguerite. There were two prominent ravines that ran all the way to the beach near Vasterival, the hamlet overlooking the water between Varengeville and Cap d'Ailly; one had cement steps, though these had been blocked off by barbed wire.

Lovat's plan of attack called for two groups of Commandos to land ashore at different points near Vasterival and Quiberville—dubbed Orange Beach 1 and Orange Beach 2. The force at Orange Beach 1 would land close to the lighthouse and use one of the ravines to climb the cliff and attack the battery from the front, engaging it with small-arms fire and mortars. Meanwhile, the group landing at Orange Beach 2 near Sainte-Marguerite-sur-Mer and the river would

sweep up and around from the west. This group, led by Lovat himself, would attack from behind the battery while the defenses were
occupied by the other force.

With his plan set, Lovat put his unit to work conducting mock
raids that simulated the plan. He planned no fewer than eight landings under conditions that would duplicate their actual objectives;
these would be followed by a week's worth of drills in specific areas
such as marksmanship before the raid was launched. The British
commander liked to train his men like a football team, getting them
into the proper shape so that they peaked just at the right moment.

"GLAD TO HAVE YOU ABOARD"

Stempson, Szima, Brady, and Koons arrived in Portland on August 2
and were directed to the *Prince Albert,* a Belgian ship being used as
an infantry assault ship. The Americans had been given firm instructions not just to present themselves to Lord Lovat, but to use the term
lord when addressing him. Szima, anxious to make a good impression, had spent at least an hour in the WC on the train down,
rehearsing his speech.

Szima had also been warned by some of the British sergeants at
the Achnacarry sergeant major's mess to watch out for Lovat's number two man, Major Derick Mills-Roberts. The major had a reputation as a fire-eater and stickler for discipline, or so the Brits said. But
what they hadn't told Szima was that the Commandos typically
removed their rank insignia from their uniforms when in combat or
practicing for it. So when the Americans boarded the ship and spotted a beefy, gruff-looking man, they thought he was just another
Commando, and addressed him as they would any other grunt, with
the 1940s equivalent of "Yo, where's the lord at?"

Amused, the man directed them to Lovat's cabin. Their guide
turned out to be Mills-Roberts, who'd either "lost his horns," as

Szima put it later, or was actually much more easygoing than his reputation made out.

As for Lovat: Szima barely got the word *lord* out of his mouth before the lieutenant colonel jumped from his desk and pumped his hand.

"Glad to have you aboard," said the Commando leader. He waved away the men's attempts to produce their orders and sent them to find quarters. From that moment on, they were part of the team.

The *Prince Albert* (or *Prins Albert*) had been launched in 1937 as a three-thousand-ton ferry, plying the English Channel. A Belgian craft, she was taken over by the Royal Navy after the German Army rolled through the lowlands en route to France. Converted to an assault ship, at her heart the 330-foot-long vessel was still a civilian craft, and retained her original cabins, albeit without elaborate decor. She'd been equipped with cannon and carried six small landing craft on the davits at her sides. Even with these boats and the guns, she looked like a small ocean liner to the American eyes.

The landing craft were Assault Landing Craft or ALCs, a designation later changed to LCAs. They were roughly thirty-five feet long, with a nine-foot beam. The LCAs were plated with armor and mounted machine guns for close support near the beaches or as anti-aircraft weapons. Crewed by three sailors and an officer, in theory they could hold thirty-five men but more often were limited to about twenty-four Commandos. A ramp at the bow allowed for quicker exits when landing. The craft drew just over a foot and a half when fully loaded, allowing them to get very close to a beach. They could do about ten knots.

The first two nights after they arrived, Szima and the others practiced clambering into the boats in the dark. Once they had that mastered, the Rangers and Commandos rehearsed landings, finding their way to the rocky English shores in daylight and at night. The shores were covered with barbed wire, mines, and tank obstacles against a possible German invasion; local guides were needed to show them ashore and through the obstructions. The exercises mimicked their eventual goal, though they had not yet been told that they were doing anything more than general training. In a typical drill, the Rangers and Commandos would cross about forty yards of beach, advancing as the lead team took out a simulated pillbox. They would then climb the cliff, often with the help of portable ladders, carried in five-foot sections. Moving through woods at the top, they would march to a mock battery, where they would make their attack. Two- and three-inch mortars were used for support during the exercises.

The Number 4 Commando section formation typically had a leading scout carrying a Thompson submachine gun and wire cutters at its head. Twenty-five yards behind him would be the second scout, armed with his rifle. The main body, ideally separated by another twenty-five yards, would be headed by the platoon's lieutenant or platoon sergeant, followed by a "batman" or assistant with a submachine gun. Then came the section leader—ordinarily a sergeant—who had wire cutters as well as his rifle. Half a dozen riflemen would fill out the body of the group. The Bren gunner, walking behind his assistant, and the corporal or platoon second would take up the rear. The Bren gunner would have at least 250 rounds for his light machine gun with him; everyone else in the section carried a clip or more of Bren ammo for use either when he ran out or went down. Besides their own ammunition and six grenades, the men carried a mortar round apiece.

The two-inch mortars were simple weapons; the flight of the small bombs was changed by adjusting the angle of the tube. It was not particularly easy to aim the weapons, but Lovat's best two-man team could put nine of ten shots into their target at 250 yards. Besides firing a heavier projectile, the three-inch weapon was more accurate and had a longer range; Lovat had a team that could hit targets at 600 yards. A forward spotter would send corrections over a field telephone to the mortar crew, which adjusted accordingly. Each company also had one Boys antitank weapon, a large bolt-action rifle that fired .55-inch rounds. Closer in concept to a powerful sniper rifle than to the later bazooka, the Boys could fire a round through the plates of light tanks and armored vehicles. In 4 Commando, two men would be teamed to use the weapon, allowing for a replacement if the first gunner was killed.

The Rangers and Commandos spent eight nights practicing the assaults. On the last exercises, live fire and mock casualties were added, increasing the stress and emphasizing the need for flexibility. The Rangers had to help carry "wounded" in stretchers to the boats as smoke wafted in the air and gunfire erupted nearby. Toughened by their stint at Achnacarry, Szima and the other Americans nonetheless had to work hard to keep up.

The training here had a different pace than at Achnacarry; the exercises were more specific, repeating the same problems over and over again. The location, too, made it clear that something was coming up. Though they hadn't yet been told where they were going, it was obvious to the Americans that they were going to get a chance to draw blood, and very soon.

WITH NUMBER 3 COMMANDO

At Seaford, a hundred and thirty or so miles to the east, Sergeant Kness, Private Sweazey, and thirty-eight other Rangers were going through very similar training. Led by Captain Murray, a Reserve Army officer who had become one of the key battalion commanders, the Ranger contingent had been divvied up among Number 3 Commando and begun practicing assaults across beaches and up cliffs at the Isle of Wight.

Commanded by Lieutenant Colonel John Durnford-Slater, Number 3 Commando had seen action in Norway and loaned demolition experts for the raid at Saint-Nazaire. While not as flamboyant as

Lovat, Durnford Slater was also an experienced and accomplished leader who had led the raid against Vaagsö Island, Norway, the first against an armed harbor. During the assault, Durnford-Slater had emptied his revolver at a sniper who was holding down his men's advance and narrowly missed getting killed by a grenade.

Durnford-Slater and his Commandos were assigned to strike a four-gun battery at Berneval similar to the battery at Varengeville. His plan would also split his group roughly in two, landing at beaches roughly a mile and a half apart. Each group would move up separate fissures in the cliffs and meet at the battery, dubbed Goebbels after the German propaganda minister, Joseph Goebbels.

The Rangers were split across the Commando. Besides Captain Murray, the officers included Lieutenants Charles Shunstrum, Leonard Dirks, and Edwin Loustalot. Loustalot, who'd impressed the Commando trainers at Achnacarry with his high standards, continued to practice them here. Assigned to Number 6 Troop, he pushed both Brits and Yanks through the drills like the more experienced Commando officers. While Loustalot was aggressive on the training field, he was often quiet away from training. Like many of the Ranger officers, he had a close bond with the enlisted men, and spent his off-hours hanging out with them.

The training was very similar to Number 4 Commando's. Kness, Sweazey and eleven other Rangers were distributed among Troop 4, where second Lieutenant Charles Shunstrum was the ranking American officer. Kness found himself paired with the company's sergeant major; the rest of the group were spread out so that overall they would have a good idea of how the entire company functioned. They began with two daytime landings, then worked at night, practicing the assault until they could do it, if not in their sleep, at least in the dark. The Commandos would undertake a speed march every few days, to keep their leg strength up.

Though the Americans were using M1s, they also had to make sure that they were familiar with the British weapons. Sweazey admired the mortars and later in the war would head a mortar squad. *Pow, pow, drop*—the weapons were devastatingly effective.

Unlike Lovat's Commandos, who wore watch caps, Number 3 Commando wore helmets but had fabric netting on them to keep them from making noise. Silence was an important ingredient; the landings and advances were to be made as quietly as possible. To communicate, the Rangers tapped on their rifle stocks, with the number and beat signifying different things. They learned to focus their attention on specific areas immediately around them, and trust that their comrades would do the same.

Sweazey suspected something was up as soon as he realized that the "problems" they were facing were the same each day. Then he and some of the Commandos he was bunked with saw Canadian tanks being loaded into a landing craft for their own drill. Rumors started—they were going to do a job that involved tanks. But no one knew for sure what was going on.

One other Commando group was to be involved in the raid—Royal Marine Commando A (a few months after Dieppe, the designation was changed to Commando 40). The raid on Dieppe was to be the first time the unit, which had been formed in February 1942, saw action. Working under the direction of Navy commander R.E.D. Ryder—who had been the naval commander on the Saint-Nazaire raid—the Marines were assigned to enter the inner harbor of the city a little more than an hour after the initial landings. There they were to steal forty landing craft and take them back to England. No Rangers joined the Marine Commando, training at the time on the Isle of Wight.

MOVING ON

Sergeant Szima made sure the bayonet was fixed to his M1 rifle, then glanced over at his Commando pal Jim Haggerty. Smoke was wafting over the battlefield; the order to withdraw had just been given.

Haggerty moved out. Szima followed. The two men and the rest of their section leapfrogged past a group of Number 4 Commandos holding the edge of the cliff and began descending toward the beach. Nearby, two Commandos were carrying a stretcher bearing a wounded comrade.

Something moved around the bend in the path. Haggerty tensed, bayonet ready, but it was just a rock tumbling from above. An officer at the foot of the cliff waved frantically at the men, urging them to pick up their pace. Szima and Haggerty, already puffing, hustled to the waterline and waded out to the waiting landing craft.

"Quiet!" hissed one of the Navy men inside. He gestured for them to stay undercover.

Szima huddled next to the Commando as the rest of the men in their section arrived. Boat full, the landing craft began backing away. The engine had a dull, mechanical sound that echoed in the hull. Waves slapped against the plywood sides. The boat heaved around, then gradually began to pick up speed, heading back to the *Prince Albert*.

Szima began to relax. He and the others had been at this now for more than a week. They were about as practiced as they were going to get.

Back on the ship, their officers called them together and told them they were moving on to Weymouth for more training. Everyone knew they were going to be involved in a raid—they knew it in their tired bones. But the officers were adamant that they were only training for an exercise. And so they moved on to Weymouth, adrenaline continuing to build.

IN TOWN

Once the night-assault practices were finished, the Commandos and Rangers billeted with local families and small bordering houses. This was a common practice through the war for the Commandos, since they didn't have permanent quarters in the area. In some cases the men became fairly close to the families who were boarding them, many of whom had husbands or sons in the service; they might be treated as surrogate sons—and once in a while as replacement lovers. But in most cases the relationships were fleeting and superficial; the Commandos were just passing through, and experience had taught the women opening their homes that it wasn't wise to get too close to people they might miss when they left.

The Americans were given allowances to cover their necessities, which were often stretched for the benefit of their allies. Szima treated his Commando pal Haggerty, an Irishman who'd joined the British Army, to regular beers when the unit broke from training for lunch at a local pub. The Rangers also went out after hours with their Commando "hosts." Sweazey and some of the other Americans billeting with 3 Commando found themselves in demand with the local women when training knocked off some evenings; the Yanks were something new. There was a decent amount of friction between the Commandos and the Canadian members of the 2nd Division staying in the same area. Unlike Rutter, which called for Canadian force to gather at the Isle of Wight for several days before the invasion, Jubilee called for them to leave from a number of ports in the area where their units were part of the defenses. The two forces did not mix easily; many Canadians felt the Commandos were full of themselves, while some Commandos thought the Canadians were less than professional in their approach to war. Many years later, Commandos would complain that the Canadians had been openly talking about

Dieppe before the operation; they still regarded this as an unforgivable sin.

The Rangers and Number 4 Commandos at Weymouth were supposed to report to a gathering place in town every morning at 7:30 for physical-fitness training; exercises were done with their weapons. Physical-fitness training would include a half-mile run with arms and generally finished off with a swim. They were then released for breakfast—usually provided at the houses where they stayed—returning for three hours of exercises ranging from climbing cliffs to attacking urban areas. The afternoon saw more drills and work on the firing range.

Szima was surprised to see how poorly most of the Commandos did with their guns. After all the stories of prowess in the newspapers, the Brits turned out to be something less than crack shots. He doubted more than 10 percent would have made it past basic training in America if rifle skills were all that was considered.

"Our marksmanship on the rifle range destroyed their morale," Sergeant Szima said, half seriously, in a letter to friends many years later. "My range record of five shots in an eight-inch group had Major Mills-Roberts accusing me of being a member of the U.S. Army rifle team."

Besides being impressed by the Americans' marksmanship, Roberts liked their gun, which was superior in many ways to the Enfields the Commandos were using. In fact, the M1 was so popular with the Brits that over in 3 Commando, Captain Murray gave one to Colonel Durnford-Slater as a present—and then found it politic to scrounge up more for the other Commando officers.

What the British soldiers lacked in shooting skills, they more than made up for when wielding the bayonet. Soldiers were trained to thrust the bayonet deeply and viciously into an opponent. The use of the bayonet by British troops had a long history; in the days when muskets were slow to load and very inaccurate, the strength of the

British Army's bayonet charge often decided the day. But most Americans seemed a bit put off by the weapon. Szima, who admired the Commandos' intensity, decided that their skill came from their hatred for the enemy.

"It was their meat," he told friends long after the war.

The Commandos weren't necessarily angry, nor was it necessary for them to hate their enemy on a personal level. Having been at war for nearly three years, they understood that the business came down to killing or be killed. If he was using a bayonet, the strength of his first thrust very literally could determine whether he survived or not. He had to strike his target not with hatred but with a ferocity that could not be manufactured, one that would come through in the way he moved, not just when facing the enemy, but at all times.

The Rangers, to this point unblooded, might have known this, too, but that knowledge hadn't yet permeated their bones. The day was fast approaching when it would.

THE DATE IS SET

The moon and tides limited the time when the invasion could take place. The tide needed to be as high as possible so that the invasion force could land close to shore; besides its effects on the tide, the moon needed to be at a minimum so they could land in darkness and go undetected.

The window in August ran from the tenth to the twentieth. Once Jubilee was approved, the planners eyed the latter part of the window to give themselves and the troops enough time to prepare. To help cut down on the possibility that German aerial reconnaissance would once again spot the invasion fleet before it sailed, the troops were to be gathered at the very last minute. Supplies had to be requisitioned and then routed to ships. A special depot was set up on a commandeered estate in Hampshire, England. Train after train arrived, beginning August 5; it took nine days for all of the gear and ammunition to arrive.

On August 16, the Canadian commanders met for a final review of the plans. The same day, Mountbatten was informed that the invasion was ready to proceed. The force commanders eyed August 18 as the target date.

But the weather deteriorated as the winds on the Channel kicked up. August 19 looked more promising, and a final staff meeting was set for the morning of August 18 to decide.

JUBILEE—THE PLAN OF ATTACK

The Commando attacks were vital to the plan to invade Dieppe, but they were nonetheless supporting operations, taking place on the far east (3 Commando) and far west (4 Commando) of the main show. Canadian units from the 2nd Division were tasked to do most of the work, striking at three separate areas, including the main seafront at Dieppe.

To the east of Dieppe—on its left when looking at the city from sea—high grounds rose over the city and harbor. There were a number of gun emplacements here, most notably a battery with four 75mm field guns dubbed the "Rommel battery" by the planners. The artillery pieces were actually captured French guns from World War I, Canon de 75mm; they were still quite effective and a number were deployed around the Dieppe area and in the city itself. As it happened, some members of the Rangers were familiar with the gun from maneuvers and their own batteries stateside. Their sixteen-pound shells could be fired to an effective range of seven thousand meters, or roughly four and a third miles. They had a distinctive sound that veterans who had been near them quickly recognized in combat.

These guns and the smaller weapons on the eastern headland were to be taken by the Royal Regiment of Canada. The regiment would land at "Blue Beach," a narrow, rocky stretch of perhaps two hundred yards below Puys (called "Puits" in the plans). After landing and climbing the steps at the side of the seawall, the Canadians would move up through the steep streets of the village and then strike inland. After taking the Rommel battery, they would move on to the guns and mortar positions closer to the city on the eastern headlands. A "prize crew" of artillerymen and antiaircraft operators would accompany the regiment in hopes of using the weapons against the Germans after they were taken. After these objectives were met, elements of the unit would hook up with soldiers from the main beaches at Dieppe who would cross through the city and over to the eastern side of the harbor.

A total of 554 men from the regiment were tasked to this attack; a company from the Black Watch Regiment was assigned to accompany them, protecting their eastern flank as they moved inland.

The landing was designed to take place in three waves, with H Hour—the time the first unit hit the beach—to take place at 0450, a half hour before the landings on the main beach. Surprise and the cover of darkness were considered key to the assault; the small ships accompanying the landing would not fire until the troops were ashore.

Puys was a small village, perched over the sea. Like Berneval and Pourville, it was a rural community, even though it was just over a mile from the city. Unlike them, there was only one way up to the village from the beach; there were houses on both sides with a good view of the seawall and the area around it.

High ground also protected Dieppe to the west, just to the right of the city when viewed from the sea.

This would be dealt with by a landing at Pourville, dubbed "Green Beach." About two miles from Dieppe, the village of Pourville sat at the mouth of the Scie River. While a single bridge ran across the river at the exit from the village, the river valley gave a wide opening to the assault force. Like Dieppe itself, the Pourville seafront was covered on both sides by high ground; the beach and seawall defenses were not nearly as extensive, however. It was estimated that only a small number of Germans—in the area of fifty—were defending the beach and the immediate area nearby, though the marked defenses indicated there should be more troops on the nearby hills.

Jubilee called for the South Saskatchewan Regiment to land and secure the beach as quickly as possible, with a company (about 120 men) taking the high ground to the east (closest to Dieppe). After destroying the guns protecting the Pourville beach, the unit would capture the nearby radar station, then make contact with infantry proceeding through Dieppe. A second company was tasked to take additional antiaircraft guns on the high ground. A German strong-point at a farm known as Les Quatre Vents (Four Winds) farther inland would be assaulted by the companies after their initial objective was achieved. A third company would strike to the west, taking the high ground there, while other units held the beach and village area.

H Hour at Pourville for South Saskatchewan was also 0540. Like Blue Beach, the landing at Green Beach depended entirely on darkness and surprise; the small ships nearby would not shell the defenses ahead of the landing.

The Cameron Highlanders were to arrive at Green Beach thirty minutes after South Saskatchewan. They would then pass through the village and the areas secured by their countrymen, bypassing any enemy opposition to rendezvous at Bois des Vertus (today the vicinity is marked by a traffic circle at Vertus) two miles south of Dieppe with tanks from the main landing. Together, they would attack the aerodrome another mile farther inland at Saint-Aubin, and if time allowed—"in accordance with developments"—strike the German infantry headquarters believed to be near Arques-la-Bataille.

The South Saskatchewan Regiment was to land 523 men at Pourville; a total of 503 Cameron Highlanders were set to follow.

Jubilee's main assaults would take place at Dieppe itself. The seafront was arbitrarily divided into two beaches, east (Red Beach) and west (White Beach). The Essex Scottish Regiment would land on the east and the Royal Hamilton the west. After landing, a company of Essex Scottish would move along the western side of the harbor channel to one of the bridges near the Bassin du Canada, crossing and capturing the antiaircraft guns on the east bank of the city. Another company would take the guns on the west bank of the harbor channel and pier, near the main part of the city. Other units would attack and capture armed trawlers in the harbor and hook up with the troops from Blue Beach.

The harbor jetties would be to the immediate left of the troops as they landed; on the right or west side of the beach, a major landmark was the Tobacco Factory, a large building with two smokestacks on the boulevard de Verdun, across the beach and esplanade.

The western portion of the Dieppe seafront, or White Beach, was dominated by the Casino, an old complex of buildings that extended to the esplanade. The Royal Hamilton Infantry would land here. One company was to scale the cliffs on the western part of the beach and capture guns there before moving on to hook up with the South Saskatchewan Regiment from Green Beach. Other companies would strike into the city, taking batteries on the high ground near the old castle and farther to the south.

Royal Hamilton had a total of 582 men in the invasion force; the Essex Scottish had 553. A third regiment, Les Fusiliers Mont-Royal, with a total of 583 men, was to be held in reserve at sea, committed to the battle on the main beaches after a breakthrough.

To accomplish their tasks, the infantry regiments would be

assisted by the Calgary Tanks, which would land nearly fifty new Mk 1 and Mk 3 Churchill tanks and a number of lighter vehicles for support on the main beach in several waves, the first (nine tanks) hitting the beach with the first infantrymen and the second (nine tanks) landing fifteen minutes later. Another flight with twelve tanks would land at 0605. After assisting the infantrymen in clearing fortified positions at the beachhead and with their objectives in town, the tanks—reinforced by two more waves—would proceed through the town south, hooking up with infantry units from Pourville. They would strike the airport and other targets in the area before retreating back to the beachhead. The main force and the troops from Pourville would be taken off through Red and White Beaches.

About a year old but untested in battle, the Churchill was the Allies' main battle tank, developed from a prewar design and rushed into production following the heavy loss of British armor at Dunkirk. At 102mm or about four inches at its thickest, the Churchill's armor was a substantial improvement over that used in earlier British tanks. Weighing over thirty-eight tons and crewed by five men, the design became the basis for several different models, and would be operated until the end of the war. All members of the family, however, suffered from the original design's two major drawbacks: the vehicle was slow, and its main guns were relatively weak.

The early Churchills were equipped with two large-caliber guns, one in the turret and one in the front hull. One of the few significant differences between the Mk 1 and Mk 3 was the size of the turret weapon; in the Mk 1 tank it was a two-pounder that fired a 40mm armor-piercing shell. Though ostensibly an antitank weapon, the gun was far too light to be of much use against German tanks in battle, and was superseded by a six-pounder in the Mk 3.

The howitzer fired a high-explosive shell intended to be used against infantry. Both variants included a 7.7mm BESA machine gun in the turret, and a few of the Calgary tanks were equipped with flamethrowers instead of howitzers.

To keep the tanks from taking on water, rubber fittings were placed in and around openings, with a large socklike cap on the main gun. The engine exhaust was directed through "lourve extensions"— a pair of pipes shaped like a *U* that stuck up from the rear of the tanks and looked like a pole for a small clothesline. Because a seawall separated the beach from the esplanade at Dieppe, several tanks were equipped with a device to climb over them. This was simply a roll of three-foot-wide chestnut planks of wood called "chespaling"; the planks were connected to one another like fencing and dropped in front of the tank, which would climb upward over the wood. The tanks following would use them after the first tank passed, or take advantage of wooden ramps that engineers were supposed to haul and mount against the seawall.

Concrete barriers blocked all but one of the streets leading from the seafront into the town. The entrance at rue de Sygogne, a metal fence, was eyed as the most vulnerable, and the plan called for the tanks to use this street if possible. Engineers were assigned to blow the tank obstacles there, and any others, as necessary.

The tanks were to be carried in new assault vessels called Tank Landing Craft or TLCs; the designation was changed a short time later to Landing Craft Tanks or LCTs, which was used for the rest of the war. The boats—LCT Mk 2s—could beach themselves, allowing tanks to get off on dry land or in very shallow water; the TLCs then used a kedge anchor and winch to pull themselves back out into the sea. About 160 feet long, each LTC would carry three tanks, along with an additional vehicle, either an armor car, scout car, or a bull-dozer, assigned to different tasks during the invasion, along with supplies.

Besides the LCTs, the invasion force was transported by an

armada of ships and small boats, escorted by eight destroyers and seventeen smaller gunboats of different varieties. The bulk of this fleet consisted of small landing craft; there were sixty LCAs and seventy-four LCP(L)s. There were also twenty-four tank landing craft and an assortment of other landing craft and motor launches. Nine infantry landing ships, including the *Prince Albert,* would transport the bulk of the men to a boarding point just off the beaches, but a number would have to ride directly to the beach in landing craft, including the troopers in Number 3 Commando, who were sailing in LCP(L)s.

The assaults at Puys and Pourville were to begin at 0450 under the cover of darkness; neither landing would get advance shelling from the fleet. At Dieppe, the destroyers were to provide covering fire for the landing parties beginning at ten minutes before H Hour, which was set for 0520. At the same time, RAF fighters were to buzz the beach, dropping bombs, firing their cannons and machine guns, and laying a smoke screen to help cover the approach of the landing craft.

The *Calpe* and *Fernie* were to act as headquarters and backup headquarters ships respectively; they would not participate in the shelling. The radio gear at the time was considered too delicate to withstand heavy bombardment.

The Canadian plans for the invasion included an elaborate schedule for each unit that would hit the beaches. Objectives were laid out in detail and certainly appeared impressive. There was only one problem: the plans seemed to assume the Germans who held Dieppe wouldn't have much of a say in the matter.

UNDERESTIMATING THE GERMANS

Aircraft had continued their reconnaissance flights over the Dieppe area, and the planners had made some minor corrections to their plans. In a few instances, misled by camouflage, they found some guns where none existed, and inexplicably thought there was no barbed wire on the seawall at Puys. But except for missing the fact that the caves overlooking the beaches on the flanks had been set up as strongpoints for machine guns and defenders, they correctly mapped the defensive positions protecting all of the beaches.

The earlier intelligence estimates identifying the German unit holding Dieppe were not altered, nor were the assessments of troop strength. Most significantly, the Canadian and Combined Operations planners continued to have an especially dim view of the German troops manning the defenses, expecting not only that they would be surprised but that they would not be able to react sufficiently to defend the city. While the presence of the panzer division several hours away had caused a major change in plans—shortening the operation to a "one tide" or few hours' stay—the defenders themselves were considered little more than sleepy garrison neophytes who would be brushed aside as the men and tanks hit the beaches and roared into the city.

Many of the troops around Dieppe were, in fact, replacements, but when it came to combat they were no greener than the Canadians. A proportion of the enlisted men were Poles and ethnic but noncitizen Germans. It's not clear now how many of the enlisted men fit this category; though estimates have run from 10 to 40 percent. But many of their officers and noncoms had combat experience, and they had been undergoing defensive drills for some time. Compared to the assault troops, their tasks were relatively easy: they had to fire from fixed positions at an enemy they could see. The most difficult thing about their job in many cases was getting to their positions.

For months, division commander Major General Conrad Haase had been working to improve his men's skills and to decrease the possibility that they could be taken by surprise. His task was urgent, because starting in the spring he had received a steady stream of intelligence indicating that the Allies were planning an invasion. Aerial photographs of southern England showed a gathering invasion fleet, and spies sent back information pinpointing the target. Unfortunately for the Germans, the reports contradicted one another, naming the targets as the Hague, La Rochelle, and Le Tréport. Only Le Tréport was in Haase's defensive zone, but the general was nonetheless apprehensive, and even told his men that "reliable sources" were predicting an attack, probably a white lie intended to keep them motivated.

Whatever their spies said, news stories in the Allied media calling for a second front had convinced the Germans that landings were imminent, and as the summer continued the Nazis were on high alert. Haase called every officer in his division to Dieppe and made him swear to die rather than give up his position. The ceremony ended with his own oath.

In early July, the Germans were alarmed by fresh photographs of a possible invasion force in southern England—Rutter, though the Nazis didn't know that, of course. More mortars and antitank guns were trucked into Dieppe as well as other strongholds along the coast. July passed with no attack, but as mid-August arrived, Haase once more ordered his men on high alert, knowing that the moon and tide favored an invasion.

Neither Haase nor his boss, General Field Marshal von Rundstedt, believed that the Allies would actually attack Dieppe. The harbor was relatively insignificant, unsuitable to sustain a sizable army ashore once seized. More importantly, they recognized that the natural geography would make it very difficult for an invader to get off the beaches. The high grounds to either side of the city provided intersecting lines of fire and a natural advantage for anyone who held them. The rocky beach had no natural cover, while the line of buildings before it would give defenders plenty of vantage points during an attack.

But the Germans would not relax. Studying the tides and moon, General von Rundstedt told Haase to place his sector on alert from August 10 to 20, the dates most favorable for an invasion. Haase, who'd conducted regimental and division exercises earlier in the month, immediately did so. He ordered that the defenses be manned every night until dawn.

FIVE

BEFORE THE DAWN

Newhaven
November 2006

* * *

After spending the day wandering across the beach and cliffs and exploring the old battlements at the edge of Newhaven, I venture into one of the local pubs and order a Guinness. The patrons are divided up into several cliques, seemingly arranged according to age; all are gathered around televisions, watching a soccer match.

I find myself watching the game with a group of young men who would have been the same age as the soldiers I'm writing about—a Yank amid the Brits, as the Rangers would have put it. Imagination and memory sift together; the present becomes the past. I'm sitting not with young men watching a soccer game but with a room full of soldiers nervous about the mission they know is coming, even though they haven't received their orders yet. They express their apprehension in familiar ways—drinking more than they should, vying for the attention of the few women left in the town, boasting and cutting up. A few get into mild shoving matches.

An even smaller number sneak away, to a corner or to their rooms, alone with their fears. They've made the mistake of thinking too much about what they'll have to do soon, and will have trouble falling asleep.

I have the same problem once I leave. I'm thinking too much: about Dieppe and a past that doesn't actually belong to me, no matter how the imagination wanders. But there's no way to turn it off. I'm anxious to see the beaches, anxious to connect the real place with what I've heard and read. It's only seventy miles away—nothing compared to the distance I've traveled to get here.

I have to get up before dawn to catch my ferry to the city, but it's impossible to sleep. Instead, I reach into my already packed bag and take out Robertson's The Shame and the Glory—Dieppe. *I've already read the book, but as I go through the pages tonight every sentence seems new, every fact a revelation. I'm not nearly as close to Dieppe as I thought.*

Dieppe, France and Southern England
August 18, 1942

■ ■ ■

ONE DAY TO GO . . .

August 18, 1942, dawned dim and gray on the English Channel. The high winds of the day before had calmed somewhat, but they remained strong enough to foam the wave tips white.

At Dieppe, the sky turned the water a darkish blue green. The forecast did not predict rain, but the horizon seemed so gray and uninviting, General Haase couldn't help but relax. The tides still favored an invasion, but the winds on the Channel made it unlikely. The danger period would pass within two days; more than likely they would slip by without action.

. . .

Alex Szima and Zip Koons exchanged glances as they hustled to their spots on the Weymouth waterfront. It was barely 5 a.m., still dark, but every member of Number 4 Commando had managed to make it to the assembly point on time.

Not that they'd had any doubts.

The men had been told the night before to settle their bills because they were going on a two-day exercise. But most knew better; they were heading for a raid. The Americans were filled with anticipation, unsure what to expect, but ready—beyond ready. Or at least they thought so.

A row of trucks drove up. Szima watched, not sure why they were hesitating.

The trouble was the officer who was supposed to command the trucks hadn't arrived. The head of Number 4 Commando, Lord Lovat, stalked near the vehicles, impatient to get moving. Finally one of the drivers pointed to a man approaching who'd just lit a cigarette. It was the officer they'd been waiting for.

Lovat slapped the cigarette away—and caught enough of the man's cheek in the process to send him rolling to the ground.

"You step to the rear, my lad," the Commando chief snarled. "And go in to report for being late for parade."

The Commandos and Rangers boarded the trucks quickly, still unsure of their final destination.

Number 3 Commando had spent the past two days confined to their billets. Officers, including the American Rangers, had been briefed on the plan, going over the maps and aerial photographs. A scale model of plaster of paris was prepared. On the morning of August 18, the officers and NCOs were briefed on the plan. Lieutenant Loustalot examined the plan closely, mentally ticking off the landmarks as the briefing continued. When the officers were finished, they began breaking the plan down with their men, explaining to the privates like Sweazey and Edwin Furru what they were going to do. The Americans were split up among the Commando; groups of three were assigned to different Commando subsections, ensuring that the Rangers were mixed in well with the more experienced Commandos. For the most part, they retained the organization and assignments they'd used over the past several weeks of practice.

With grenades and the rest of the ammunition passed out, the brigade mustered for a final check. Lieutenant Colonel Durnford-Slater looked over each man, officer or private, personally. Lieutenant Loustalot stood ramrod straight as the colonel came to him, as always squared away just so.

"Would any man like to leave now?" the colonel asked. If so, he could do so with no penalty or regrets.

Loustalot was a little shocked that the question was even asked, but not surprised in the least that no one took up the commander's offer.

STRANGE FELLOWS

While Loustalot and the others attached to 3 Commando were studying scale models of the area they were to assault, First Lieutenant Robert Flanagan was leading a group of six Rangers in search of a Major Stockley at East Bridge House in Farnham, England. The five men with Flanagan had completed training at Achnacarry and were training with the Commandos at Shiel Bridge, Scotland, when Major Darby had them pulled aside. Told that they'd been assigned to a special school, they got up early on Saturday morning, August 16, and began the long journey to southern England, where the training was supposed to be held.

When Flanagan found Stockley on Sunday afternoon, the British major was confused and told Flanagan to return in the morning. When the Americans came back, the British major told them to make themselves at home, but seemed still unsure about their assignment. They left Stockley and began wandering around the house, looking for a place to wait.

One thing seemed clear—this wasn't going to be a normal training session. They met an odd assortment of characters in the rooms and hallways—Frenchmen pretending to be Canadians, Germans pretending to be French, and even a group calling themselves phantoms who were pretending not to exist.

Unknown to the Americans, the men at the house were all waiting to join Canadian units in the Dieppe invasion. Each group represented a special mission that had been added, first to the Rutter plans, and then to its successor. Some of the Frenchmen were to act as guides for the invaders; others were probably on their way to join members of the French Resistance. The Germans were apparently Allied spies who were to be infiltrated onto the continent with the invasion force. And the phantoms—possibly these were radio operators who were to be assigned to one of the Commando units, but their identity remains a mystery to this day.

The most interesting special mission belonged to a young radar expert named Jack Nissenthall, who at that moment was using his shaving razor to rip the insignia off his RAF uniform and waiting for a car to take him to Combined Operations Headquarters in London. Nissenthall had been selected to inspect the German radar station near Pourville; sitting on high ground at Caude-Côte, the station's radar—known as Freya—was an early warning radar that the Allies were interested in studying. Nissenthall's assignment was to get into the station, examine the radar, and take back some parts if possible. He would make the journey to the beach accompanied by guards under orders to shoot him if capture was imminent.

The six Rangers—Flanagan, Lieutenant Joseph Randall, Sergeants

Lloyd Church, Kenneth Kenyon, Marcel Swank, and T-4 Howard Henry—had no part in any of these special operations. They'd been assigned as observers to the Canadian units taking part in the main raid, though neither they nor Stockley knew that yet. Swank, for one, still believed the story he'd been told at Shiel Bridge, that they were going to a new school.

It took Stockley a few hours to sort out the confusion and find the Americans transportation to Canadian units. He gave Flanagan a list of the ships the Rangers would join, but nothing else. A short time later, a bus came to pick them up. It began driving them around the local area, then letting a single Ranger off at a time without further explanation.

The last men on the bus, Sergeants Swank and Church, found themselves dropped off together in a large field. Members of the Queen's Own Cameron Highlanders, a Canadian unit with a Scottish tradition and bagpipes to match, were scattered around the field, smoking and silently waiting. Only now realizing what was going on, Swank and Church kept uneasily to themselves.

"We better ditch these helmets," Swank told Church, taking off the new-style bucket helmets that they'd just been issued. "We look like we're the enemy."

They managed to find a pair of Canadian helmets, and did their best, if not to blend in, at least to seem innocuous.

NEWSMEN AND GENERALS

American newsman Quentin Reynolds was by nature a late riser, and the late hours he kept in London made it especially difficult for him to rouse himself from bed much before noon. But the freelance writer and correspondent for *Collier's* magazine found himself wide-awake at 9 a.m., August 18, stepping into an office at Combined Operations, where an American member of the staff, Jock Lawrence, was waiting for him. Lawrence and Reynolds had known each other before the war; Lawrence had been a Hollywood assistant producer and public-relations flack pushing stories Reynolds's way.

Lawrence called in a colonel, who told Reynolds he'd been tapped to accompany a Combined Operations raid. Reynolds, who'd been hoping for months to be granted permission to join the Commandos, nodded as the major told him he would be aboard the destroyer *Calpe,* which was to be used as the floating headquarters for the raid. He readily agreed to the ground rules, which called for him to keep the operation secret and to stay in Lawrence's apartment until a driver came to take him to the ship. The men sealed the agreement with a quick gin on the terrace.

Asked by acquaintances at the headquarters what he was up to, Reynolds replied blithely that he was about to undertake a tour with General Eisenhower. It was a lie, of course, but there was more truth in it than the newsman knew. Eisenhower, anxious for the American participation in the raid to gain publicity, had pressed Combined Operations to allow American correspondents to cover the raid. The presence of newsmen during military actions, especially those undertaken by the Commandos, was not unusual, though the number of reporters on this raid was high compared to earlier ones. In this case, Combined Operations allowed five men to go, rather than the two Reynolds expected based on past practice.

In another corner of Combined Operations Headquarters, Lucian Truscott had begun the day much as he had done over the past few weeks, working on Torch, the operation for landings in northern Africa. But the general soon received word that Jubilee was on; if he wanted to observe it, he had to be in Portsmouth by 8 p.m.

There was a slight holdup when one of his superiors told him his role in Torch meant he couldn't observe the operation; Truscott immediately appealed to General Eisenhower, who gave him his blessing. Truscott rounded up several other American observers at Combined Operations and together they headed for Portsmouth.

Ham Roberts had spent the night of August 17 tossing and turning in bed, worried about the invasion. Despite his assurances to the men in his command that surprise was all that was needed to take Dieppe, Roberts had nonetheless continued to press for concentrated bombing before the invasion. He remained unwilling, however, to accept the small raids offered, contending that they would do little besides alerting the defenders and causing rubble that would interfere with the tanks as they rushed through the streets.

Whatever doubts he had, Roberts pushed them away in the morning. Confronted by one of his lieutenant colonels, who said the destroyers' shelling would be inadequate, Roberts offered to have him relieved. The officer assured him he would do his duty.

The weather was a final holdup. A fresh storm looked to be brewing. But after consulting the weather maps, the meteorologists decided it would hold off long enough for an invasion to be launched.

At 10 a.m., Roberts issued the order: the Jubilee force was to board its ships. The attack was on.

Order of Battle

■ ■ ■

Yellow Beach—Berneval
Objective: "Goebbels" Shore Battery

Number 3 Commando
Rangers:
Captain Roy A. Murray
Sergeant Edwin C. Thompson

Sergeant Tom Sorby
Private First Class Howard W. Andre
Private First Class Stanley Bush
Private First Class Pete M. Preston
Private Don Earwood
(all with Headquarters Troop)

Second Lieutenant Charles M. Shunstrum
Staff Sergeant Lester E. Kness
Sergeant Theodore Q. Butts
Sergeant John C. Knapp
Sergeant Dick Sellers
T-5 John H. Smith
Private First Class James O. Edwards
Private First Class Donald G. Johnson
Private First Class Charles F. Grant
Private First Class Clare P. Beitel
Private First Class Charles Reilly
Private First Class Owen W. Sweazey
Private First Class Charles R. Coy
(all with Number 4 Troop)

First Lieutenant Leonard F. Dirks
Sergeant Harold R. Adams
Sergeant Mervin T. Heacock
Sergeant Marvin L. Kavanaugh
Sergeant Gino Mercuriali
T-5 Michael Kerecman
T-5 William L. Brinkley
T-5 Joseph C. Phillips
Private First Class Howard T. Hedenstad

Private First Class James C. Moseley
Private First Class Ervin J. Moger
Private First Class William S. Gridley
Private Jacque M. Nixson
(all with Number 3 Troop)

Second Lieutenant Edwin V. Loustalot
Staff Sergeant Merritt M. Bertholf
Sergeant Albert T. Jacobson
Private First Class Walter A. Bresnahan
Private First Class William B. Lienhas
Private First Class Donald L. Hayes
Private First Class Edwin R. Furru
(all with Number 6 Troop)

Blue Beach—Puys
Objective: Shore Battery & headlands overlooking Dieppe beach

Royal Regiment of Canada
Ranger: Sergeant Kenneth G. Kenyon

Red Beach—Dieppe beach, eastern half
White Beach—Dieppe beach, western half
Objective: Dieppe and beyond

Essex Scottish Regiment
Royal Hamilton Light Infantry
Fusiliers Mont-Royal
Royal Marine Commando
14th Canadian Army Tank Regiment (Calgary Tank Regiment)

RANGERS:

Second Lieutenant Joseph H. Randall (with Royal Hamilton)*

T-4 Howard M. Henry (with Essex Scottish)*

Green Beach—Pourville
Objective: Shore batteries, radar station, western headlands near Dieppe, airfield

South Saskatchewan Regiment

Cameron Highlanders of Canada

RANGERS:

First Lieutenant Robert Flanagan

Sergeant Lloyd N. Church (with Cameron Highlanders)

Sergeant Marcel G. Swank (with Cameron Highlanders)

Orange Beach—Vasterival
Objective: "Hess" Shore Battery

NUMBER 4 COMMANDO

RANGERS:

Staff Sergeant Kenneth D. Stempson

Sergeant Alex J. Szima

Corporal William R. Brady

Corporal Franklin M. Koons

---

* As explained in Chapter 9, Lieutenant Randall may have landed with the South Saskatchewan Regiment on Green Beach; according to one eyewitness, T-4 Henry landed with an engineer's group attached to Calgary Tanks.

Southern England
August 18, 1942

■ ■ ■

A SEND-OFF

Someone pulled back the canvas side on the truck and the Commandos and Rangers piled out. Szima's Commando buddy pointed over toward the edge of the street, where a group of spectators were watching, some smiling, some waving, a few gaping. Southampton's residents had come out to see what the fuss was all about as truck after truck pulled into town and disgorged gear-laden men. One of the Commandos saw a convoy of Canadians and noted that the canvas at the sides of their trucks hadn't been unfurled. Anyone the truck passed had that much more information about what it was carrying, that much more to go on when guessing that something was up. It was a small thing, but it bothered the Commando.

Rangers Stempson, Szima, Brady, and Koons made their way from the trucks over to the docks, where the *Prince Albert* was waiting for them. The men had had a large lunch at Warnford, a town used as a gathering point a little farther inland. Lunch had included British pints all around, but any mellowing effect of the beer melted away as the men clambered onto the deck of the landing ship. The tension had slowly ratcheted up over the past three weeks, each notch barely perceptible amid the hard routine of training. But now the tension jumped tenfold. A *few* men might still believe the talk that all they were doing was going on an exercise, but most didn't. The sweat gave them away.

Lord Lovat and his officers busied themselves with final preparations. Watches were synchronized. Not everyone had one, but there was at least one per section or work team. Major Mills-Roberts sported one on each wrist.

Around 5:30—1730 in military time—the Rangers and Commandos were mustered to attention to hear a visitor speak. It was Lord Mountbatten, who'd come aboard ship to give them a pep talk.

Mountbatten tried breaking the ice with a few off-color jokes, then got to his point. No matter what happened, he told them, they needed to hit their objective, the big guns behind the cliffs near Varengeville. The job was critical; if they didn't take the Germans out, the mission would fail. The guns had to be taken out. The guns. He couldn't emphasize that more.

The commander of Combined Operations was candid about the fact that the raid wasn't intended as the start of a second front, but what he called "a reconnaissance in depth."

There'll be plenty of firepower, he added; you'll have airplanes backing you up. One for every five men going ashore.

The ratio was correct, more or less—upward of a thousand planes had been tasked for the raid—but the majority of them were intended to be dogfighting with the Luftwaffe. Six squadrons were tasked to strafe the beaches at the start of the attack; another three would set up a smoke screen. Additional aircraft would strafe the city later in the day. Still, this attack was small compared to the overall number of squadrons committed to the raid—at least seventy-four.

The Commandos had no way of knowing this, but some may have sensed it. In any event, there were a few frowns as the general continued. To some of those who'd seen action, the commander's words sounded distant, too rehearsed, insincere. When he said he wished he could go with them, a number thought of offering their place.

He made a few jokes. Koons laughed. For a moment, he was in a good mood. Then reality set in.

"Tomorrow we deal the Hun a bloody blow," Mountbatten told the men. "We expect over sixty percent casualties. To those of you that will die tomorrow, may God have mercy on your souls."

Whatever his purpose might have been, Mountbatten's dire prediction hit many of the men like a kidney punch. Speechless, Szima, Koons, Stempson, and Brady made their way to the cabin they'd been assigned, stunned by the enormity of what they were about to undertake.

IN THE LCPs

Assigned to accompany the South Saskatchewan Regiment, Lieutenant Flanagan boarded the *Princess Beatrix,* a small landing ship of about a thousand tons. Still in the dark about what exactly was going on, he searched out a Canadian officer who could tell him. The officer explained the overall plan and told the American that their assignment was Pourville, where the troops would neutralize defenses and move up the cliffs. Flanagan was to go ashore as an observer with an intelligence officer, an interrogator, an artillery officer tasked to watch the destroyer's salvos, and a newspaperman. The officer didn't know much else; clearly, the Canadians hadn't been expecting "guests."

Privately, the Ranger lieutenant bridled at the lack of information he'd been given. There was nothing to be done about it now, however, and around midnight he went below decks to try to grab some rest.

At least there was a "below" for him to go to. In another part of the convoy, Sergeants Swank and Church were trying to find a place to grab some rest in the well of the landing craft. Because there weren't enough landing ships, a portion of the invading force had been boarded directly onto their landing craft for the several-hour journey across the Channel.

The regiment they were with, the Cameron Highlanders, had problems getting their truck convoy to the docks because of the traffic, and the delays added to the tension and the confusion as Swank and

Church did their best to keep up with the others while still staying out of the way. Led to an LCP, the two men still had no real idea where they were going or what they were supposed to do. Finally, they managed to find the Canadian lieutenant in charge of the boat. Shocked that they hadn't been briefed—and probably lacking as much information about them as they did about him—he gave them a quick rundown of the assignment: land at Pourville, climb the cliffs, march to Dieppe.

The LCP(L)s—also called Eurekas and R boats—were American-made landing craft that could carry as many as thirty-six troops, though that was a fairly tight squeeze. Unlike later landing craft, the LCP(L)s did not have ramps at the bow; to get out, troops jumped over the side. Made of plywood with armored bulkheads, the boats had been invented by Louisiana native Andrew Higgens before the war. Higgens had designed them to operate in swamps, for which their shallow draft was well suited. While the design was excellent for landing troops on shallow beaches, the boats were intended for short hauls, such as a few-mile hop from assault ship to shore, not a Channel crossing. They lacked seats, not to mention any other amenities, and were anything but comfortable.

Church and Swank found a place in the bottom to rest with the gear, and tried getting some sleep. The Americans, not knowing any-one in the units they'd been assigned to, remained strangers to the others in the boat. A few of the Canadians nearby exchanged friendly words, but the news of their target had given most something besides conversation to focus on.

NUMBER 3 COMMANDO

Number 3 Commando was also making the crossing in landing craft. Some twenty LCP(L)s and a flak boat carrying the brigade's Troop 4 left Newhaven and the English coast behind at roughly 8:30 p.m. and headed out into the Channel. The winds had mercifully calmed; still, the small vessels had some difficulty finding their places and then holding their position in the flotilla.

Steam Gunboat Number 5 led the convoy. Though "steam gunboat" makes the craft sound like a relic from before the turn of the century, SGB 5 was actually only a few months old. She was a fast little ship—her top speed was thirty-five knots—and was equipped with a three-inch cannon, three two-pounders, and a number of 20mm cannons and machine guns. A little more than half the size of the *Hunt*-class destroyers, she had a thirty-four-man crew.

Ranger Captain Roy Murray was aboard the gunboat, assisting Lieutenant Colonel Durnford-Slater and the group's Navy commander. SGB 5 also carried a reporter from the Associated Press, Larry Meir, who'd come aboard specifically to write about the Rangers. A small number of enlisted Rangers were also aboard; they were to transfer to landing craft a few miles off the beach for the run in.

Behind the twenty LCP(L)s, arrayed in a procession of five across and four deep, was a motor gunboat, ML Number 346, and a landing craft outfitted with flak guns to provide air cover. Kness, Sweazey, and eleven other Rangers were aboard the flak boat, which carried all of the brigade's 4 Troop. Designated an LCF, the vessel had begun its days as a Landing Craft Tank, a wedge-shaped floating barge roughly a hundred and ninety feet long and thirty-one feet wide. Between the superstructure at the stern and the ramp at the bow sat a deep well large enough to carry several tanks. A deck had been welded over the well, and antiaircraft weapons—20mm Orelikon cannons and 40mm pom-pom guns—were mounted on top. To Sweazey and some of the other soldiers who hadn't had much experience with naval warfare, the LCF was an awesome ship; Sweazey thought it had more firepower than a destroyer.

Number 3 Commando's target was the Goebbels battery, which sat at the edge of the village of Berneval about a quarter mile from the sea. The plans for the attack called for two pincer movements, each with roughly two hundred men.

Led by Lieutenant Colonel Durnford-Slater, one group would land at Yellow Beach 1 to the east of Berneval and proceed up through one of the two cuts in the cliff toward the small hamlet above. At the same time, a similar group led by Major Peter Young would land to the west on Yellow Beach 2 and attack from that direction, climbing through a wedge shaped ravine toward their target. The battery was situated near farm fields at the edge of the town; there were buildings behind it at the northeast, as well as a sprinkling of houses and yards near the cliffs where the Commandos would land.

Sweazey and the others aboard the LCF were to land as a second wave in Young's group, picked up and transported by LCPs returning after they dropped off the first waves of men. The troop had practiced making the attack on the battery several times. As Flanagan described it, their role was to act as a flanking element to the main attack; because the spearhead would be moving in a wide circle toward the rear of the battery, they were to actually move in an almost direct line. This would protect the other group, and would bring Troop 4 toward the side of the objective as another part of the pincer.

Sweazey tried to get some sleep as the boat plunged through the darkness. He pulled the blanket he'd been given over him and hunkered down, but his mind and heart were racing, stoked by adrenaline. He didn't feel fear, just anticipation and a crazy energy that kept him from drifting off.

In theory, the LCPs could cruise around ten knots even when fully loaded. But theory wasn't working that night, and when Steam Gunboat Number 5 tried to set a ten-knot pace, the columns began to lose their shape. Engine problems hit four of the boats; within a few hours they were forced to turn back, out of the battle before it began.

ABOARD THE *CALPE*

The ships left from different ports along the coast to avoid the sort of preinvasion buildup that had given the fleet away during Rutter. As they headed toward a rendezvous, minesweepers prepared to clear a channel through a minefield between the English coast and their destination.

Aboard the destroyer *Calpe,* American war correspondent Quentin Reynolds made his way toward the wardroom, looking for a drink. He was one of some sixty or seventy men, mostly Allied officers, who'd come aboard the small destroyer to either help run or observe the operation. The drinks were customarily offered to visitors, and the crew saw no reason to break with that custom now—though most of the officers Reynolds squeezed past had nothing stronger than tea.

A lieutenant from the naval staff of Combined Operations took Reynolds in tow and led him up to a large room stocked with radio equipment so it could be used as the operation's floating command headquarters. As soon as Reynolds entered, General Roberts rose and shook his hand. The American had never met the raid's commander, though he did know the Canadian by reputation as a "fighting general"; the wounds Roberts had received during the First World War added to the general's stature. They exchanged a few words, then Roberts told Reynolds he planned to go ashore at 8:30 and invited him to come along. The reporter eagerly accepted.

Reynolds's next stop was the formal briefing, which was to be given on the bridge by Hughes-Hallett. On the way, the lieutenant asked if he'd ever been to Dieppe. Reynolds said sure—two weeks before.

Actually, the correspondent had been in the glass nose of an A-20 Douglas Boston, used by the British as a night fighter. A number of Bostons had been tapped to provide support for the Dieppe mission.

Reynolds's A-20 had flown over the area, hoping to prey on German bombers returning to the nearby aerodrome. While they hadn't engaged any bombers, they had spotted a downed pilot in the Channel and sent someone to save him. The reporter had never found out whether he'd been saved; the pilot he'd flown with had told him it was best not to bother. Reynolds decided he was right: if you worried too much about individual lives, you wouldn't be able to do your job.

Hughes-Hallett gave Reynolds and the other correspondents aboard an overview of the operation, calling it a historic undertaking and pointing out that there was a wide assortment of vessels in the assault fleet. He also said that all available fighter aircraft would be involved. As is often the case, however, what was important about his briefing were the things he omitted—the significance of the fleet including nothing larger than a destroyer, the absence of heavy bombers from the air armada. The reporters, of course, didn't know the background of the raid's planning and weren't equipped to adequately judge the plan anyway. Even if they had pressed him, the wartime censors who had to clear their stories would have taken out anything significant—or anything that would have made the commanders look bad.

The briefing included a map of Dieppe with its defenses, and reconnaissance photos that had been taken the day before. Reynolds peered at the pillboxes and obstructions, shown in remarkable detail.

The lieutenant who'd been assigned as a guide took out a schedule of the invasion and handed it to Reynolds. The reporter read through it in amazement, admiring the punctuality of the document. Something was scheduled to happen every ten minutes; bombardments were calculated down to the number of shells. To the man who just a year before had been covering entertainment, it read like a play.

Thoroughly impressed, he handed the schedule back to the lieutenant, then went to get his lifejacket as word came that they were approaching a minefield.

DIE LIKE AN AMERICAN

Mountbatten's prediction that 60 percent of the brigade would be killed and the reality of what they were up against had had a big effect on the Commandos and four Rangers aboard the *Prince Albert*. The Americans were shocked; even if the rounding went in their favor, two of them weren't coming home.

Szima, prowling through the ship and making friends as usual, came upon a sailor willing to sell a bottle of rum for a pound. The Ranger sped back to his companions to share. But the mood remained somber, despite the drinks. Koons was convinced he'd been selected for the mission because his company commander had it in for him.

"Captain Miller never did like me and just wants to get rid of me," he blurted, referring to Alvah Miller, who he thought had selected him.

"Nah," insisted Szima. "We're going to be the forty percent that survives."

Just then, a man came in with Commando uniforms for the men to wear. Szima gave the clothes a frown and said the hell with getting changed.

"We're going to wear American uniforms," he told the others. "And if they get me, they'll know I'm a sergeant, and an American."

The others agreed.

Szima kept on the pair of rubber-soled British boots he'd gotten, figuring they would be good for climbing. And like everyone in 4 Commando, he wore a soft watch cap; Lovat believed strongly that helmets, even when covered with cloth like those at 3 Commando, were too much of a potential for noise and decreased a Commando's ability to see and hear in battle. But Szima's sergeant's chevrons were easily discernible on his shoulder, a break with Commando practice, where no ranks were worn so that snipers could not cherry-pick their targets.

Before they knew it, the order came to board the landing craft. The small boats had to be swung out as the assault ship passed through the minefield. It was 2:30 a.m. They'd all been up for twenty-two hours.

Faces blackened, the Rangers filed into the corridor and headed for the galley where Lieutenant Colonel Lovat gave them a parting speech. To the Americans, he cut a suitably eccentric figure, with corduroy pants and a monogrammed sweater visible beneath his Commando tunic; he would sling a sporting rifle over his shoulder to lead the troops ashore. Lovat's speech mixed optimism—the Germans were not good in the dark—with dire warnings—wounded men would have to be left behind. In some respects, his words were even more desperate than Mountbatten's, but there was a critical difference— Lovat was going ashore to lead the men, and everyone aboard was fully aware that what he said to them applied to himself as well. Privately, Lovat had some doubts about the mission, but didn't share them with his men.

"Crew to the boats!" said the ship's captain, and the men began filing toward the waiting LCAs.

THROUGH THE MINEFIELD

Out ahead of the LCAs and other landing craft, General Truscott paced on deck of the *Fernie*, the backup flagship for the assault. The night had turned cool, but Truscott wanted to stay topside anyway; he was too excited to go below. His mind waxed poetic as he stared into the darkness. The infantry ships were "dark gray ghosts" in the water nearby. The landing craft, low to the waves and seeming to crawl along, "great dark water beetles" with "snout-like ramps." It would be an experience he would remember through the rest of his life, vivid even after years of other hard-fought campaigns.

A force of fifteen minesweepers moved ahead of the armada as it gathered a few miles off the coast. Together the sweepers cleared a straight path toward France, the way marked with small marker buoys that glowed against the dark water. The *Calpe* and *Fernie* entered the minefield first. Roberts had made a point of this earlier with some of the men, saying the mines were all he really worried about, and that he would take the risk ahead of them.

Two hundred and thirty-seven vessels were soon slipping past the mines. The nine small infantry assault ships carried a bit over a thousand men between them, but the bulk of the men were in the over one hundred small assault craft that made their way behind the larger ships. Also in the armada were two dozen tank carriers, crammed with Churchill tanks and men.

Besides the eight destroyers, there was a seven-hundred-ton sloop named the *Alresford* with a 4-inch gun, and the five-hundred-ton *Locust,* a gunboat that sported two 4- and one 3.7-inch weapons. Four steamboats, a dozen motor gunboats, and seven French Chasseurs— patrol boats of about a hundred feet armed with a 75mm cannon— were to provide additional firepower.

Once clear of the mines, the ships' captains checked their positions. By now the moon was out, and the men aboard each ship could see the black shadows of their companions fanning out around them.

There were several cases of nerves, including a few that led to accidents. Someone aboard the troop ship *Invicta*, heading toward Green Beach, took out a box of grenades and started to clean them. One of the grenades exploded, and seventeen men were wounded. In some of the small landing craft, soldiers accidentally discharged their weapons. But for the most part, the sea was quiet, the dull drone of diesel and gasoline engines barely rising above the lap of the waves.

At 3 a.m., the go–no-go point, the commanders huddled. The latest weather report predicted that fair weather would begin to disintegrate by noon, with rain to follow later in the afternoon. But by then they'd be back on the ships, heading for home.

The raiders were committed. There was no longer a chance of turning back.

Newhaven
November 2006

■ ■ ■

The lights glow a dull gray in the low-slung building wedged between the dock and the train tracks, the light so feeble it can't even make it to the puddles that line the sidewalk at the entrance. The building is the terminal for foot passengers taking the Transmarche Newhaven–Dieppe ferry; it has all the charm of a bus station in Poughkeepsie, New York, especially before six in the morning. The place is empty, except for a harried-looking woman at the counter.

"The ferry's been delayed," says the woman as I walked across the scuffed linoleum-tile floor.

"How delayed?"

She smirks. "See the ferry out there?"

"Yeah, is that it?"

"That's the two-thirty a.m. ferry. It hasn't left yet. The wind is up on the Channel."

The ferry captains have decided not to brave the crossing until the weather calms, and there's nothing anyone can do about it. The Transmarche employee has no idea when the next ferry will leave.

"Maybe at three," she says. "Can you call at noon?"

Someone has ripped the pay phone from its stand, but I manage to commandeer a taxi and make my way back to the bed-and-breakfast where I was staying. I have breakfast and brood about my bad luck. Leaving at three means that the ferry won't arrive in Dieppe until sometime around 8 p.m., Dieppe time. The city and beachfront will be dark. I'd arranged to take the ferry because I wanted to see the city from the water. I had a perfect image in my head: *the city would be spread out before the ocean, a few tourists walking along the beach, the sun high and bright. I'd stand on the deck at the front of the ferry, take a few pictures, then watch the city growing larger and larger, the way the Rangers must have done.*

But that's not going to happen. And now I have to worry that the carefully orchestrated plan for my visit in France, with its elaborate time schedules and multiple appointments, will prove more noose than aid.

The wind remains high all day, and the ferry is delayed several more hours, until at last we leave Newhaven well after dark. It's ironic, in a way, though—I'm on the water at roughly the time the Rangers were.

Unlike the terminal, the ferry is almost brand-new, with private cabins, a sleek bar, and other modern amenities. I grab a beer and sit near a large window, looking out at the black night. In the middle of the Channel the boat feels utterly isolated, a world unto itself: a comfortable one, far removed from plywood-sided landing boats.

It's not just the time that separates me from the past, or the fading memories of those who have lived through it. Our experiences limit how far we can go when reimagining other people's past. Whatever hardships I have had, they're imperfect analogues for those faced by the men crossing the Channel on the night of August 18, 1942.

Does it mean that I can't understand what they felt at all? How far do I really have to go to understand and communicate what they experienced?

Would I have understood more if I'd gone to Dieppe in an open boat? Can any of us understand what it means to come under heavy gunfire without the bullets and bombs whizzing over our heads? Can we try to emulate our heroes without knowing precisely what a hero feels in his gut?

I stare out at the black water and sip my beer. One thing's for sure: the Rangers would have preferred the ferry as well.

The English Channel
August 19, 1942
• • •

AT THE LAST MOMENT

The amazing thing about the assault to this point, thought Captain Murray as he surveyed the ocean from the deck of gunboat SGB 5, was how quiet it was. The ships seemed eerily silent. With its lights out and the sailors absorbed at their duty stations, SGB 5 felt almost like a ghost, lonely and alone, drifting across the water. The invasion fleet around them moved quietly away, each vessel its own dark island.

Once they passed through the minefield, the ships spread out for the run to the beach, becoming something akin to a football team at the line of scrimmage. The sheer variety of types caused the formation to buckle and fall off schedule. Their bit over, the minesweepers turned back toward England, only to cross into the path of the LCPs carrying 3 Commando. The columns of landing craft slowed, then fell into disarray as the captain of SGB 5—the gunboat leading them—tried to make up time. Within minutes, eight of the landing craft that had been following SGB 5 were split from the main group.

Captain Murray listened as Commander D. B. Wyburd, the Navy group officer, explained the situation to the Commando leader, Colonel Durnford-Slater. The eight boats carried more than 150 men—a good portion of the 460 planned for the raid. And they'd already lost about 50 in the boats that were forced to turn back.

There was nothing to do but hope they'd show up, Wyburd told them. Murray crossed the deck, waiting to speak to the men aboard the flak boat as it drew alongside.

Out in his LCP, Lieutenant Loustalot checked his wristwatch. It was 0330. They were due at the beach at "nautical twilight"—0440, a good three-quarters of an hour before dawn. Loustalot glanced around the landing craft, checking not just on the Rangers with him but the Commandos as well. He felt a mixture of nerves and pride. To the west, the Ranger lieutenant saw dark shadows on the horizon—the rest of the fleet. Up ahead, SGB 5 was barely visible on the water.

Then there were other shadows to the east, near the lead ship. They looked like different boats. No sailor, the Louisiana native wasn't sure at first. Then he realized they were moving across the path of the convoy, not with it.

Who were they?

In the next moment, something exploded behind them, and tracers filled the air. Reflexively, Loustalot threw himself down for cover.

SIX

YELLOW BEACH

Off the Coast of Dieppe
August 19, 1942

* * *

THE GERMAN CONVOY

Group 5, the vessels containing 3 Commando, had run smack into a German convoy. A German escort taking cargo ships to Dieppe harbor noticed shadows on the water off its port bow, and sent a star shell into the sky, illuminating the gunboat and several of the landing craft. The Germans began firing at the nearest craft; the three other escorts with the Nazi convoy joined in.

"Get below!" Wyburd told Captain Murray and Commando leader Lieutenant Colonel Durnford-Slater on SGB 5. As the two soldiers scrambled for cover, Wyburd ordered his helmsman to take the ship directly at the Germans, hoping to shield the fleet of plywood-hulled craft behind him. The gunboat's deck guns swung into action as her gunners began answering the cannonade erupting from the German escorts. LCF 1 veered forward from the rear of the column to help.

The German combat vessels are generally described as E boats, the English name applied to the *Schnellboot,* a 114-foot high-speed raider that carried two torpedoes and a 20mm and a 4mm gun on her deck. The German report on the incident, however, calls them *Unterseeboots-Jäger*—submarine hunters. The term was applied to a class of ships converted from other uses, generally small merchant vessels or trawlers, and outfitted with a variety of guns. These would have been somewhat bigger than E boats, not as quick or maneuverable, with bigger guns, but without the crack crews that typically manned the E boats.

Whatever the escorts were, SGB 5 and the flak boat should not have had to face them alone. The crossing plan called for two destroyers, the *Brocklesby* and the Polish *Slazak,* to be ahead of the group and on its flank, almost directly in front of the German convoy as it approached. But the destroyers had gotten off course and were five miles away, well behind the assault group; when the captain of the *Slazak* saw the gun flashes in the distance, he assumed the landing had started and the firing was on shore. Another destroyer also saw the flare-up, but thought it was coming from ships in the fleet.

Les Kness had just brought up some ammunition from below when he saw lights arcing across the water. His first thought was that they were actually pretty. Then he realized they were tracers—and not only that, but they were coming toward him. He jumped into one of the nearby gun turrets, only to be showered by hot shells. Kness managed to get them off and hunkered down while the battle raged.

Sweazey, who'd been sorting out equipment and getting ready for the landing, threw himself to the deck. A strip of steel running around the railing provided some cover, but shells ricocheted everywhere, even a few inches over his head. As the gunners aboard the LCF began firing back, Sweazey hugged the deck, thinking buckets of lead were being tossed back and forth.

The Navy crews in charge of the smaller landing craft, meanwhile, began taking evasive action, zigging and zagging out of the way. For the soldiers, it was the worst sort of battle—they were helpless passengers, unable to do anything more than tighten the chin straps on their fabric-covered helmets and hope for the best. Others grabbed their Bren guns and fired in the direction of the enemy tracers, more for effect than with any hope of hitting anything.

The flak boat's gunners zeroed their weapons on one of the German ships, *UJ 1404*. Sweazey raised his head in time to see flames erupt from the ship, which looked to him like an armed trawler. Within moments, it lit on fire and exploded.

Cannon and machine-gun bullets from the other German boats raked the bridge and superstructure of SGB 5, knocking out the ship's radio and cutting her off from the rest of the fleet. The forward gun was disabled. Then a shell hit the engine room; steam escaping from the damaged boiler added a shriek to the screams of the wounded.

With the black night now red and gray, Roy Murray tried to help some of his men who'd been wounded. Rangers Stanley Bush, John Knapp, and Charles Reilly had all been hit; so had a good number of the Royal Navy crew. With SGB 5 stopped dead in the water, the sailors expected their attackers to close and finish her off. Instead, the gunfire suddenly stopped and the German ships slipped away. Battered themselves and sure that they had encountered a force of fast raiders, the Nazis had decided to retreat toward Le Tréport, several miles to the northeast.

It is one of the great myths of Dieppe that the encounter between the German convoy and the Commandos alerted the defenders at Dieppe and the other beaches, and therefore caused the mission to fail. But while the gunfire may have shaken up some of the troops near Berneval, it did not have any effect in the other sectors. The German logs make it clear that the only troops that responded to their posts because of the clash were at a Luftwaffe post to the east of Berneval. Other units were already at their posts as part of the standing watch. In no case were units alerted that this was part of an invasion. It was not until landing craft were sighted at Puys at 0430 that the defenders began responding to the threat of a seaborne attack.

The myth seems to have started because of the initial statements given by the military commanders soon after the raid that indicated that surprise had been lost. Certainly that must have seemed a logical assumption for them to make at the time. From the very first drafts of the official Canadian history, several historians have tried to downplay any connection between the convoy clash and the main operation, but the notion has lived on.

The engagement had lasted only a few minutes, but it had utterly wrecked the assault plan. Four LCPs had been badly damaged; they turned back toward England and limped home. Five others closed in around SGB 5, which was still dead in the water.

On LCF 1, Kness climbed out of the turret and was handed a bucket through a scuttle hole by someone below.

"Hand me that bucket, you fawking Yank," yelled a British sergeant. Kness did so, and found himself as part of a bucket brigade attacking a fire that had started in the galley below. Water was pulled from over the side and passed down to the galley. The buckets were filled with silver kippers as well as water, a school of fish apparently among the victims of the battle.

Having something to do focused Kness, taking him away from the chaos and worry for a moment. He concentrated on the buckets, grabbing and passing, urging the others on as the fire was put out.

Battered but still afloat, SGB 5's crew worked to get their engines back online. Up on the bridge, Lieutenant Colonel Durnford-Slater called Murray and Wyburd together to assess the situation. They had started the operation with twenty-three landing vessels and a little over four hundred men. As far as he could tell from surveying the water around him, he now had five landing vessels with roughly a hundred men, some of whom had been wounded or were already dead.

Durnford-Slater could also no longer count on surprise. With less than a quarter of his force, unsure of where his second-in-command Major Young was, he concluded he had no chance of taking out the Goebbels battery. He called off the attack.

Besides everything else, the German cannonade had wiped out SGB 5's radio, and there was no way of communicating what had happened to the force commander or the command ships. Knowing they had to be alerted, Durnford-Slater boarded a landing craft with Wyburd and set out to find the *Calpe* while SGB 5 turned toward home, leading three landing craft in a slow limp toward Newhaven. Before it left, Captain Murray clambered down from the deck to the flak boat, hoping to find a way to get to one of the other beaches, or at least observe what was going on.

With dawn rapidly approaching, it appeared that 3 Commando's attack had been completely thwarted. But in fact it was just getting under way.

3 COMMANDO'S ATTACK

At almost the exact moment Captain Murray got aboard the landing craft, Lieutenant Loustalot and a force of about a hundred Rangers and Commandos were crouched in their LCPs, trying to figure out where they were. A small combat craft, ML 346—little more than a speedboat with machine guns—had managed to find and lead five LCPs away from the fray and was heading with them toward Yellow Beach 1, the beach to the east of the gun battery where Durnford-Slater had intended to land. Without radio contact from the commander, both the sailors and soldiers assumed they were to go ahead with the landing. And so they did.

It seemed amazing, but no gunfire greeted the first of the boats. The men in the Goebbels shore battery and the lookouts near the beach had been alerted to the naval clash, but they thought it was simply a particularly nasty confrontation between naval vessels, a common occurrence on the Channel. The pillbox closest to the ravine had not been manned, and there were no German soldiers at all on the beach.

Besides the men who manned the battery itself, there was only a small guard force and a handful of soldiers from a nearby Luftwaffe air station in the area. When someone finally spotted a landing craft below, the defenders rallied and began firing a machine gun from the cliff top. ML 346 returned fire, holding them off as the Commandos and Rangers dashed from the water to the shelter of the cliffs.

Ranger Edwin Furru made his way to one of the gullies, waiting behind the scouts and section leader clipping through the barbed wire with hand cutters. The original plan had called for the men simply to blast their way through using bangalore torpedoes. Unfortunately, all of the torpedoes were back on the flak boat, which was nowhere in sight. Cutting the wires by hand was slow going, but the Germans hadn't figured out where the invaders were, and Furru was able to get past and then walk his way up, hugging the side of the rocks, until he and the Commandos he was with reached the top of the passage.

Still walking—albeit quickly—they moved through a backyard, passing a garden and a small cottage. Sprinting across the road, they headed in the direction of the hotel at the center of the hamlet to the east of the battery. Lieutenant Loustalot, Sergeant Albert Jacobson, and Private Bresnahan were behind Furru somewhere, the Commandos fanning out as they tried to find the big guns. It was getting light now, and the Germans were rushing to defend the battery.

MAJOR YOUNG

As Furru and the others worked their way past the barbed wire, a
small band of their comrades was racing toward the guns from the
west.

Major Peter Young, second-in-command of 3 Commando, had
continued to Yellow Beach 2 in LCP 15 after the convoy ran into the
German escorts. A veteran of two Commando assaults in Norway,
Young had spent time as a planner with Combined Operations
before rejoining the Commando. He had been responsible for much
of the unit's training, and he had a reputation for setting a tight pace.
He had no way of knowing that Durnford-Slater had called off the
attack, and in fact believed that his orders were to land even if his
was the only boat that made it.

So did the landing craft's captain, Sublieutenant Henry Buckee.
Buckee found Yellow Beach 2 and delivered the boat's section
unscathed five minutes ahead of schedule at 0445. Young, limited to
a tenth of the planned manpower, a handful of mortar shells, and
without bangalore torpedoes, decided he would make the attack anyway. They found the path leading to the village of Berneval blocked
off by barbed wire but undefended. Fearing that the walkway that
ran up the cut had been mined, Young abandoned the heavier of his
mortars and told his men climb up the side of the gully.

It was slow going. The Germans had cut pegs into the rocks to
hold the barbed wire in place. The Commandos used these as hand-
holds, but the chalky walls were slippery and wet with spray. Nearly
everyone, including Young, fell at least once as they worked their
way up. It took a half hour to cover the hundred and fifty feet to the
top; by the time they reached the empty field at the top the sun was
up and they were easy targets. Fortunately, no Germans had been
posted nearby, and after a short break, Young split his group into

three small bands. They set out in the direction of the battery—not hard to find, for it had just started to fire at Dieppe. Young ordered the men to run, hoping to get to the guns before they did too much damage.

A surprising number of residents were in the narrow streets of the village. They mostly kept their distance, though a few waved encouragingly at the Commandos. Shells from one of the ships or perhaps something from the flight of Hurricanes detailed to drop smoke on the battery just prior to touchdown had started a fire in the village. A local fire brigade worked to put it out as the Commandos ran past.

Young's group still hadn't encountered any Germans. That changed as they approached the church at the heart of the village. A machine-gun battery on the roadside began shooting at them, and the men scrambled behind the building for cover. Setting up the two-inch mortar, they managed to silence their enemy after a few salvos.

Their route into Berneval had taken them behind the battery, and Young at first thought that the steeple in the church might give his snipers a vantage point on the men manning the guns. But the church was small and its tower mainly decorative; the ladder had been taken away years before and Young couldn't find a way in. The troop began advancing through an apple orchard in the direction of the battery's rear, only to come under heavy fire. Stymied once more, Young decided to backtrack and come at the guns through the cornfield they'd passed earlier.

By now, the ground reverberated as the heavy guns threw their shells at the ships offshore. Closer to home, some of the battery's guards spotted the Commandos and began firing at them.

From the field, the Commandos could see the rear of the battery. They began showering the gun crews with gunfire and lobbed two-inch mortar shells into the battery; their supply of the latter was limited to half a dozen, all that they'd carried with them from the beach.

One of the gun batteries turned out to be a decoy, and it appeared that only one of the weapons was being fired when Young's men began their attack, firing the last of their small horde of mortar shells as well as their guns. Young wasn't sure whether his men's bullets hit anyone or not, but the Germans scrambled away from the artillery for cover, halting their bombardment.

Major Young and his men kept up their attack on the Goebbels battery for about an hour. The Commandos would fire, then move to a new position, then move again, trying to make it as hard as possible for the Germans to strike them. The major had taken the M1 the Rangers gave him on the raid, but he regretted it, for he had some difficulty loading the unusual weapon.

Exasperated by the steady stream of bullets raking their position, one of the gun crews turned its weapon 180 degrees, lowered its barrel, and sent a shell toward their tormentors. Young was surprised, but then realized they'd achieved their goal—shells being fired at them meant the weapon couldn't be used against the invasion force. The Commandos were so close to the weapon that it presented no harm; the barrel simply couldn't be depressed far enough to aim at them. It took the Germans a dozen salvos or so before they realized this and gave up.

By 7 a.m., the Commandos were running out of ammunition. Young ordered his group to withdraw. But by now the Germans had brought reinforcements into the area, and a patrol of German soldiers moved to cut them off. Young's men fought a running gun battle to the top of the cliffs, moving with the same precision they'd practiced just a few days before. Two men would leapfrog back, then cover the others. The withdrawal went well, with no casualties, until they started back down the ravine.

Here the Germans had the advantage. Rushing to the cliff edge, they began peppering the ravine and beach with machine-gun fire. But ML 346 had been watching the engagement offshore, and now rode to the rescue. The tiny gunboat unleashed a barrage of covering fire at the Nazis. While they backed away from the cliff, Young got the rest of his men down to the beach, where they sprinted toward their returning landing craft. With ML 346 blasting away at their German pursuers, the men hopped aboard and waited for it to back out of the shallow water.

The craft groaned, shifted, and groaned again. It shook and rumbled. The one thing it didn't do was budge off the beach. With the tide going out, the Commandos weighed too much for it to float in the shallow water.

Guns were tossed overboard in a desperate attempt to make it lighter. The craft's commander tried using the kedge anchor to help pull them out, but couldn't get off the rocks. Finally Young, one of his lieutenants, and a Bren gunner clambered over the side and the landing craft pulled free.

The three men grabbed hold of ropes and did their best to keep their heads above water as the boat veered out to sea under fire. The Germans at the top of the cliff now had easier shots. They emptied their rifles at the landing craft, sending a steady stream of slugs out after the boat until it reached deep water. Young and the others were pulled aboard, wet but intact.

The gunfire wounded one of the sailors; another of Young's men had been shot and injured near the ravine. But otherwise, the entire section had returned from the engagement unharmed.

The landing craft rendezvoused with ML 346. Young and the rest of the Commandos climbed aboard the patrol boat, where the gunboat's sailors gave them coffee and a bit of whiskey and rum to go with it. Then they headed toward Newhaven, their part of the battle already done.

LOUSTALOT FALLS

As Young and his men were scrambling down to the beach, the other members of 3 Commando who had made it ashore found themselves enmeshed in a fierce firefight with the German reinforcements up on the cliff to the east.

Private Furru and the dozen or so Commandos he was with had climbed into the backyards of the houses near the cliff, and then cut across toward a large house that looked like an inn dominating the small settlement above the water. A scout entered the building; after he made sure it was clear, the group ran up the hill and found a path that led in the direction of the gun battery.

But they didn't get very far before a barrage of heavy German gunfire stopped them cold. The section returned fire, but within minutes it was clear that they were outgunned and wouldn't be able to advance. On the contrary, they were in danger of being overrun. A squadron of Nazi soldiers had arrived by bicycle to immediately shore up the defenses; other reinforcements were on their way with field guns. Moving in from all sides, the Germans pinned the Commandos down, threatening to slice them into isolated groups and annihilate them. The battery unreachable, Furru's squad had no option but to try to fight their way back to the beach before they were cut off completely.

One by one, the other sections came to the same conclusion. The Germans, knowing there were only a few ways down to the water, moved to cut them off.

Lieutenant Loustalot and a small group of Commandos found themselves pinned down not far from the path they'd taken up from the beach. German machine gunners had taken up positions at the end of the field, cutting off the way down.

Loustalot rose and beckoned to the men to follow. Firing his rifle, the Louisiana native leaped forward in the attack, his field glasses thumping against his chest as he ran.

The machine guns concentrated their fire on the khaki-clad figure rising from the grass. Within seconds, he was falling. At least two of the Commandos with him also fell, but the bullets from the attackers either killed or wounded the machine gunner, and the firing stopped.

One of the Commandos glanced down at the American officer. Blood covered his midsection. The field glasses he wore around his neck lay to one side of his chest, the glass smashed by the German bullets. He was already dead; there was nothing anyone could do for him. The Commando and the others ran forward to the ravine, grateful for Loustalot's courage, their attention once more focused on the enemy.

Ranger Walter Bresnahan dropped to his knee, lingering for a moment, when he saw Loustalot's dead body. But fresh gunfire nearby convinced him to move on, and he scrambled toward the beach.

The rest of the Commandos who'd made it to the cliff came down the same path a few minutes later. Furru, now at the tail of his section, did his best to run at a controlled pace, remembering everything he'd practiced over the past few weeks. As he reached the path that Loustalot and the others had cleared, he came upon a pair of injured Commandos, too wounded to get up. Private Furru slid in next to them, but the men told him to move on before he, too, was shot. He jumped up and ran toward the lip of the ravine to the beach. A short distance away, he saw a body clad in a GI uniform limp in the field. He ran to it, and found it was Loustalot, already dead.

Another round of gunfire convinced him to move on again. As he began clambering down toward the beach, Furru saw something whiz by. The Germans had brought a field gun to bear on the raiders. Furru, who'd been in an artillery unit before joining the Rangers, could tell from the sound that it was a captured French 75, an old but still-devastating artillery piece.

Scrambling into the wide ravine to the beach below Berneval, the private spotted fellow Ranger Sergeant Albert Jacobson. Pausing for a moment, the two men shared a quick smoke, then descended the last twenty or thirty feet to the beach. Three landing craft were stranded nearby. One had been abandoned, its crew dead. Another had sunk in the shallow water not far offshore. The third was on fire.

Furru and Jacobson ran toward a nearby cave at the foot of the cliff. There were already a dozen or so men there; the Americans asked the others where their landing boat was. No one knew. The men hunkered down, hoping the craft would show up soon.

It would be a long wait.

SEVEN

ORANGE BEACH

Off the Coast of Dieppe
August 19, 1942

*   *   *

WITH NUMBER 4 COMMANDO

Several hours before on the far western flank of the convoy, Ranger Alex Szima had inflated his Mae West lifejacket and promptly fallen off to sleep after the LCA cleared the minefield. He was suddenly woken by the sound of gunfire off in the distance to the east. Roused, he saw flashes of star shells in the distance.

The sailors leading the boats spotted what looked like three German ships between them and the shore. The V-shaped flotilla changed course to the west to evade them, hoping to preserve the element of surprise by avoiding a fight.

The assault on the Hess battery near Varengeville called for two columns. One would land directly in front of the coastal battery near the lighthouse at Pointe d'Ailly on a beach dubbed Orange 1. The second would land to the west near Sainte-Marguerite-sur-Mer at

Orange 2, swinging in a semicircle to attack the battery from the rear. With the lighthouse flashing its beacon ahead, the landing craft split into two columns, each going to a different side of the lighthouse. SGB 9 (later given the name *Grey Goose*) led LCAs 3, 5, 7, and 8 toward Sainte-Marguerite and Orange Beach 2 at the west. Rangers Stempson and Brady were in this group, which was under Lord Lovat's direct command. LCAs 2, 4, and 6 sailed behind MGB 312. Szima and Koons were in this detachment, which was led by Mills-Roberts.

The lighthouse's beacon stopped flashing. Star shells flew into the air from the tower nearby. The light caught the small boats, illuminating everyone, holding them for a long moment as the flares burned down. Worried that they had been spotted, Mills-Roberts told himself it was too hard for people onshore to see the low-lying boats.

Koons had calmed down considerably since his outburst aboard the ship. Or maybe he was just tired. He hadn't gotten much sleep the night before, and between his fatigue and the rhythmical rocking of the boat, he, too, dozed off as the boats headed toward shore. Suddenly, seawater splashed on his face, and he woke to the buzz of two Spitfires racing overhead. The airplanes, only a few hundred feet over the ocean, began firing their cannons at the lighthouse. Antiaircraft batteries began to respond.

I'm really in the war, Koons told himself.

While the attacking aircraft took the attention of the defenders, the LCAs plodded relentlessly toward the beaches. The cliffs were still in shadow, and besides the lighthouse and two white buildings visible above the rocks and trees, it was difficult to make out landmarks. The sailors looked for a pair of V-shaped cuts in the chalky cliff where they'd hope to land. But the shadows made them difficult to discern. The evasive maneuvers earlier had taken the force farther west than they'd wanted; the sailors came east, looking for the ravines or the stairs at the base of the crevices that would give them a way up. Finally, someone spotted one of the cracks in the cliff and began racing toward it. A Commando counted down the distance.

And then they were there, the boats stopping with a rough grumble against the stones. The ramps fell and the men in the LCAs leaped forward. Training had taught them that there was no time to waste in the first moments on the beach. Szima and his Commando partner, the Irishman Jim Haggerty, splashed through two feet of water and ran quickly to the shadow of the cliffs, hunkering down as the team responsible for clearing the ravines scouted the two openings nearby, deciding which to take. As at most of the other cuts along the coast, the Germans had strung their spools of barbed wire across the ravines. The obstructions appeared less formidable in the wider gully to the west; a pair of bangalore torpedoes were put into place, and the concertina wire blown up.

As at Berneval, the soldiers feared that the main path up the cut—a set of concrete and stone steps—had been mined. Clambering up the sides, they slipped on the wet rocks and mud, crawling at times just to keep moving. A reinforced German machine-gun position with supporting trenches sat at the intersection of the ravine paths at the top, arranged to catch both in its sights. Fortunately, there was no one in it.

Spitfires continued to strafe the lighthouse area, where a group of Germans were manning gun posts. Antiaircraft weapons near the battery opened fire, but so far, the Commando group had not been engaged.

Now that they were off the beach, the different sections and subsections began taking on their assignments. Szima and Haggerty ran past a stand of pine and fern to the narrow road that ended near the path to the beach. Small houses and buildings dotted both sides of the road; there were small gardens and open fields. Near one of the houses, Szima saw his first dead man—a German soldier whose grenade had exploded when he'd been shot. The man was in pieces; steam rose from his broken body.

Working with some Free French Commandos, the Rangers' section began moving through the yards and checking the houses, looking for Germans. Going through the first house, Szima found a locked bedroom door. He gathered himself, then took a step, raised his leg, and stomped his foot against the wood. The door flew inside; a dead German lay on the bed.

Something moved in the corner; Szima jerked and fired, so tense that his finger clicked off two rounds.

His target crumpled to the ground. When he regained his breath, he realized it was a blanket that had been tossed in the corner.

The French Commandos accompanying the raiding party assured the locals that they would not be harmed. The assault was aimed only at the Germans and would last just a few hours; they must be careful not to expose themselves to retaliation. The residents, scared but not unfriendly, gave them some information about the German defenses. One offered the Commandos fresh eggs—it was, after all, nearly breakfast time.

STEMPSON AND BRADY

Things didn't start as smoothly for the Commando detachment landing on the western beach near Sainte-Marguerite. German machine-gun fire opened up on the landing craft as they touched down. Sergeant Stempson leaped from the LCA, running with a twelve-man section along the steep beach toward a barbed-wire obstruction that blocked the path upward. As they ran, a machine gun pulled them into its sights; four men fell, but Stempson and the others were able to toss a "rabbit netting" or metal blanket over the barbed wire that allowed them to cross. A pair of Commandos carrying tubular ladders followed the riflemen, slapping their ladders together so they could climb. Under heavy fire, the point team scaled a cliff about thirty feet high. Three more Commandos had fallen by the time Stempson discovered that the machine gunners were firing, not from a pillbox as he'd thought, but from a position about twenty yards away. While they weren't in a position to take out the gun, they had a clear shot on the gunner's ammunition bearer as he ran forward with ammo. Stempson took aim and fired as the German ran forward, boxes of bullets in both hands. At twenty yards, it was a no-sweat shot. The man tumbled over like the jackrabbits Stempson had once hunted back home.

The machine gunner still had plenty of ammo left. He continued to fire, pinning the Commandos down.

Somewhere to Stempson's right, Private Brady and the team he'd been assigned to headed toward a local road, aiming to cut it off so it couldn't be used to reinforce the battery. Brady carried a bag of grenades; he was the fifth man in the section behind the ladder carrier, the bangalore specialist, a scout, and the section sergeant. As he started to climb up the cliffside, machine-gun bullets began cascading around him. The assault party had been caught in a cross fire from a pair of guns above.

Brady's grenade pouch came undone, and he had to stop and cinch the bag so he wouldn't lose the grenades. The man just ahead of him slumped to the side, shot; as Brady tried to squeeze past, a bullet passed through the rear of his pants. The man behind him was hit in the face, perhaps by the same bullet, or at least the same burst of fire.

Brady kept moving.

By now the rest of the landing force was coming ashore behind the advance teams, streaming through the path Stempson had taken. The group's success depended heavily on their getting off the beach as quickly as possible, and the men ran for all they were worth, dashing across the twenty or so yards to the ravine. MGB 312 engaged a pill-box just to the west, between the landing area and the village, eliminating it as a threat. At some point, the defenders began peppering the area with mortar fire. A Boston attack aircraft flew in overhead, the four cannon in its nose blazing. Two more followed in quick succession. The attack from the air seemed to fluster the German gunners for a moment; a few turned their weapons toward the plane in a vain attempt to shoot it down.

Stempson and the others on the ridge pressed their attack against the machine gunner who was pinning their men down. Under covering fire, one of the Commandos ran forward and threw a grenade into the position. A low thud announced it had done its job; the gun lay silent, its master dead.

Commandos sped through the gap. Speed was everything now; with the defensive line breached, they raced to take advantage. Ignoring the gun positions to the right, the Commandos raced into the gap they'd created. The woods, with low bushes, brambles, and fern, helped shield the breech. Under attack from the air and with the motorboat's cannon firing in their direction, the Germans did not immediately realize that their defensive line had been pierced.

Brady and his Commando pal crossed through a wooded copse and field, reaching the road. The men ran to the nearest telephone pole, and then began what looked like a circus act—the six-foot-six Brady boosted his five-foot-four companion up his back and onto his shoulders, steadying him as he began to cut the phone wire. Bullets filled the air, splintering the pole but miraculously missing both the Ranger and Commando. Wires cut, they dove to the ground and began returning fire.

The German who was shooting at them suddenly stopped; he'd

either been shot by someone in the team or decided it was time to retreat. Brady got to his feet, joining the others as they sprinted toward the road they'd been tasked to secure.

AHEAD OF SCHEDULE

As his men cleared the hamlet near the beach and moved into position northwest of the German battery, Mills-Roberts took stock of the situation. Two LCAs had been sent to ferry additional ammunition and men from MGB 312. A party had set out to cut the local telephone wires. Defensive positions had been established. The sun was rising, but thus far the operation was running incredibly smoothly. The plan called for Mills-Roberts's team to engage the gun battery from positions directly in front of it at 0630; this would draw the Germans' attention away from the rear and side of the gun battery as Lovat's team approached to make the main assault. It was now 0540. They were well ahead of schedule.

Suddenly the ground shook with the report of a heavy gun going into action. The Hess battery had been manned and begun to fire. With the shells a threat to the main assault fleet, Mills-Roberts decided to attack the battery immediately. He ordered his companies to advance on the gun emplacement.

What Mills-Roberts didn't know was that the German defenders were regrouping on his right flank, preparing to attack the Commando group from the rear.

LIKE PUPPETS, FALLING ON A STAGE

The German battery sat in front of a run of buildings nestled on the north side of the main road. It was bordered on the west by fields and yards. The Commandos approached from the west and southwest, moving from the hamlet they had just secured to the one just behind the battery, and to the fields that were on the west of the big guns. Low hedges and wire fences marked the boundaries of the generously spaced yards; dirt lanes ran at the sides. Some of the fields were filled with apple trees, and a number of Commandos grabbed apples as they advanced, stuffing them into their pockets.

Germans sniped from the houses and fields. Running through the orchard, Szima heard a buzz and threw himself to the ground. A bullet grazed his watch cap—one of at least two that would knock it off during the engagement. Pulling up his rifle, the Ranger spotted the man across the road; as the German took aim at a Commando, Szima squeezed off six rounds of black-tipped, armor-piercing bullets into the man, blowing him to pieces.

Farther up the road, a sniper sat on a rooftop, dousing the road with gunfire. Once more, Szima worked himself around to a firing position; his second shot sent the man crashing to the ground.

Even if he'd forgotten the maps and model he'd been shown, Szima would have known he was close to the battery by the report of the guns as he ran. The big cannons made a heavy *ther-ump* as they fired, tossing their shells in the direction of the invasion fleet. Crossing the road in their direction, Szima spotted a stable in one of the yards and ran for it. As he reached the archway, someone yelled, "Watch out, Yank!" He ducked inside just as a German potato masher—a hand grenade with a long handle to make it easier to toss—flew into the courtyard.

After it exploded, Szima caught a glimpse of Haggerty sighting on the German nearby. He didn't stop firing until he'd run through his Thompson's fifty-bullet drum magazine.

Szima burst into the farm building. Seeing it was clear, he climbed to the second story and found what he was looking for—an unobstructed view of the rear of the battery. The white work clothes and shiny helmets of the gunners ferrying shells to their guns made obvious targets.

The Germans were like puppets, Szima thought, watching them

fall as he pumped the trigger. He sighted, pressed the trigger, sighted again. The bang of the gun as it fired was followed by a loud ping as the armor-piercing bullet hit the helmet and went through the soldier's skull. He hit another man, his helmet flying upward, spinning twenty-five feet or more in the air.

Koons's squad found a similar vantage point in a barn nearby. He zeroed in on the battery and began shooting. A German went down; then another. Then another and another. It was almost surreal. He had a perfect vantage, and he became almost like a machine, firing at the enemy. The words of the men who'd trained him, the instructor who'd taught him to shoot, the experience of the range, and years of hunting—all of that was working somewhere on an unconscious level. He was just doing his job, sighting and firing so quickly he lost track of how many men he hit.

As the harrying fire began to have an effect, German snipers began shooting at the buildings. Szima moved to another spot, and began firing again. The snipers chased him from the second spot. This time the Ranger jumped down and landed in a manure pit. He had a hell of a time clearing his gun, but managed to do so quickly and resumed firing.

The antiaircraft gunner at the rear of the German battery lowered his sights and began firing at the attacking Commandos. The Boys-gun team had moved into the fields at the northwest. Hearing the gun start to fire, the Commando got close enough to see the antiaircraft tower. He zeroed the long barrel of the heavy gun on the flak cannon and sent a 55mm shell into the weapon. The mechanism on the German antiair gun jammed, limiting its field of fire.

By now a German 81mm mortar crew had rallied to their weapons, and began lobbing their large bombs just beyond the battery's defensive perimeter. The heavy shells killed more cows than men, but for a moment the starch seemed to go out of the Allied attack. Then a Commando two-inch mortar crew in the field near

Koons set down their weapon and zeroed in on the German coastal battery. The first shot went wide right, landing behind the big guns. The next was a direct hit in the middle of the battery—but the small bomb seemed to explode without doing damage, its burst absorbed easily by the sandbags protecting the emplacements.

The third sailed closer to the perimeter. It just missed Gun 1—and instead struck the sacks of cordite stacked nearby. The charges exploded with a shriek. Flames leaped from the battery as the ground shook. The men nearby were killed; when other Germans rushed to help them or put out the flames, they were cut down by Koons and the others firing from the buildings behind them. Secondary explosions rocked the battery, and the big guns fell silent, their crews either dead or scrambling to protect themselves from the onslaught.

LOVAT ARRIVES

To the west, Lord Lovat's Commandos had been slowed by the line of machine guns at the top of the cliff and had trouble gaining momentum. The Colonel pushed them on fiercely, finally directing them to run rather than march toward their target. They ran over a mile and a half, trying to get back on schedule. The headquarters group briefly got tangled with another troop, which began firing at it. Fortunately, the confusion was straightened out before anyone was wounded. As they moved ahead once again, some of the Commandos spotted German soldiers boarding a truck in a field. It was the German counterattack, preparing to ride in behind Mills-Roberts's group. The Commandos fired from close range and then used bayonets, obliterating the force of thirty-five.

Minutes later, advance elements of Lovat's group reached Mills-Roberts's perimeter. The Commandos began organizing for the final attack.

While the coastal guns had stopped firing, they had not been completely destroyed. The only way to guarantee that they would not be used against the invasion fleet was to spike them. Specialists within the Commando troops were carrying explosive charges to do just that; in order to use them, the attackers had to get through the barbed wire and machine-gun positions that formed the inner ring of the battery's defenses. German mortar shells were still falling, there were snipers in different positions around the hamlet, and several machine-gun nests continued to pepper the Commandos arrayed around the perimeter. Every so often, an aircraft would roar overhead, guns blazing.

The Germans, with some of their telephone lines cut off, were confused about the size of the enemy attack; at one point, headquarters received information that the invaders had been repulsed. Though far better organized, the Commandos, too, were caught in the confusion. Mills-Roberts's decision to attack early meant that not all of the German soldiers had been rousted from the houses on their flanks. The narrow lanes and undulating terrain presented many places for a soldier to hide or approach an enemy; the trees and houses presented cover and unseen vantage points. Grenades and rifles were used at close range. Rather than a huge, finely coordinated mass, the engagement was a collection of intense, bloody splinters, fought in twos and threes, occasionally fives and sixes; many of those who died on both sides never knew where the man who killed him was.

Others saw him eyeball to eyeball. A German sniping near the battery shot a Commando, dropping him nearby. Thinking the man was alone, the Nazi soldier came out from his hiding spot, kicking the Commando as he passed. Unfortunately for the German, the Commando's comrades were nearby. He was gut-shot, then bayoneted, dying not far from the man he'd only wounded.

As Lovat's forces searched for a good place to breach the barbed-wire ring around the battery, the Commandos' mortars began lobbing smoke to cover them. A dozen Spitfires—harried by Focke-Wulfes that dove at them from above—arrived around 0630, firing their cannons at the battery and its defensive positions. Some of the aircraft also took aim at the buildings the Commandos were using to fire at the battery. At least one Commando was heavily wounded in the pass.

Lovat's after-action report included information that "two Ranger sergeants" were in the building hit by Spitfires, and that bricks fell on their heads. But the Rangers were never near the houses, and in fact the only two Ranger sergeants with 4 Commando—Szima and Stempson—were never together during the entire battle. The story has nonetheless been repeated in many places.

One of the troops discovered a path through the barbed wire— possibly a shortcut used by the battery members—and the Commandos flooded through. Just outside the gun pits, they paused and fixed bayonets. And then with a yell, the men leaped forward, running into the position.

They caught a group of Germans by surprise from the rear. The Nazis were cut down. A lone German coming out of the bunkers was sliced practically in half by the bullets.

The fight reached a furious crescendo as the Commandos overran the German position. Men screamed and cried, both in victory and death, shouting for strength and wailing as a hail of bullets and steel cut them down. Guns, bayonets, knives, and even fists flew in the mad tumult. The dead and dying, some blackened by fire, others almost immaculate in their white work clothes, lay in crumpled heaps on the ground. The Commandos did not take prisoners.

With the battery now secure, charges were set against the guns; others were tossed into the bunkers. Lovat ordered the men to set everything on fire.

A NEAR-DEATH EXPERIENCE

Stuffed full of high explosives, the six French cannons at Varengeville exploded in quick succession as the fuses set by Number 4 Commando went off. Their barrels split; jags of metal flew through the air, showering the woods and nearby fields.

With the battery overrun, Corporal Koons gave up his sniping position. His Commando buddy had been wounded slightly and was being treated by the medics. Koons moved back through the small hamlet. He met up with one of the Free French Commandos, and went with him to one of the houses. The Frenchman attempted to calm the two old ladies in the house, assuring them that the raiders meant no harm. He pointed to Corporal Koons and explained that he was an American. The family didn't seem impressed—perhaps because the woman's son was a French officer who was collaborating with the Germans in Berlin.

Koons rummaged through the clothes of the dead Germans nearby, grabbing wallets and papers, anything that would give the Allies information about the unit. He was still on an adrenaline rush.

The guns had been destroyed, but Lord Lovat's Commando groups were still under fire from the mortars and stragglers from the troop assigned to protect the battery. They were also a long way from shore. Before Lovat could give the order to withdraw, a flight of Messerschmitt 109s came in low over the battery. Lovat waved, and the Germans—probably assuming the troops in the battery were on their side—held their fire.

Brady and his group of Commandos were still holding the road to the west near Sainte-Marguerite against possible reinforcements. Things had been relatively quiet in their sector since they'd seized the road.

But now two groups of Germans came up the highway, each in a knot flanking the hedges at the side of the road. Brady and three other soldiers waited until the enemy was within fifteen yards, then opened fire. Several of the Germans fell; the others quickly retreated.

"Back to the beach," ordered their lieutenant. The men began leapfrogging back, moving to the east to rendezvous with the main group at the beach near the lighthouse.

Back near the battery, Szima had taken up a position with a Commando manning a .55 Boys antitank gun at the edge of one of the lanes back to the beach. Acting as rear guard, they took shelter behind a thick wall in one of the yards. The men who had charged the battery fell back first; then came the members of Mills-Roberts's sections. Szima spotted Koons's Commando buddy, patched up and helping another wounded man back to the beach. But he didn't see Koons.

The Ranger steeled himself, and continued to keep watch, scanning the Commandos as they came through, worried now about his friend. Finally, the stream of Commandos ebbed. Then there was no one left, no one except the dead.

"Come on, Yank," said the gunner.

Szima knelt, getting ready to ignite a smoke grenade to cover their retreat. Then he heard someone running on the road. They'd waited too long. The Germans had rallied and were on their way.

Szima signaled for the Commando to step back, then aimed his M1 point-blank at the small gate in the wall. His finger pulled back about three-fourths of the way on the trigger, just to the point where it would take a slight tremor to fire.

But something Szima would never be able to fully explain kept him from shooting. The door swung open and Koons came through. They stared at each other in surprise.

It took Szima several heartbeats before he could growl at the corporal and tell him to get below.

A few minutes later, finally satisfied that there were no more stragglers, Szima and the British Commando once more got ready to go. Just then a German troop truck drove up. A soldier got out, checked the area, then hopped back inside. The truck started toward them.

The Commando fired his Boys gun point-blank at the truck's engine. The truck stopped dead—and Germans poured out from the rear. Szima emptied his clip, then turned and tried to help the corporal with the long-barreled weapon as they retreated. They scrambled into each other and fell, German rifle fire passing over their heads as they slid down a small ravine. Back on their feet, they ran until they reached the next Commando checkpoint, just barely remembering the password when challenged.

By 7:30, Number 4 Commando had accomplished its mission, with considerably less loss of life than either Mountbatten had predicted or its commander had feared. From the perspective of the men leaving the beach below Varengeville, the Dieppe Raid had been a stunning success.

But their perspective was severely limited. By the end of the day, Number 4 Commando's exploits would stand in stark contrast to the raid as a whole.

EIGHT

DISASTER ON THE FLANKS

Puys, East of Dieppe
August 19, 1942
...

BLUE BEACH

There is no better example of the magical thinking involved in the Canadian planning for the raid than the plan for Blue Beach, the assault of Puys and the surrounding area to the immediate east of Dieppe.

The Dieppe Raid was conceived as a series of interconnected landings. The success of the main landing at the city depended first and foremost on the success of the landings on the flanks—first those by the Commandos and Rangers at Berneval and Varengeville, and then much closer to town by Canadian forces at Puys and Pourville, respectively east and west of the city. Puys and Pourville both had German artillery batteries that could be trained on the Dieppe beachfront, and while the caliber of the weapons was somewhat smaller than at Berneval and Varengeville—105mm and 75mm—the targets were closer and could be easily seen from the nearby cliffs. The beaches were also supposed to be the gateway to a flanking maneuver whereby Canadian troops, besides dealing with the guns, would swing toward Dieppe and launch attacks on the defenders there.

Puys (or Puits) is located just two miles east of Dieppe. Unlike Berneval and Varengeville, a single cut through the cliffs leads to the hamlet and the streets beyond. Though the cut is described by historians as narrow, it was actually wide enough for houses to be located on its sides, with two small streets running up from the beach to form a "V." A network of smaller lanes and yards crisscrossed the steep hillsides that flanked the crevice. Separating these streets from the beach was a seawall between ten and twelve feet high. Two sets of steps ran down from the top.

The Germans had strung barbed wire across the steps to cut off access to the water. More importantly, they had located pillboxes and other defenses on the higher ground, covering the seawall area and beach as well as the ravine and nearby streets. German 81mm mortars had been zeroed in on the beach area, and there were howitzers within range as well. Two platoons, a total of ninety-four men, were assigned to guard Puys.

The Allied intelligence analysts seem to have missed the fact that there was barbed wire at the top of the seawall, but had found most of the other German defenses. The lieutenant colonel who was to command the attack theorized that the barbed wire must in fact be in place, given usual German procedures, but was assured by General Roberts, the division commander, that he was mistaken.

Roberts seems to have believed that the assault force could run past the pillboxes and compromise the other defenses quickly. His assault plan depended on it. According to the plan, roughly 550 men from the Royal Hamilton Regiment would secure the beach, wipe out antiaircraft batteries on the slopes above, capture a German barracks, march about a mile and a half, neutralize the German guns overlooking Dieppe, meet the forces landing in front of the city, and help blow up the gasworks there.

Not only were the tasks fantastical, but the time line was incredible as well; the heavy guns were to be taken out before the tanks hit the beach at Dieppe, which would give the troops a little more than an hour from touchdown to subdue the battery.

Of course, nothing went right. The troops took longer than planned getting from their transports to LCAs. Then some of the craft began following the wrong gunboat to the beach. Once they were rounded up, the naval commander tried to make up for the delays by increasing his speed to the beach. This split the invasion force in two. Then, rather than going straight into the beach, he sailed westward toward Dieppe and came back east—either by mistake or in the hope of bringing the landing craft toward the land in the shadows, depending on whose eyewitness version of the assault is believed.

The German records show that the Puys defenders spotted the Canadian landing craft and called for a bombardment at 0430. By most Canadian accounts, however, there was no gunfire from shore until the nine boats of the first wave actually landed around 0510, roughly a half hour late—which meant they could be seen relatively easily from shore. A handful of men had already reached the seawall when the first machine gun began firing from the eastern side of the beach. Firing from the hillside above, the machine gunner and another on the western side of the beach, had an interlocking field of fire on the men scrambling to get out of the landing craft. A good number of Canadians were killed or wounded in the shallow water before they could get to the seawall near the cliff.

The man who should have led the first wave, Major G. P. Schofield, was fatally wounded by a Bren gunner in his own boat who'd fired the heavy machine gun without properly aiming and securing it, spraying his bullets around the boat. Between the withering fire toward the beaches and the loss of their leader, a number of the Canadians lost their nerve. In four of the landing craft, the Navy officers had trouble getting their troops to leave the craft, and at least one had to threaten to shoot them to get them to brave the enemy fire. Once they were ashore, the majority froze, pinned down by the machine guns and their own fear. Within minutes, German 81mm mortars began firing from above, killing the trapped men at leisure.

A second wave of four landing craft reached the beach around 0530. Royal Regiment commander Lieutenant Colonel Douglas Catto was in one of the boats; after making it to shore, he gathered the survivors and managed to cover the landing of a reserve force of five boats, which included members of the Black Watch.

Catto rallied a force of about twenty men up the western stairs of the seawall after cutting a hole through the barbed wire. It took the colonel and the three men helping him about a half hour to get through the wire. Once past it, they cleared two houses of defenders on the west side of the beach. At this point, they started back toward the beach, only to find themselves cut off by machine-gun fire from the opposite side of the hill. A German patrol then chased them to the west; below, the Germans were already rounding up the men they hadn't killed and taking them prisoner.

Catto decided that the only hope was to hook up with the Canadian troops arriving in Dieppe. He and his men got about a hundred yards away from the gun battery they had been assigned to neutralize, but seem to have decided that it would have been suicide to attack it. By 11 a.m., they had resorted to hiding in the woods, not sure what to do next.

FAILURE

A single Ranger, Sergeant Kenneth Kenyon, was assigned as an observer to the Royal Regiment. The sergeant waited with the others as his landing craft approached the beach. Heavy machine-gun fire drove it off. The coxswain, following directions from a lookout in the bow, came in and tried again, only to be driven off again as a hail of bullets chewed into the hull. The sailor gave it one more chance before retreating again, this time for good. Even though the boat hadn't landed, there were several wounded; they went in search of a destroyer to get them help.

By 6:30 or seven o'clock, the attack on Puys had been completely broken; a sizable number of soldiers remained on the beach, but they were in no shape to launch an attack. The objectives Roberts believed essential to his main assault—the guns on the eastern headlands over-looking Dieppe—were out of reach and would never be taken. If the landing had ever had a chance of succeeding, it evaporated on the stones below Puys.

The failure of the assault plan at Blue Beach is often blamed on the lack of surprise there; the plan called for the attack to be made under the cover of darkness, and when the first boats were delayed, the mission was doomed to failure. Surprise and darkness might have helped more men escape the machine-gun fire as they landed, but even if the first wave had been able to breach the barbed wire at the stairs and then take on the positions, the plan itself would have been exposed as deeply flawed. There were simply too many tasks for the Canadians to accomplish in too short a time for them to have any realistic hope of success. They would have been slowed by positions in the village, and then met stiffening resistance from reinforced positions and fresh troops arriving from the south.

The Canadian plan seemed to believe there would be little resistance from the Germans. Indeed, the schedule of objectives on *all* the beaches appears several times more ambitious than anything the regiments were able to accomplish in training, when they weren't being fired upon.

It has been estimated that there were only 150 Germans defending the area; they had the high ground and took advantage of it very well. Two machine-gun positions were able to cover the area at the seawall; with the Canadians bottled up there, the assault was stillborn.

Heavy firepower might have neutralized the defenses, but the assault teams were without any. There was nowhere on the Puys beach to safely operate the mortars that the troops managed to bring in from the boats. Offshore bombardment against the positions, supported much more lightly than at the main beach, was equally ineffective. The fact that the Germans were operating from what looked like—and may in fact have been—private houses probably complicated the role of the supporting craft, as did problems of communications between the landing parties and the ships. The paucity of naval support—the destroyers were to the west covering the main landing—was undoubtedly a factor as well.

One of the great difficulties in describing the battle at Puys is trying to judge the effects of cowardice. A sizable number of soldiers refused to leave their boats and, after they did, froze at the seawall. The fact that they lost their nerve is apparent from all of the eyewitness accounts, but it is something most historians have skipped by. No one has asked why, if Colonel Catto made it up the stairs into the hamlet above the beach, a much larger group couldn't have done so before him, or followed afterward.

Part of the answer probably has to do with the murderous machine-gun and mortar fire that shredded the troops huddled by the seawall; the German photos taken after the raid show a good portion of the men dead by the stairs. It's also possible that the several

hundred other men on the beach were huddled around an indenta-
tion in the cliff where they couldn't see him to follow.

The greatest part of the answer, though, is probably that many of
the troops landing at Puys became terribly, and understandably,
scared when they came under fire for the first time in their lives. They
stopped moving, and for many that sealed their fate.

The truth is, though, that even if they hadn't stopped moving, the
odds are high that they would have died or been wounded anyway.

POURVILLE

The troops landing at Pourville, the other Canadian flanking operation, had a major advantage over those landing at Puys: the beach
they were landing on was much wider, and the cliffs were set farther
away, making it more difficult for machine-gun nests to catch troops
in a cross fire there. The first wave of troops also arrived on time in
the dark, as planned. Charged with securing the beach, 525 men of
the South Saskatchewan Regiment hit the rocky shore at 0450,
quickly spreading across the wide landing at what had been dubbed
Green Beach.

The only problem was, half of the regiment landed on the wrong
side of the beach. While they moved eastward, the other half had to
fight their way over a bridge to reach their first objectives. The
assault lost valuable time and left the second wave of troops, about
five hundred members of the Canadian Cameron Highlanders, vulnerable to the German defenders.

Rangers Marcel Swank and Lloyd Church had spent the night
with the Canadian Cameron Highlanders, sailing with them in
LCP(L)s, which the Canadians they were with generally referred to as
"R" boats. Swank had fallen asleep somewhere around midpassage,
and didn't wake up until about 5 a.m., when he heard the sound of
gunfire and saw flashes of light in the distance. The Ranger got his

gear and joined Church, waiting anxiously with the Canadian sergeant they'd been told to shadow.

German mortar shells landed in the water as they came in. Though the troops that had landed earlier had taken out the pillbox and other defenses on the seawall and near the beach, machine-gun positions on the cliffs hadn't been touched, and their low rumble formed a counterpoint to the boom of the mortar shells and heavier weapons. By now it was about 0540 and full light; the Germans were firing everything they could at the beach, and the air smelled of cordite and death. Suddenly over the din came a sound so strange that neither Church nor Swank could decipher what it was. A bagpiper, wearing the Highlanders' regimental cap and ribbons, had risen and was playing the regimental theme, "The 100 Pipers," on a nearby landing craft.

Swank felt a swell of pride and inspiration as the landing craft hit the beach. He and Church jumped out of the craft behind their Canadian sergeant, running with him toward the seawall perhaps fifty yards away. Within only a few steps, the sergeant was cut down and killed; Church and Swank, continuing on their own, climbed up to the promenade at the top of the seawall and went through one of the holes that had been blown in the barbed wire. Still under fire, they ran toward the nearby buildings, looking for a group to join.

The Canadians at Pourville had a number of different objectives. After landing, the South Saskatchewan Regiment was to send a company east and take the high ground above Dieppe, about three miles away. This portion of the mission was vital for the assault on the city, for the positions there posed the same threat as those on the eastern side of Dieppe that were to be taken by the men landing at Puys. The company's objectives included a number of light antiaircraft guns and machine-gun positions as well as the radar station Jack Nissenthall had been tasked to inspect. After they reached these, it was to help another company capture a farm in the valley behind the coast; the farm, known as Les Quatre Vents, was the German regimental headquarters and had an antiaircraft battery. Other Saskatchewan companies were to secure the small city of Pourville and the surrounding area, cutting off reinforcements. The Camerons were to go up the Scie Valley and take the airfield at Saint-Aubin, several miles inland.

The German force at Pourville at the time of the raid has been estimated at about fifty men, not counting soldiers in the defenses above the village or the nearby regimental headquarters. A reserve battalion rushed toward the city after the assault began.

By the time Swank and Church came ashore, the assault had stalled. Cement pillboxes on the hillside—still visible today—and other gun positions on the hill choked the rush to the radar station and the defenses near Dieppe. A single machine-gun post on the bridge leading from the beach slowed the rest of the Canadians trying to move from the village toward the farm; while this was eventually overcome, it took a heavy toll in casualties.

Seeing the situation, the Camerons' acting commander Major Tony Law—the colonel who headed the regiment had been killed—left a number of Camerons to help subdue the town. He assembled the rest and started up the western side of the Scie Valley, aiming to swing toward the rendezvous with the tanks at Les Vetus Wood. The path would have taken them around Quatre Vents Farm, bypassing the stronghold.

Church and Swank joined one of the Cameron companies marching up out of the town along the road. Within minutes they were being sniped at; then mortar shells began falling. The Rangers and the Canadians dispersed into the woods, moving up undercover. But the woods ended abruptly, and the Camerons found themselves facing entrenched German positions on high ground. Swank and Church joined an assault on one strongpoint; after a bayonet charge, they gained the trench, leaving seven Germans dead.

One of the Canadian force's main complaints during the entire raid was the trouble they had with their Sten guns. The 9mm submachine guns were meant to give small units extra firepower in the same way that the Thompson did with the Commandos. But the guns were in short supply, and while some of the Canadians had trained with Sten guns before Rutter, the weapons had been returned when the raid was called off. New weapons were issued just before the raid; they came straight from storage and were well clogged with grease. There was no time to refine the guns, which had a tendency to jam easily; some Canadian soldiers had discovered during the rehearsals for Rutter that this could be fixed by adjustments to the firing mechanism and honing down the hammer. Major Law said later that no one in his regiment had actually had a chance to fire the weapon during the rehearsals before the raid because of the shortage of ammunition.

The assault by now had ground down. Law decided to cross the river and attack Quatre Vents Farm directly. But the Germans had blocked the bridge, and under withering fire, the Camerons broke off their attack.

For just under an hour, the two Canadian regiments held on to their positions, unable to advance. Around 1015, word came to fall back into Pourville to wait for withdrawal.

Swank, who by now had lost track of Church, retreated with the others, reentering the village and then dropping back to a street corner not far from the beach, crouching with a Bren gunner behind some bushes. Suddenly the gunner started firing like crazy. Swank didn't think the man even had a target until suddenly a burst of machine-gun fire rattled through the bushes next to him, slicing the tops off.

Silently, something inside the Ranger gave way. He turned and lay down on his back. Stretched full-length, the Ranger stared at the clouds gathering overhead. Unable to move, utterly possessed by fear, he did the only thing he could manage at that moment: he started to pray.

NINE

DIEPPE

Dieppe
November 2006

． ． ．

Walking across the beach at Dieppe for the first time has more of an effect on me than I'd thought it would. Perhaps it's because I've stolen into Dieppe well past midnight, more ghost than tourist. Lit only by a few streetlamps and a string of lights in the harbor, Dieppe belongs to no specific time, past or present; it's more theater stage than city. As the sun gradually makes its way toward the horizon, the mist becomes smokelike and thick, wrapping itself around the smooth rocks on the beach. There is no sudden burst of light this dawn; it sneaks its way in, seeming to peek in under the turquoise ocean that reveals itself in front of the city.

It's obvious walking across the beach how murderous the landing must have been, had to have been, in 1942. The surrounding cliffs, the wall of buildings hiding the movements of the German reinforcements, the well-prepared defenses—these are all things I've known about for a long time, and yet I haven't really known them until now, shifting and sliding on the stones.

In the dawn twilight the parked cars have disappeared; the construction crane fades into the clouds. It's August 19, 1942.

I step over the bodies of the brave Canadians who ran through the surf only to fall at the water's edge. The tanks are scattered, facing in different directions, most with their tracks shredded. U.S. Army Ranger Howard Henry is lying against the rocks, facedown; in a few hours, a German patrol will check his body, turning him over to stare at the sun. A passing photographer will capture him on film, making it seem as if he died that way, preserving a false moment for all time.

And then the beach is empty again, and I'm in the present.

Off the Dieppe Coast
December 19, 1942

* * *

TRUSCOTT

Standing on the deck of the destroyer *Fernie*, General Truscott had seen the flashes of gunfire when the boats carrying Number 3 Commando clashed with the German escort. Red and green tracers had crossed in front of white flashes two or three miles off the port side of his ship. They'd been too far to render any assistance, and in any event the flashes died within a few minutes.

Truscott and the British officers who were with him in the backup command ship realized that surprise had been lost, at least in that sector, but there was nothing to do but press on. The loss of the radio aboard SGB 5 meant there was no information on what precisely was going on; radio problems would continue to mar the entire operation.

Less than an hour later, a fresh round of cannon fire broke the stillness of the night. This time, the gunfire was part of a plan, not an accident: the destroyers escorting the invasion fleet began firing at the defenses on the Dieppe beach. Truscott thought the bombardment was pitifully small, much less than he'd expected. The *Fernie* wasn't firing; her communications gear was considered too delicate and liable to be disabled by the reverberations of the ship's own guns.

Ahead in the distance, the cliffs were a dark gray smudge on the horizon, just visible in the predawn shadows. A flight of aircraft passed overhead. Truscott could see their outlines dropping toward the shore as the gun batteries below sprang into action, the sky flashing above them. There were explosions, a flood of light, and then a curtain seemed to come down as a heavy smoke screen was laid for the assault boats to hit the main beach.

Unable to see anything more, the American general went below to the operations room, listening as the Canadian and Combined Operations officers tried to sort through the confusion. The messages from Number 4 Commando were good, but there was still no word from 3 Commando. Truscott couldn't help but think about the large contingent of Rangers he'd sent with them.

The news from Green Beach indicated Pourville was under control; the Canadian troops were moving on and were about to subdue Quatre Vents, the strategic farm nearby. The main assault was under way. Everything seemed hopeful.

His energy level ramping up and with nothing purposeful to do in the headquarters space, Truscott went back out on deck. The smoke had cleared somewhat, and the night that had been so quiet had given way to a furious morning. The main beach at Dieppe spread out before him, magnified by his binoculars.

What had seemed so hopeful in the compressed quarters of the communications area now looked much less so. Truscott saw one of the large landing craft—probably TLC-3—swinging helplessly with the tide, ramp down, its interior and deck littered with dead and dying men. On the rocks beyond, he could see tanks burning. While the first waves of British planes had not met any resistance, either from the flak guns below or interceptors above, an air battle was now raging over the city and sea; flak flew everywhere. Aircraft wheeled through the sky above. With a shock, Truscott realized that most of them were German. The fight the RAF had hoped for was in its beginning stages; planes would appear in waves over the beaches for much of the rest of the day. But the fight would not go as the RAF had hoped—the British would lose 106 planes to the Luftwaffe's 48. A good number of the German fighters were FW 190 Focke-Wulfes, at the time the most capable planes in the war. The Butcher Birds, as the 190s were known, flew faster and were more maneuverable than any of the British planes they were flying against, including the Spitfire. The free-ranging fight allowed the German pilots to choose tactics that suited their aircraft; the 190s' performance edge allowed them to break off an engagement if things started to get too hairy.

The German Air Force had another advantage—they were operating on their home turf. The British planes could spend only a few minutes over the battlefield before having to return to their airfields for fuel. That greatly restricted the fleet's air protection, as flight after flight of Junkers 88 and Heinkel He 111 bombers would soon show.

As he was watching the Spitfires and FW 190s twist above him, Truscott was suddenly thrown against the railing. A shell had hit the destroyer so hard that it knocked some of bolts from the superstructure loose; one bounced against the general's foot. Men screamed from the side of the destroyer where the shell had hit. A total of sixteen men had been killed or wounded in an instant. The destroyer turned back from the beach, sending smoke in its wake as a screen against more bombs and shells.

ABOARD HMS *CALPE*

The *Calpe* had also gone very close to shore. Quentin Reynolds, the American news correspondent, was in the operations center, watching and listening as reports came in to General Ham Roberts, the commander of the 2nd Division. Though the *Calpe* was supposed to be the nerve center of the raid, Roberts was handicapped by communications problems; many of the radio messages that reached *Fernie* never made it to *Calpe*. Besides interference and the normal mechanical difficulties associated with the equipment at the time, in some instances the specialists ashore who were supposed to be keeping the commander informed had been killed and their equipment wrecked, though there was no way of knowing that aboard the *Calpe*.

Reynolds watched Roberts shifting back and forth uneasily, desperate to know what was going on but stymied by the lack of information, especially from the main beaches. Finally, information arrived that Royal Hamilton had gotten over the seawall at Dieppe and was in the Casino. The information seemed to signal that the raid was going well.

In fact, the information meant just the opposite. The raid had been under way on the main beach for nearly an hour. The seawall was the first objective; it should have been breached within minutes. The Casino was the most prominent building on the western side of the beach. By this time in the raid, it should not only have been taken but should have been to the rear of the advance; the assault plans had called for the headquarters of both infantry regiments to land at 0605 and set up stations in the town's two churches, several blocks from the seafront.

Reynolds, even though he'd been shown the timetable for the raid, didn't realize that. But then, the commanders didn't interpret the information that way either.

Despite the fierce bombardment from German guns on both flanks of the city, the mood in the command center on the *Calpe* grew more and more positive. A report arrived around 6:30, indicating that troops had entered the city itself. The report came from the brigadier general commanding the 6th Brigade, William Wallace Southam, whose forces included the Fusiliers Mont-Royal on Red Beach, the western half of Dieppe. A short time later, the commander of the forces on the other half of the beachfront reported that White Beach was also under control.

Sensing momentum was on his side, Roberts committed his reserves to exploit the advances. It was an enormous, though understandable mistake. For the information he based his decision on was wildly incorrect.

MAIN DIEPPE BEACHES

Contrary to the messages that reached the *Calpe,* the landing at the main beaches of Dieppe had gone wrong from the very start. The plan had always heavily depended on the batteries and gun emplacements bordering the city being wiped out as the main forces arrived. But the timetable for doing so had proven ridiculously optimistic; even Number 4 Commando was not able to reach its objective until after the landing had begun. And the stalled attacks at Pourville and Puys meant that the guns close to the beach remained in action the entire day.

The main beach ran some two thousand yards from the long jetty at the end of the protected harbor on Dieppe's east to the cliffs dominated by the old castle on the west. An escalade ran the entire length to the old Casino at the western part of the beach; the seawall separating it was ten to twelve feet high. There were several defensive positions on the beach itself, including a pillbox in front of the Casino; there were Germans in the houses to the west of the Casino.

Rangers training for an amphibious operation with Royal Navy personnel in Scotland
Reproduced from the collections of the Library of Congress

Major William O. Darby
Courtesy of the U.S. Military Academy at West Point

Lucian Truscott, assigned by Marshall and Eisenhower to write the blueprint for an American "commando" group. The photo was taken later in the war. *Reproduced from the collections of the Library of Congress*

Lieutenant Edward Loustalot (left) and Don Fredericks, then a private. Fredericks would go on to receive a battlefield commission. The photo was taken just before the Dieppe battle. *Courtesy of Ranger Don Fredericks*

Owen Sweazey was one of the Rangers who never got ashore in the battle; he won a promotion to sergeant later in the war. *Courtesy of Ron and Paula Sweazey*

Then-Captain Roy Murray (right, with baseball glove) relaxes with fellow Rangers during the war. *Courtesy of Ranger Gerrit "Ted" Rensink*

Canadian troops training for Jubilee, the invasion of Dieppe
Library and Archives Canada, PA 113243

The Jubilee invasion force sets out.
Library and Archives Canada, PA 171080

One of the destroyers in the invasion force lays smoke to cover the assault force.
Library and Archives Canada, AA116291

Landing craft near one of the Dieppe beaches
Library and Archives Canada, PA 183770

Bodies and abandoned tanks litter the main beach at Dieppe after the withdrawal. The photo is looking northeast, toward the entrance to the harbor. The northeastern headlands can be seen in the background. *Library and Archives Canada, C 17296*

Some of the dead in front of the Casino following the battle. The second man is an American; though some sources have identified him as Lieutenant Joseph Randall, the Rangers who survived the battle came to believe it was T/4 Howard Henry. *Library and Archives Canada, C 14160*

Allied prisoners being marched through the center of Dieppe. More than two thousand Canadians were taken prisoner, about a quarter of them wounded. *Library and Archives Canada, C 14213*

German troops examine a tank and Canadian dead on the beach following the battle. *Library and Archives Canada, C 17293*

The tank "Bert," disabled during the battle, managed to provide cover for the handful of men who made it into the city streets behind the Casino. Contrary to what has been written, no tanks made it into the city itself. *Library and Archives Canada, C 29878*

Safe at last, part of the invasion force crowds the wharves at Newhaven, England. *Library and Archives Canada, C 210152*

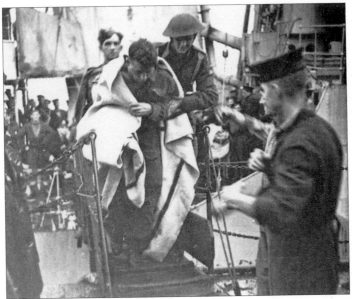

One of a handful of German prisoners is helped off a ship after reaching England. *Library and Archives Canada, C 183765*

Lord Lovat (left) confers with his men in Newhaven following the battle. *Library and Archives Canada, C 183766*

Alex Szima (left) receives a cigarette from a British commando in Newhaven after returning from the battle. The shot—staged for war photographers—was printed in newspapers all over the world and made the Americans celebrities. *Library and Archives Canada, PA-183790*

Promoted to sergeant following the battle, "Zip" Koons received a medal and congratulations from Lord Mountbatten (right) after the Rangers took part in the invasion of Northern Africa. *Reproduced from the collections of the Library of Congress*

A monument to the British and Americans who landed at Berneval. Lieutenant Loustalot died somewhere near this spot. *Jim DeFelice*

The monument stands at the top of the path up from the beach that the Rangers and Commandos used during the assault. The cut in the cliffs was wider than most of the others used that day. *Jim DeFelice*

A monument to the dead at Berneval; the church that once stood here was destroyed during a bomb raid later in the war. *Jim DeFelice*

The "cut" in the cliffs used by the Commandos and Rangers to assault the Hess battery near Varangeville. *Jim DeFelice*

The beach below Varangeville
Jim DeFelice

The beachfront before Pourville, taken from the German pillbox
Jim DeFelice

The remains of German defenses near Pourville, France, today,
forgotten by the roadside
Jim DeFelice

The sea front at Pourville, today a playground. Sergeant Swank lay paralyzed here for a short while during the battle. *Jim DeFelice*

The seawall at Puys, where numerous Canadians were cut down by gunners in the white house at the top. The remains of German defenses can still be seen around the area. *Jim DeFelice*

The caves to the west of the main beach at Dieppe provided some temporary shelter for soldiers during the height of the assault, but once reaching there they were trapped.
Jim DeFelice

Among the many plaques to the fallen Allies at Dieppe is one commemorating the Rangers; many other memorials are scattered throughout the area.
Jim DeFelice

The Allied cemetery just outside of Dieppe. The bodies of three American Rangers who were buried here were returned home after the war. *Jim DeFelice*

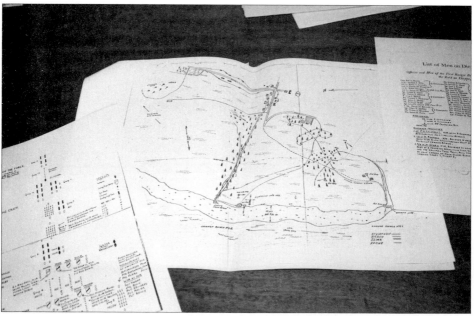

Some of the original Dieppe Rangers' handwritten notes and maps about the battle, including annotations on printed accounts and a copy of the force composition orders. *Jim DeFelice*

There were also gun positions on the hillsides east and west, up on the promenade, and at the entrances to the city, which except for one had been blocked by large slabs of concrete. Farther back, mortars and heavier weapons were zeroed in on the beach.

The Royal Hamilton Infantry and Essex Scottish were assigned to attack the main beach, but the main show was to be provided by the tanks of the 14th Canadian Army Tank Regiment—better known among the Canadians as the Calgary Regiment. The name reflected the area where most of the crews came from; many of the men had grown up on farms, which supposedly made them familiar with the engines and heavy machinery used by an armored unit.

Companies of the two infantry units landed first, beginning at 0520. The Royal Hamilton Light Infantry came in on the west side of the beach, between the Casino and the cliffs. They were immediately caught in a cross fire. A single soldier was able to crawl toward the pillbox in front of the Casino, under and through the barbed wire, and then destroy it with a hand grenade. But that still left the fire from above. Nearly half of the 580 or so members of the regiment were killed or seriously wounded during the course of the battle. A good number of these casualties occurred during the initial phase of the assault, in effect stopping it before it could really get under way.

On Red Beach, the eastern half of the landing front, the Essex Scottish got to the seawall but had trouble blasting through the thick barbed wire with their bangalore torpedoes. Not only were they easy prey for the guns on the eastern headlands, but the German 37mm gun and other positions on the pier next to the beach were able to pepper them as well.

For the next ten to fifteen minutes, the infantry along the beaches huddled in the small pockets of rocks or near the seawall while the Germans rained shells and machine-gun bullets down on them. Then the Nazis had new targets—a wave of landing craft carrying tanks were making their way to the beach.

Though they had intended on landing with the infantry, the first wave of tanks didn't arrive until 0535. The first landing craft came in on the western end of the beach. As its three tanks and small scout car drove across the rocks in search of a way up the seawall, the Germans zeroed in on the LCT. Heavily damaged, the vessel ended up sinking in the shallow water off the beach.

The second LCT landed on the opposite end of the seafront. A number of engineers who were supposed to clear obstacles when the tanks landed were killed on the way in, but the tanks themselves managed to get off the boat. Shortly after landing, the first Churchill climbed over the seawall with the help of its chespaling and took on a 75mm cannon firing across the harbor. The German gun scored a hit that locked the Churchill's turret, but the tank was still able to fire, and disabled the gun.

The third and final LCT in the first wave had the worst luck of the group. Trying to provide a better view for the tank commander, one of the sailors lowered the ramp when the boat was still a hundred yards from shore. The tank commander misunderstood; thinking they had arrived, he ordered his driver to move out. The ramp was only halfway down, but the weight of the Churchill forced it open. The tank sank in ten feet of water. The LCT managed to back away; all but the tank commander were saved.

The boat approached the beach again and landed the second of its three tanks, but the third found itself unable to go forward. Reversing, the tank crushed two wounded men who'd been lying behind it. The problem turned out to be a chuck that hadn't been removed from in front of the tank's treads, perhaps because the men tasked to do so had been hurt by the heavy fire engulfing the LCT. The last tank managed to get off, but the boat had been so heavily damaged that it was derelict. It drifted westward, finally beaching near the middle of the beachfront.

If anything, the gunfire had increased when the second-wave

tanks hit the beach. The crew of one of the landing craft in this wave was wiped out, but all of the tanks managed to disembark. Several three-inch mortar teams from the Calgary Highlanders, about twenty-one men in all, refused to disembark from one of the vessels because of the fierce shelling and gunfire; the LCT was also unable to get its large, D7 bulldozer on the beach.

By 6 a.m., seventeen tanks had managed to come ashore. All had been heavily engaged by the Germans. But their armor had held well under the onslaught, and a handful of tanks had managed to breach the seawall. Others were helping the infantry troops who had landed earlier press an attack against the Casino on the western part of the beach and a tobacco factory farther back on the street at the east.

At 0605, the third and last wave of tank carriers came in. This wave had four craft and included the two brigadier generals in charge of the brigades making the assault.

It also seems to have included Ranger Howard M. Henry.

Pine Island, New York
November 2006

■ ■ ■

I'm up late one night working when I decide to do a random Internet search, just to see what else I've missed. At some point, I come across a Web site identifying one of the dead soldiers on the main beach at Dieppe as an Army Ranger. I've seen the photo several dozen times in other places, but never once noticed that the man is wearing the leggings or gaiters that were part of the standard U.S. Army uniform at that point in the war. (Most of the Rangers with the Commandos wore British boots.)

The Web site identifies the man as Lieutenant Joseph Randall, and I set out to verify the identification.

Three Americans died at Dieppe. Lieutenant Loustalot fell at

Berneval, and while the exact spot can only be guessed at, it's clear he was miles from the main beach when he fell. That leaves T-4 Howard Henry and Lieutenant Joseph Randall, both of whom were with Canadian units. (The T-4 designation would be roughly equivalent to a specialist today; for practical purposes, Henry was a corporal, and that's how he's often been referred to.)

Lieutenant Robert Flanagan's after-action report says Randall boarded the landing ship Glengyle, which carried the Royal Hamilton Light Infantry; the unit came into Dieppe on the western or White Beach. Flanagan put Henry on the Prince Charles, which carried the Essex Scottish Regiment, the unit assigned to land on the western half of the beach—Red Beach. The dead man lies just to the east of the Casino, on what technically was White Beach. But given the chaos of the day, the current, and the wide spread of the landing craft from their designated touch-down positions, either man could have come ashore near there.

The problem is, Lieutenant Flanagan didn't actually witness any of the men get onto the ships. The Rangers were transported separately to their ports; there's no way to verify that they actually made it to the assigned ships, or reached the units the ship assignments seem to indicate.

Years after the battle, the Rangers who had been on the raid set out to determine once and for all where their friends had fallen. They, too, had the after-action reports, but while comparing notes, they came to believe that Lieutenant Randall had accompanied not the Royal Hamilton Light Infantry but the South Saskatchewan Regiment. South Saskatchewan was part of the same brigade within the Canadian 2 Division, but it landed at Pourville—Green Beach.

It turned out that Marcel Swank, who landed on the same beach with the Queens Own Cameron Highlanders, had spoken to a man immediately after the battle who'd seen a dead American lieutenant in the woods beyond the town. Swank—who did most of the *sleuthing—discovered a researcher for the Canadian Broadcasting Company in the 1970s who had interviewed a member of the South Saskatchewan Regiment who also remembered a dead American— and had, in fact, taken the man's .45 Colt pistol to use after he fell. Then, while helping a film crew working on the Dieppe story, Swank met a tank captain from the Calgary Tank Regiment who said that he'd seen an American enlisted man on his landing craft (TLC-7), who'd been with a Canadian demolition crew. The man told him he'd seen an American fall near the water. Swank looked at the photo, but it wasn't clear enough for him to identify the man.*

"Near the water" does not quite describe where the American Ranger is in the photo. Even at high tide, he'd have had to run at least ten or fifteen yards to get to where his body is shown in the photo; at the time of the landing, the water would have been even farther out. But it makes sense that an American was assigned as an observer to this landing craft—if not to help (or watch) the demolitions team, then to tag along with the brigade signals team also aboard. The signals unit was assigned to come out with a small scout car. There a "tourist"—as the Americans with the Canadian units called themselves—would be in a good position to observe what was going on, without getting in the way.

Randall or Henry?

It could be either. Swank's evidence rested on memories that were decades old—but then, the after-action reports were a matter of memory and hearsay as well. I also know from Szima's correspondence that the reports were heavily edited and amended, and contain a number of errors.

Long after the battle, many of the surviving Rangers retained a strong bond. They worked hard to preserve the details of what had happened to them and their friends at Dieppe. Whether that should influence me or not, it does—and so in the end, I finally decide to side with their interpretation that the man was Henry.

But the question of who it was leads inevitably to another: What was his time on the beach like?

This time, I consult eyewitness accounts of the battle and some detective work by historians, including Hugh G. Henry Jr., who worked out the fate of every tank and most of the LCTs that launched them. Henry did the work for a master's-degree dissertation, speaking to many members of the Calgary tank regiment as well as relying on traditional sources. With Jean-Paul Pallud, he published part of his findings in Dieppe Through the Lens.

Finally, I begin to answer my question.

TLC-7 came under heavy fire when it attempted to land near the center of the beach around 0605. Hydrogen was stored in canisters at the port side of the landing craft, intended for barrage balloons. A shell from the east side of the city blew up several canisters, spraying the men with shrapnel and setting some on fire. The tanks got off; the second one drove to the right, toward the Casino, looking for a place to get up on the promenade. The other two eventually followed. TLC-7 backed out from the beach, only to be sunk as the German gunfire continued.

Wounded, Henry fell by the water but then managed to get up, helped by some of the Canadians on the landing craft. They ran toward shelter, behind the tank going toward the Casino. By this time, the Canadian troops had silenced the pillbox in front of the Casino and were pressing their attack on the building. Groups of soldiers were clustered near the tanks and the damaged LCTs here, the able-bodied firing, the wounded trying to tend to their injuries. The battle to take the Casino would rage for over an hour. In the meantime, the area between it and the beach became a comparative shelter, where the wounded were gathered.

Henry, trained for a battle he had never been allowed to join, looked for something to do. He volunteered as a stretcher bearer, helping the wounded. He watched as shells continued to land around him, wondering which one would bring death.

All of this is speculation, built on secondhand accounts and photos that are so blurry that it's impossible to tell if the dead man has Henry's trademark thick mustache. It's also built on the expectations of what Henry might have done given his background and training, the role he'd been assigned, and what I know the other Rangers did. It's based on my identifying with the Rangers trying to piece together what had happened to their comrade many years before, my sense that their concern for the truth of what happened to their friends helped them make accurate assessments.

And to be honest, it's based on what I hope happened, the way I want to think about the Rangers and the other men who died at Dieppe that day. I want Henry to have been brave even when wounded, want him to have persisted even when bewildered. But there are many ways the narrative might have gone, many things that might have happened before the photographer snapped the picture, and Henry's—or Randall's—body was carted away with the rest of the dead.

Our own feelings filter all of our interpretations of history, whether we want them to or not. Historians as well as generals fall victim to emotion and preconceived ideas, and many times their decisions are guided more by emotion than truth. To find good in something horrible, to celebrate a hero, is such a strong emotion that it can overcome not only good sense but even memory.

The first wave of reports after Dieppe included an account by a soldier that was nothing short of fantastic. After landing on the beach around 0700, the man remained on the rocks, mostly spellbound. Then suddenly he came to life. Looking for a safe vantage where he could fire his Bren gun, he ran to a tank. Finding it unoccupied, he climbed inside. With the help of another man he turned the gun toward the cliff and fired all of the two-pound ammunition—thirty rounds— before leaving. He then ran to the west near the cliffs and, with another group of men, entered the city, running past the roadblock at the rue de Sygogne and passing a group of Germans who had no weapons. They made it all the way to rue Claude-Groulard—a major east–west road about a half mile from the beach. There they found a machine-gun pit manned by three Germans in a park. One of the sergeant's men threw three grenades into the pit. While the Germans were stunned, the grenades did not kill them; someone in the party dispatched them with a submachine gun. The sergeant and his group then ran along the street until they came to the inner harbor. When they came to the Bassin du Canada—named after the many who left the port for Canada when it was a French colony—they found two men lying in the street talking to some Frenchmen. After a gunfight with some men aboard a vessel in the harbor, they were surrounded by fifteen Germans at the southwest portion of the basin. (This is the corner farthest from the seafront, roughly a mile away from the ocean.) The Germans ordered the men to strip, first in German and then in English, and finally in French. After they had done so, most of the German patrol left, leaving only one man to guard them. The sergeant asked for a drink of water, then, seeing that the man had turned away, jumped on him. Another of the sergeant's partners picked up a nearby pipe and cracked open the skull of the German. Escaping, the sergeant ran toward the seafront, eventually reaching the promenade, which by that time had become eerily quiet. He was somewhere to the west of the Casino and was able to join his commanding officer on a spot east of the Casino. He helped the wounded officer to a landing craft, went back, and helped another solider, finally escaping with him.

The story is truly amazing and incredible, and it's no wonder that he was awarded a Military Medal after the battle.

But photos taken the day after the battle of the only tank that was abandoned by its crew—it went off its landing craft in eight to ten feet of water and was "drowned"—show the waterproof sock on its barrel intact; it hasn't been fired. The man claimed that he saw the crew abandon the tank; that would have happened around 0530, an hour and a half before he himself landed. While no one else did it, it's still conceivable that he made it past the snipers in the houses to the west of the Casino, and then the machine guns and barbed wire covering the gap between the Casino and the western headlands where he claims to have entered the town. But why did an earlier party report the road there into town was impassable because of heavy barbed wire? What happened to the other men who were with him, none of whom was ever found and none of whom he knew? Why would the Germans leave only one man to guard prisoners, or make the prisoners take off their clothes? How did he manage to make it back down the promenade to the beach without going through the Casino? How was he able to get into the tank, fire all of its shells, run down the beach, get into the city, be captured, escape, and then come back to roughly where he started in the course of three hours?

Men took off their uniforms to swim out to the boats. There are no other reports of prisoners being ordered to take their clothes off; those seen in German photos appear to have done so after trying to swim out to the landing craft but being forced back.

The account suggests many more questions. Undoubtedly the historical officer who recorded it asked some of them. But he accepted and wrote down the man's account, including it as an appendix to his original report on the operation. From there, the story has been printed in several accounts of the battle, accepted completely as true. Ironically, most accounts leave out the one part of the story that does ring true—and that, by itself, would have been heroic enough to win a medal: helping a wounded man from the beach under fire and getting him safely aboard one of the few landing craft to escape.

At the end of the war, Lieutenant Colonel R. R. Labatt, who'd commanded the soldier's unit during the operation, returned from the POW camp where he had been interned. Reading the account, he termed it false from start to finish. Another officer of the same unit said that he doubted anyone from his company made it. The historical officer discounted both opinions, though in the body of his report noted that perhaps there was some "embroidery" of details in the soldier's account.

As printed in the official report, most elements of the story that would most readily lead one to doubt its validity—the episode with the tank, for example—were removed. It is therefore difficult for a reader who doesn't have a deep understanding of the battle—and access to the earlier statements—to judge whether what is printed in the official history is true.

Is it important? Does one individual story add that much more or less to the collective memory of an event? Should we believe in a "relative" truth, or an absolute, however unknowable it may be?

Does it matter if it is Randall or Henry dead in the photo? One might argue it doesn't to them. But somehow it doesn't feel right leaving the matter entirely open. There is a difference, I think, between admitting that I cannot give a definitive answer and not making the attempt at all.

Dieppe
December 19, 1942

■ ■ ■

BREACHING THE CASINO

The Casino on the western part of the beach became a focal point of the battle. Several small groups of men were able to enter during the early stages of the assault. Battles ensued inside as well as outside; the labyrinth of halls and rooms made it possible for German soldiers to hide and even continue shooting at the beach as the Canadians entered elsewhere. Fighting went on room to room; one Canadian bayoneted a German sniper to death, then threw up on the man before he could get his bayonet out.

A small group of men under the direction of George Hickson, a sergeant who had been assigned to blow up the telephone office in town, cleared out one sniper post and used their charges to blast through the main floor of the hotel, killing German soldiers holed up there and taking a total of twenty-three prisoners.

Outside, the tanks provided cover for the infantrymen who had survived the initial onslaught. Several climbed up the seawall, either using their chespaling mounting apparatus or finding spots where the seawall was not that high. Once they were on the esplanade, their guns helped neutralize some of the less fortified positions, and pounded the buildings being used by German snipers.

But the goal of the tanks was far beyond the grass separating the boulevard de Verdun from the seafront. In order to get into the city, the tanks had to have a way blasted through the obstacles or the heavily protected roadblock. A trio of sappers ran through the Casino, across to the roadblock in front of the rue de Sygogne. But the team could not blow up the barrier. All three men were injured or killed in the attempt.

Unable to get beyond the parklike area between the buildings and the beach, the tanks drove back and forth, suppressing the machine-gun nests and providing cover for the infantrymen, most of whom were still down below the seawall. It was not quite 7 a.m., but already the battle had been decided. The Churchill tanks were not going to stream through town and hook up with the troops in Pourville; several were nearly out of ammunition. Their treads were proving particularly vulnerable to the German fire, and their greatest use over the next several hours would be as strongpoints for the infantry to rally behind while waiting for the order to retreat.

TEN

SLAUGHTER

Dieppe
August 19, 1942

* * *

SENDING IN THE RESERVES

A number of tanks and the Fusiliers Mont-Royal had been held in reserve, to be used to exploit the breakthrough from the beach. Sometime around 6:30, acting on what he thought were the positive messages from the groups ashore on the main beach, General Roberts decided to send the reserves into battle. The Fusiliers were to land on Red Beach, the eastern portion of the beach. The Royal Marine Commando, unable to sneak into the harbor and steal the German landing boats after the alarm was sounded, were also available, and Roberts instructed them to head for Red Beach, too. Finally, acting on a garbled message that seemed to indicate that the Royal Regiment had not been able to land at Puys, he ordered them to proceed to Red Beach as well.

Roberts's decision would rank as one of the most controversial of the war. While the messages he had received to this point were overoptimistic in the extreme, they were still at variance with the goals Roberts himself had set in his plan; many argue that he should have realized he was reinforcing failure rather than exploiting an advantage. Evidence that the battle wasn't going well was all around the ship—landing craft with wounded were sailing around the *Calpe* and the other destroyers, trying to get medical attention for their men. It was clear from the deck if not the radio that the guns on the cliffs at both sides of Dieppe were still working.

What Roberts didn't know—and apparently couldn't imagine— was the size of the debacle unfolding on the Dieppe beaches. It has been estimated that 75 percent of the men in the Essex Scottish Regiment had been killed or wounded by the time he decided to send in the reserves. And things would only get worse. The regiment ended the day with 86 percent casualties—and the percentage only appears that good because some of the men never made it to shore.

The Fusiliers cheered when they heard that they were going in. Assembling behind a smoke screen offshore, they boarded twenty-six LCP(L)s and headed toward shore. With two hundred yards to go, the wooden-hulled boats burst through the smoke screen into a thick hail of artillery and mortar shells, and the cross fire of machine guns firing from both the east and west ends of the beach. The worst fire was coming from the east side, their left as they went in. Between the current pushing to the west and the mad torrent of gunfire, the boats sailed well off course, toward White Beach at the west. Two were sunk, and probably all were hit several times on the way in.

A little more than half of the 584 men in the regiment landed on the extreme western side of the beach, far beyond the Casino. As they ran up the rocks toward the cliff they were gunned down by positions in the caves as well as by machine guns above. When they reached the chalky cliffs, they were pummeled by grenades tossed over the sides.

. . .

The "A" Commando of the Royal Marines was the equivalent of 3 or 4 Commando, except that the men making it up had been drawn from the British Navy's Marine force. Like the other Commando brigades, the force specialized in small-unit infantry tactics and was designed for tasks such as infiltrating enemy territory and striking prize targets under the cover of darkness.

Roberts told the Marines they were to attack Red Beach near the long jetty that entered the Dieppe harbor, cross into the city there, and then swing up and around to the eastern headlands and attack the guns there. This was to be done in broad daylight under murderous direct fire, without the benefit of preplanning, let alone covering fire. The goal was even more far-fetched than their original mission of grabbing the German landing craft.

Three hundred and sixty-eight Marines boarded five LCAs and two larger LCMs, Landing Craft Mechanized, which were well-shaped landing craft big enough to carry a single vehicle ashore. Like the Fusiliers, they met a typhoon of bullets and bombs once past the smoke screen, and their boats veered west as well. One of the LCAs was hit and sank; the men were picked up by a boat that was itself hit and began to sink.

The A Commando's leader, Lieutenant Colonel J. Picton-Phillips, finally realized the landing was hopeless somewhere around a hundred yards from shore. Without any other means to signal the other craft, he pulled on a pair of white gloves, climbed onto the rear deck of his LCM, and tried to signal by hand semaphore that the force should retreat. A bullet found him quickly.

The colonel's LCM grounded in shallow water. Now that it had stopped moving, the enemy zeroed in, and within seconds it was taking on water. The front ramp refused to go down. Some men began returning fire. One of the Marine Bren gunners threatened to shoot anyone in the boat who retreated. But even without his threats, going over the side would have been suicidal, as the boat now seemed like the most popular target in the surf.

The chaos reached a new level when the water flooding into the boat suddenly ignited. The Bren gunner who had threatened the others caught fire; he jumped up with his gun and plunged over the side. Everyone else who could went over the side as well. About half of the platoon managed to escape, swimming in the direction of the sea, some going miles before they were picked up. Others, already seriously wounded or confused by the sheer hell that surrounded them, swam toward shore and were apparently killed on the way in.

The other LCM turned back, but the colonel's semaphore wasn't seen or interpreted properly by the LCAs, and the three remaining craft continued toward shore despite the gunfire. One ended up grounded so far from the rocks that the men inflated their life jackets when they got out into the water. Most went back toward the ships rather than be slaughtered on shore.

The Marines who did reach the beach—sixty-nine would die or be captured there—were scattered in small groups. Even if they'd had a realistic goal, they had lost their commander and a good portion of their weapons and equipment. They were no longer an effective fighting force. Like the other men huddling amid the stones, clustered behind the tanks and seawall, the only thing they were capable of was trying to stay alive—and doing that depended much more on luck than the battle skills they'd trained so hard to obtain.

INTO DIEPPE

As bad as the situation was on the beach, a few handfuls of men did manage to make it into the town streets.

On the western side of the beach, the Casino building not only provided shelter for the Canadians who could get there, but it gave them some cover toward the city streets. By moving through the southeast wing of the building, soldiers could get relatively close to the boulevard de Verdun without coming under direct fire. A group of about fourteen Royal Hamilton Light Infantry soldiers under the leadership of Captain A. C. Hill had rushed through the Casino not long after landing on the beach, running toward a small alley east of the rue de Sygogne. The alley itself was blocked with thick barbed wire, but the men were able to get into the theater next to it, moving from a storeroom and then around and out the east side to the street. Within minutes, they were near the Church of St. Remy, which dominated a small square on the eastern half of the city. Finding only light and unorganized opposition, Hill's men saw what they thought was an enemy headquarters on the rue de la Barre, a main east–west cross street south of the church. After a brief firefight, they retreated back past the church, fought with a gun crew using a dual-purpose antiaircraft and tank weapon on rue de Sygogne, and then made it back into the theater.

The Dieppe they encountered in their roughly hour-and-a-half foray was a bizarre mix of death and everyday life. A handful of French citizens were going about their business seemingly oblivious to the gunfire. An elderly custodian calmly swept the theater as the Canadians crouched near the windows.

A second party led by Sergeant Hickson—the engineer tasked to destroy the phone lines at the post office—reached the Church of St. Remy sometime after Hill. After storming the Casino, Sergeant Hickson gathered about eighteen men with him. They crossed boulevard de Verdun and ran into one of the buildings facing the seafront, helped by covering fire from a tank that had positioned itself behind the Casino buildings. The men went through the building, came out on a side street, and then ran about a block into town, arriving at the square where the town hall sat. Germans fired at them from the windows of the buildings; at the same time, civilians milled around in the streets. Hickson, seeing some of the civilians pointing out where the

Canadians were, decided they were actually Germans, and the force cleared the area by firing a Bren gun.

Those few blocks were as far as they got. Bogged down fighting German soldiers in one of the buildings, Hickson's force nearly exhausted their ammunition and was forced to retreat back the way they came, eventually reaching the Casino.

Gradually, the tank commanders realized that there would be no chance of getting into the town, and that the best they could do was protect the men who were still alive. The tanks moved back down to the beach, waiting with the infantry for the order to withdraw.

THE RANGERS AT SEA

Still on the flak boat, Ron Sweazey, Les Kness, and the dozen other Rangers had a ringside seat for the air battle and the disaster on shore. After the landing at Berneval had been called off by the Commandos' leader, the boat sailed south in the direction of Dieppe. Sweazey set up his rifle at the side of the boat and fired along with the heavier weapons when a German aircraft would come near. Two bombs came close enough to drench him with water, but between the flak and the ship's maneuvering, the crew managed to keep from being hit. At least one artillery shell, however, did find the boat. Kness was down in the galley when the shell flew through without exploding. It was maybe four feet from his head.

By 7 a.m., the flak boat was picking up wounded men from landing craft that had returned from the beach. The hail of fire on the beaches and in the water immediately in front of them was so intense that Sweazey felt as scared as he'd ever been in his life. Captain Murray, who'd boarded the ship earlier, by now had given up hope of landing. He watched the battle, trying to remember as much as he could, hoping it would be of use in the future.

Aboard the *Fernie*, General Truscott was trying to decipher the conflicting reports. He heard the Casino reported taken, and that the tanks were moving over the esplanade and into the city. He knew the reserves were being sent in, in hopes of taking the city. A message came, indicating that the Commandos had taken the battery at Varengeville. But Truscott also knew that the headlands on either side of the city had not been subdued, and the continuing thunder from the shore made it clear that the battle was ferocious. By nine o'clock, the reports reaching the operations room had become more accurate—and desperate. An air of depression settled into the backup headquarters, the commanders beginning to sense the fiasco.

Aboard the *Calpe,* General Roberts listened incredulously to a report from one the Marine officers telling him what had happened to A Commando. Roberts simply couldn't believe it.

Or rather, he *did* believe it, but didn't want to. He ordered the tank reserve to stay at sea, then tried to find his own way to the beach to observe what was happening firsthand. One of the Navy commanders convinced him to stay aboard the ship.

The Navy commander, Hughes-Hallett, told Roberts he had to order a withdrawal—the sooner the better. The Canadian agreed, but the tide had gone out, which meant the troops would have a long, murderous dash through the surf to get to any boats attempting to land. Roberts decided the reembarkation would start at half tide, lessening the distance to the boats. He issued the order "Vanquish," signaling that withdrawal would begun at 1030. Roberts subsequently changed the time to 1100 to give time for the RAF to help cover the withdrawal.

It was now shortly after nine. On shore, General Haase and the commander of the 10th Panzer Division watched the battle from one of the houses on the western high ground. Things were going so well, they decided, there was no need to bring the tanks in.

On the *Fernie*, Churchill Mann, the Canadian brigadier general who had been responsible for drawing up much of the Canadian plan, received the order to withdraw. He told Truscott sadly that the operation would surely be remembered as a historical failure.

ORANGE BEACH

While the forces on the main beach in front of Dieppe had been slaughtered, Number 4 Commando had finished off the gun battery and withdrawn to the beach. The wounded were carried down to the water on improvised stretchers, including at least one door taken from a French house. They were under fire, but it was comparatively light. Three sailors were injured by the combination of machine guns and rifles firing from the cliff, but the gunfire was nothing compared to what they had experienced back at the battery. Then a German mortar began firing at the beach, its salvos striking near the ravine they were using to descend. The Commandos set up a three-inch mortar and began returning fire.

Spitfires and the Commandos' own two-inch mortars laid down smoke, helping cover the retreat and the landing craft as they approached. Szima, getting down to the beach, heard Major Mills-Roberts shouting and pointing out a sniper. He emptied his M1 in the sniper's direction; the smoke was so thick that he couldn't tell whether he'd hit anything, but the gun stopped harrying the Commandos.

Some of the wounded were carried out into the water to be reloaded into the boats. A number of others lay on the rocks. Szima, told to go out into the water, offered to help take the men. But the Commando officers ordered him away. In their opinion, the men were too wounded to make it back to England alive. Their only hope was to be taken to a German hospital and remain prisoners of war. Medics were moving among the men; they were staying with them on the beach, in effect volunteering to be prisoners of war.

Szima thought the men would have a better chance in the boats. But it wasn't up to him. He obeyed orders and waded out into the water, M1 on one shoulder, Boys gun on the other. The water was up to his chin before he finally reached an LCA; it was already so full that the bow looked as if it was going to dunk under the waves. Szima climbed aboard, one of the last men to leave Orange Beach.

By now, the Germans had gotten back to the lighthouse at Cap d'Ailly; they began firing machine guns and possibly a flak gun at the boats. The Commandos answered, firing as their boats moved back in the direction of the main landing force. Three miles offshore, the landing craft rendezvoused with MGB 312. The wounded were put aboard; Szima climbed up on a scramble net. The gunboat and LCAs then headed toward the *Calpe,* where the wounded could be off-loaded and Lord Lovat could give Roberts his report.

Lovat, standing on the deck of one of the boats, shouted up orders from Roberts. Eventually, a staff officer appeared and told the Commandos to go back to England. By then, the wounded had been transferred. Before the boats could start away, German bombers launched an attack; the small boats swerved back out to sea, trying to duck the salvos before setting sail for home.

YELLOW BEACH

To the far east of Dieppe at Berneval, the survivors of Number 3 Commando were still huddling against the cliffs, waiting to be picked up. Rangers Furru, Jacobson, and Bresnahan had reached the beach sometime after 8 a.m. For more than two hours, they'd watched the ocean with falling hopes, waiting for one of their landing craft to appear. What they didn't know—though by now they probably guessed—was that the commander of the landing craft assigned to them believed that all of the Commandos had been cut off on the cliff above the beach. Even as Lieutenant Loustalot was fighting his way to the machine-gun position above, the LCP commander had ordered his boats to withdraw.

The decision was understandable. Three of the six LCPs had been sunk, and several members of the crews manning the surviving boats had been injured. The landing craft had waited more than a half hour on the rocks, apparently summoned prematurely by one of the Commando officers who didn't realize the Germans had cut off his path down to the beach. But the absence of the landing craft doomed roughly a hundred men, a good number of whom had been wounded. One or two men managed to escape by swimming out to the sea, passing through the smoke and haze to be picked up by ships or landing craft passing westward, but most took positions in the ravine, on the beach, and in caves, firing desperately as the Germans pressed their attack. Despite a shower of grenades and shells from a French 75 the Nazis had brought up for support, the Commandos fought on until about 10:30. Then the ravine fell; Nazi patrols began scouring the beach. The gunfire intensified, then died. Seeing no hope, men surrendered.

Furru and the others considered resisting, but they realized that it was futile. One German "potato masher" would kill the lot of them. The only rational choice that remained was to surrender. And so as a squad of Germans closed in, the men threw down their weapons and raised their hands.

"VANQUISH"

At 1110, a flight of Boston light bombers approached the main beach at Dieppe, laying smoke for the landing craft that were coming for the men still alive. The smoke cloud made individual boats hard to target, but the Germans plastered the water in front of it with mortar and heavy artillery shells. The destroyers and gunboats moved closer to shore, trying to provide cover by bombarding the headlands and German positions as best they could. Fighters also made strafing runs. But the German attack was relentless. The landing boats were splintered before ever getting close to shores.

The troops onshore had gathered wherever they could under cover to wait for the boats. Many were near the tanks, most of which by now had had their treads knocked off but whose armor continued to protect the men inside. Two LCTs had beached on the western half of the seafront, providing shelter as well. About a hundred men were in the Casino and the seaside deck at its front.

When four landing craft made it to White Beach near the Casino, they were nearly swamped by men trying to get away. As they backed out, one was struck by an artillery shell, killing most of the men aboard and swamping the boat. On Red Beach, six of eight LCAs that managed to land were wiped out; only two made it back to the destroyers, their wells filled with wounded men.

Soldiers dropped their gear and swam out toward the smoke, figuring they had a better chance of reaching the craft there. Despite the beating they were taking, the Navy boats kept trying to make pickups, skirting in and out of the smoke and bombs. The boats and swarms of men were easy targets, and the Germans continued to pound them. A Canadian Presbyterian minister, Padre John Weir Foote, carried several men on his back down to the water and then to whatever landing craft he could find. But after the men aboard pulled him to safety, the chaplain leaped back into the water and went back ashore. His place, he thought, was with the hundreds of men who couldn't get off and would soon be taken prisoner.

GREEN BEACH

At Pourville, Ranger Marcel Swank lay on his back, staring at the sky for a long time. Too scared to move, Swank's mind locked him out of the fight. And then, as mysteriously as it had come, the paralysis left. He pushed himself back up, not without fear, but able to move.

Ranger Lloyd Church ran to him a few minutes later. Church said they needed help carrying wounded down to the beach. Swank nodded and followed. They took several men down, leaving them near a neutralized pillbox on the seawall that was being used as a gathering point.

By the time Swank was done and returned to his post with the Bren gunner, word had come to withdraw. He found Church and together the Rangers once more headed to the seafront, trotting down across the village road.

Realizing the invaders were pulling back, the Germans began counterattacking, hoping to catch the men on the beach. They pressed in, rushing past the defensive positions that had just been evacuated. As they came down the broad street in front of the sea, Church and Swank found themselves under fire from both sides and the rear. They ran for the pillbox, taking cover for a moment, not sure what to do.

The plan for Jubilee had called for the forces on Green Beach to proceed to Dieppe; they were to be evacuated from the city at the end of the raid. Obviously, that wasn't going to happen now.

Once the Vanquish order reached Green Beach, the beachmaster attempted to contact the boat pool by radio, hoping to arrange for the pickup. When that didn't work, he resorted to semaphore flags—which meant he had to stand up in the middle of the beach without cover from the German fire above. Though hit four times, he was finally seen, and two LCAs approached the beach. Both met heavy fire and retreated without picking up anyone.

Finally, sometime after 11 a.m., four boats broke through a layer of smoke offshore and came toward the beach. The landing craft had actually tried to land at Dieppe, but between the current and the confusion had ended up here. A mad rush broke out as the men who had made it down to the seawall began running through the surf to board them. The Germans began emptying every weapon they had.

Church and Swank saw the rush and the men falling under the heavy fire. Since the alternative was being taken prisoner, they decided to chance it. They slipped through the front of the pillbox, jumped down to the rocks, and ran.

Swank reached his boat. But before he climbed in, he realized Church wasn't with him. Frantic, he looked back and found that his friend was lying in the surf about halfway back to the beach. He turned and ran to him, grabbing him and dragging him all the way back to the seawall.

Church had been hit in the head, either by a bullet or a splinter; he was still conscious.

"Can you make it?" Swank asked.

Church said he couldn't.

Swank didn't know what to do. Shells and bullets were flying all around. If he stayed, he'd surely be taken prisoner. Or killed.

But if he left, he'd be leaving Church to die alone.

Go, he decided. And he ran back into the water, leaving his friend propped against the seawall as the Germans closed in.

On the Beach at Pourville
November 2006

■ ■ ■

On the way into Pourville, I pull off at a small viewing area at the side of the road overlooking the beach area. One of the German pillboxes that guarded the beach is visible a few yards away. The beach itself is in full view, the center of a horseshoe formed by the cliffs. There are houses on the slope, modern-looking boxes whose wedge shapes contrast with the curves of the nineteenth-century roofs in the village below. But they seem appropriate here, reminiscent of the pill-boxes and gun positions that would have made the hill so deadly in 1942.

Down on the beachfront—or plage *in French—I meet an older French woman who asks why I've come. I explain. She says she was only a child at the invasion, and doesn't know anything firsthand, but it's clear she wants to be helpful, and spends the next half hour or so conjuring what she can remember from the stories she's been told. She's trying so hard that it would be an insult to tell her I've heard these stories already. And beyond her generosity toward me, there's something reassuring in her need to share them; sacrifice and death have not withered from memory.*

When she leaves, I have the beach to myself. I walk along it, and think of something she said. My French is terrible, but her words were easy to understand: They were very brave, those men. Very brave.

She said it with wonder in her eyes, in a tone that asked, Why were they so brave? How could they manage it?

It is a question I have thought about many times, along with another, even harder to answer:

Would I have been so brave?

Learning about Dieppe, reimagining it through the documents and memories of others, has taught me that courage is something that comes only in individual packages, in small and large helpings depending not just on the man or woman but on the circumstances. In a real way, the question of whether I or you or anyone would have had the guts to get out of the landing craft that day is irrelevant. It doesn't matter because we weren't there, and will never be except in our imaginations, where courage and cowardice are only theoretical.

The question to ask is what can we do to make ourselves ready for the moment when courage is needed?

A month or two of speed marches? More practice on the rifle range? A Commando "pal" at our side to show us the way.

Or is it knowledge of what others have done? Not the Hollywood version, not the slick story of derring-do, but the one with the twisted stomachs and the cries of despair, the clandestine rum, the defiant gesture in the face of despair; gut knowledge of the fear, the bragging, the blind rage, the mistakes, and the triumphs.

And most importantly, the knowledge that, at the most critical moment, you won't realize it's courage you need.

ELEVEN

ACCOLADES AND DENIALS

Off the Coast of Pourville
August 19, 1942

■ ■ ■

SWANK'S ESCAPE

Sergeant Swank left Sergeant Church and ran back into the surf. A mass of men had gathered around the landing craft, and Swank couldn't find a place to board. The Germans were continuing to shoot, targeting the boats and the men who clustered around them, ripe grapes primed for picking.

Swank finally managed to push his way to the boat's gunwale, then gestured to the Canadian beside him to go ahead. As the man climbed up the side, the German bullets found him and he fell back onto the Ranger, dead.

Sensing he wouldn't get into the boat without being killed, Swank waded away, moving through water so littered with bodies that he was stepping on fallen men as he went. He stripped off his clothes, intending to swim, but left his rifle over his shoulder. He kept moving out to sea, not knowing exactly what he would do, only that it was better than dying here or being taken prisoner.

Suddenly he realized something was holding him back; he turned and saw that his rifle had hooked one of the dead, and he'd been dragging the man through the water behind him as he went.

Swank undid the gun; as the bullets continued to fly from shore, he took his rifle apart, scattering the pieces. He told himself he did it because he didn't want the weapon to fall into enemy hands.

Moving faster, the Ranger reached deeper water and began to swim. There was a destroyer in the distance, and he headed toward it, pushing himself for about two hundred yards until he saw a landing craft nearby. The vessel had just put off from shore and was going toward the same ship. Someone aboard spotted Swank, and the craft veered in his direction. Weighed down by an overload of men, still taking fire from the shore, the boat came close enough for Swank to grab onto one of the rudder guards at the stern. A Canadian lieutenant inside reached over to help pull him up. As he did, a bullet flew in and hit Swank in the shoulder. It seemed to him that the slug had ricocheted off the water, defying physics to strike him.

The lieutenant got Swank up onto the gunwale, then went to help someone else. The Ranger crawled over the brain of a man whose skull had been shattered and dropped down into the well of the boat. Water sloshed to his knees, its color deep red from the blood of wounded and dead around him.

Close to sinking, the landing craft continued toward the destroyer, struggling to get away from the shore guns.

ABOARD THE *CALPE*

The ship Swank and the others were heading for was the *Calpe,* General Roberts's operation center. Roberts was pleading for more air support, asking again that the high ground around Dieppe be bombed. Besides the horrendous gunfire, the radio problems that had plagued the entire operation hampered the evacuation as well. Misunderstood messages sent a number of the available landing craft back to England prematurely; a number were empty or nearly so when they arrived.

Swank's landing craft pulled near the destroyer, and the Ranger started to help himself up. As he did, he discovered that Ranger Ken Kenyon, who'd transferred to the ship earlier after failing to land on Blue Beach at Puys, was aboard and helping with the wounded. The two Rangers had found each other despite the odds.

They didn't get long to talk. A German plane strafed the destroyer a few minutes after Swank was pulled aboard. Kenyon was hit by one of the bullets, apparently the last Ranger to be injured in the battle.

The destroyer took on two loads of men from the Pourville area, most wounded, before heading back toward the main beaches. So many wounded were taken aboard that there was no room for them below and they had to be kept on the deck. German planes passed overhead, occasionally diving in to strafe the ship. Everywhere, men were moaning and dying from their wounds.

Quentin Reynolds, the American correspondent, stayed with some of the wounded as they were taken to the wardroom. The reporter had already seen a bit of the war over the past year, enough to know that as long as it was kept at a distance, it was easier to deal with. But there was no keeping it at bay now. The doctor gave him a bottle of brandy and bandages, and Reynolds became a nurse. His first instinct was to use the brandy as a disinfectant, but after one man's screams brought the doctor running, he realized the liquor was intended as a sedative to ease the pain.

Some of the wounded laughed at his mistake, and Reynolds bent to give them a drink and do what he could with bandages and Mercurochrome. Then he did what he did best: he listened to the men tell their stories over and over. Besides their wounds, they were suffering from the knowledge that the mission had failed; a sense of doom and depression filled the room.

Finally needing relief himself, Reynolds went up on deck. The German bomber attacks were increasing, and the ship veered left and right, laying smoke, firing furiously, and occasionally rocking with very near misses. As he walked among the wounded, he spotted American uniforms and introduced himself to Swank and Kenyon. Swank made light of his injury, and showed the correspondent the good-luck charm he'd brought with him—a Bible his father had carried through World War I. It was soaking wet but intact. Swank told him about the action on the beach; Reynolds would have trouble sorting the details later, but the impressions of the battle raging overhead and the men's bravery would remain vivid.

Swank would remember something else: Church, wounded on the beach. He could still see his friend's face as he left. It was a face he would see often in his thoughts and dreams over the next several years, and no matter how he tried to justify his decision or see it in the context of the vicious logic of war, he would be haunted by it for the rest of his life.

SURRENDER

There were still hundreds of men on shore. In the *Fernie,* General Truscott listened helplessly as Major Gordon Rolfe, the head of the Calgary Tanks Signal Corps, reported the situation from a wrecked scout car on the Dieppe beach. Again and again, the major asked for landing craft, but there were none to send.

The Canadians later estimated that 368 men were taken off Red and White Beaches; the official British Naval Staff historical report completed after the war calls this a high estimate. The historian also estimated that no more than eighteen landing craft took part in the final evacuation, and that no more than nine were able to take troops away; the rest were destroyed. Several LCAs were said to have carried upward of 70 and 80 men in them, twice their ordinary capacity.

Truscott went topside as the *Fernie* closed toward the shore. It wasn't quite one o'clock. Breaking through the smoke, the destroyer got close enough to take machine-gun fire from the gunners on shore. Smoke curled from the beach. All the American general could see were broken landing craft and the dead.

The messages from shore had finally stopped. With the Germans moving around them on the main beach at Dieppe, the last survivors faced the inevitable and began to surrender as best they could. The tank crews, who'd stayed in their tanks helping protect the infantry-men around them, squeezed from their battered vehicles and crowded near the two LCTs in the vicinity of the Casino. One crewman managed to swim out to sea, where he was picked up; along with two others who had been wounded and evacuated earlier, he was the only Calgary tanker to avoid death or capture ashore.

Leaving the area behind the armored car, Major Rolfe prepared for the surrender by starting a bonfire so he could burn his code lists and other documents. Nearby, he saw General Southam, the brigadier in charge of half the Canadian force, standing with a waterproof package of papers. Rolfe realized it was the plan for the invasion and tried to take it from the general to throw into the fire. But Southam inexplicably refused. He claimed he might need it, then pointed at the approaching enemy.

Shoot at them, demanded the general. We won't surrender.

Southam's refusal to destroy the orders was the final act of fantasy and denial on the beaches; all around him men were already putting handkerchiefs onto guns that had long ago run out of ammunition. Truscott, looking at the beach from the shore, could see no resistance.

Nor could Ham Roberts, who'd ordered the *Calpe* to get as close as possible. Still under heavy attack from the air, the Canadian commander ordered the fleet to head back to England.

PRISONERS

Taken prisoner on the beach below Berneval, Rangers Furru, Jacobson, and Bresnahan were marched back up into the town. The American uniforms made them stand out from the others, and in a few hours would give them a dubious quasicelebrity status—they were the first ground soldiers to be taken prisoner in Europe. Jacobson and Bresnahan would be taken to Berlin for questioning—or display, depending on one's point of view. For the moment, however, they were packed into trucks with the rest of the Commandos. A total of eighty-two men were taken prisoner at Berneval. Another thirty-seven, including Lieutenant Loustalot, had been killed.

Furru was in one of the trucks when he heard an odd sound from above. Glancing upward, he saw telephone wires falling toward the road. Just as he realized what was happening, a Submarine Spitfire appeared, gun blazing. Some of its bullets hit the truck, and it caught on fire. Barely escaping a fireball, the Ranger rolled onto the ground, ducking for cover as more airplanes shot up the convoy, apparently mistaking the prisoners for German troops.

The planes gone, Furru leaped to his feet and ran to help the people still in the truck. He grabbed one of the men by the door, but as he pulled him upward, he realized that the soldier's legs had been shot off.

Dazed, the Ranger went to the side of the road. He found he had to relieve himself. As he squatted, he saw holes in his pants. He checked his shirt, and saw it was ripped as well. Then, to his surprise, he found that he'd been smacked in the knee by a large piece of shrapnel.

Furru found a place to sit down near the road and waited for the Germans to find him. Eventually, they did; he was taken to a hospital and, after healing, brought to a prison camp, where he spent the rest of the war.

On Green Beach, Sergeant Church sat against the seawall with dozens of other men, unable to move as the Germans came down through the town. The shore was lined with dead bodies, and the water that came up on the rocks flowed with blood. Gazing out to sea, knowing that the boats were not coming back, the survivors surrendered.

In one way or another, every man at Dieppe was injured by the mistakes of the senior officers who had planned the mission, but General Southam's decision to bring the invasion orders on the beach—a violation of procedure—and then his refusal to burn them added one more insult. A German officer recovered the plans on the beach shortly after the surrender there. Besides the technical details of the operation, the packet included a number of orders relating to the mission. One, apparently originating with Combined Operations, directed that prisoners of war be tied before being taken away. This violated the Geneva Conventions. In retaliation, the Germans had the hands of the Canadian prisoners bound for more than a year.

Most of the prisoners reported that the Germans were very "proper" toward them on the beach and immediately afterward, treating them with a rough respect. But several captured Commandos said later they were sure they would have been shot had some officers not intervened, and even one of the medical people who'd stayed behind at Varengeville was lined up as if to be assassinated before an officer appeared and ordered that he be let go. Hitler had already authorized the assassination of Commandos, saying they were not to be treated as ordinary prisoners of war because of the way they fought. It was a vicious sort of tribute, fortunately not always followed.

The POWs taken at Dieppe and nearby were led through the city, marching toward the outskirts where a hospital and then a brick factory were turned into temporary holding areas. Curious residents watched them go by; a few offered food and water, and in most cases the Germans did not interfere. By then, German press and film crews had arrived, and some of the soldiers prodded their captives to raise their hands for the camera. A few of the POWs, almost all of them Canadian, tried to make a jaunty face or show some small but important sign of defiance. Most simply stared vacantly, tired and trying to make sense of what had gone so terribly wrong.

NEWHAVEN CHEERS

Packed with men who'd come back from the raid on Varengeville, MGB 312 headed back for Newhaven on the Sussex coast of England. Sergeant Szima, after lying on the deck for a while, got up and went down for a cup of tea. The other Rangers with 4 Commando were in the LCAs nearby. The sailors gave them cans of soup that contained candles in the middle; once lit, the candles warmed the surrounding container. The soup tasted like a gourmet meal to the men, who hadn't eaten for twelve hours. A few of the Commandos ate the apples they'd taken and forgotten back at the orchard near the gun battery. The fruit was still bitter, not sweet, perhaps needing another week or so to ripen on the tree.

In one of the boats, someone tuned a radio to the BBC and heard a preliminary report of the battle, recounting their success. The men were filled with an adrenaline-flushed excitement, riding the wave of energy that comes from a mission that goes well. At the same time, they were exhausted. Szima, like a good number of the others, fell asleep.

The flotilla reached Newhaven around a quarter to six. People lined the docks at the end of the long jetty past the fort and beach defenses. As the boats tied up, the crowd began to cheer. Climbing from the landing craft, some of the Commandos started to sing, and a jaunty marching tune rose from docks as they shuffled onto shore.

Szima found the other Rangers. Glad to be alive, proud of what they'd accomplished, they talked a bit about what they had been through. Stempson was reticent, recounting what had happened at the pillbox with very little detail, save one: the image of the ammo carriers falling like jackrabbits would be one of the first things that came to his mind whenever he thought of Dieppe.

The American journalist Walter Knickerbocker, who'd written several stories on the Commandos, was on the dock to get information for a story on the raid itself. General Eisenhower's staff had released a statement earlier revealing the Ranger battalion's existence and the fact that it was taking part in the battle; either Knickerbocker overhead the Rangers' accents or saw and recognized their uniforms, for he went over and introduced himself, asking for details of what had happened. Now Knickerbocker realized that the story of the first American ground forces going into action in Europe was staring him in the face. The men were an easy interview, still keyed up from the battle.

Szima told him how he'd gone into combat with a knot in his stomach. Koons, in an understated tone, talked about sighting on the battery and firing; probably twenty men had fallen, though he thought for sure he'd killed only two. Other newsmen gathered, British as well as American—here was an angle that hadn't been explored before, Yanks with the Brits. A photographer arranged the men and some nearby Commandos for a shot. Szima lit a cigarette for one of the Commandos as the camera flashed, then thought that the scar on his cheek would mean the picture wouldn't be used. He switched sides, and this time the Commando lit the cigarette after a bit of trouble with the wet matches. The photo would appear on the front pages of newspapers around Great Britain and the United States the next day.

SADDER AND WISER

Truscott's homecoming was much more sober. After pulling away from the shore, the *Fernie* saw her sister ship, the HMS *Berkeley*, hit by bombs from a German bomber. Heavily damaged, the *Berkeley* unloaded its men and passengers to nearby gunboats. It was so far gone that it was sunk by the destroyer *Albrighton*.

Among those wounded was an American, Colonel Loren B. Hillsinger, an Army Air Force officer who'd been observing the air operations. One of his feet was blown off by the explosion; he's generally considered the last casualty of the battle.

Loaded with wounded, the *Fernie* made her way back toward Portsmouth at a snail's pace, dodging aircraft and herding the smaller boats as it went. Fully aware of the battle's disastrous results, Truscott paced through the corridors of the destroyer. He did what he could for the wounded. In the wardroom, he handed out handmade cigarettes, rolling and lighting them for men too weak to do so on their own. When the ship finally pulled into Portsmouth, he watched the men being taken aboard trains and transported to hospitals. Then he took leave of the other officers, and found his own train to London. He was "a sadder and wiser man," as he would write many years later in his memoirs.

Staggering home with the Commandos and the small American contingent were about 2,000 Canadians. Roughly 850 of them had never landed; at least half of the rest were wounded.

The unit-by-unit tally of casualties was gruesome. The Royal Regiment, which attacked Blue Beach at Puys, sent 554 men on the raid; 56 returned. Of those 56, 30 were wounded and another 6 died of their wounds soon after getting home. No officer in the unit survived the battle without injuries.

On Green Beach near Pourville, where Sergeants Church and Swank joined the Queens Own Cameron Highlanders and the South Saskatchewan Regiment, 503 Camerons and 523 Saskatchewans embarked for the raid. The Camerons lost 54 men killed, with 174 taken prisoner; 4 of the POWs subsequently died from wounds. (These totals don't count 17 men still reported missing six months later; presumably, all died on the battlefield.) Of the 258 who returned to England, 103 were wounded. South Saskatchewan lost 65 men killed; 91 were taken prisoner, with 2 dying a short time later. Of the 350 who returned, 166 were wounded. (Seventeen men were still missing six months later.)

Of the men who made it to shore in the Calgary Tank Regiment, only three escaped capture, one because he was seriously wounded and evacuated early in the battle. In sheer numbers, the Essex Scottish suffered more casualties than any other unit—90 dead, 386 taken prisoner, including 268 wounded. Of the 50 men from the unit who returned, 28 came back wounded.

The total casualties for the Canadians were 47 officers and 760 enlisted men killed; another 2 officers and 26 enlisted men died of their wounds after being brought offshore, with 7 officers and 65 enlisted men dying as POWs. A total of 587 men, 39 of them officers, were wounded but got back to England. Men wounded and taken prisoner came to 561, with 35 officers. Another 1,312—83 of them officers ranging from lieutenant to brigadier general—were captured. The casualty rate was 67 percent; if only the number of men who made it to the beaches in the first place is considered, the ratio is even worse.

Number 3 Commando, the unit Lieutenant Loustalot was with, lost 37 killed; 82 were taken prisoner. Immediately after the battle, 12 men from 4 Commando were known killed, with 9 wounded and listed as "missing," along with 4 others supposedly missing. These missing were the wounded men and their caretakers left on the beach. Another 20 men had been wounded. When the war was over, 16 men from 4 Commando would be listed as killed.

While the Rangers did not have anywhere near the number of men that the Canadians or British had in the battle, on a percentage basis they, too, suffered greatly. Of the fifty men who left Achnacarry, three were killed, three taken prisoner, and five were wounded—a casualty rate of 22 percent. If the men who were on the boats that couldn't complete the crossing are subtracted from the total, the casualty rate approaches 50 percent.

But the percentages really don't tell the story.

MEDIA FRENZY

Combined Office released two statements about the raid while it was still going on. This was normal procedure, though the statements would evoke an unusual amount of confusion and, to some degree, mistrust and bitterness from Canadians. The first, issued at 6 a.m., identified Dieppe as the target and emphasized to the French in the area that the attack was a raid, not an invasion. A similar message had been spread by the French Commandos; it was meant as a warning so that the French residents would not do anything that would draw reprisals from the Germans.

A longer press release came out at 1 p.m. This one said that the main force was Canadian, adding that "British Special Service troops"—the Commandos—and American Rangers were involved. It also mentioned that the troops on the right flank—without identifying them, but referring to 4 Commando—had succeeded in smashing the six-gun battery. The statement claimed that forces on the left flank had been repulsed but re-formed and took their beach.

The reports were clearly based on incomplete information and spun—as were all dispatches during the war—to favor the Allies. They naturally roused press interest, which wouldn't have been avoided anyway, given the number of correspondents that had been taken along and the vaunted German propaganda machine, which could be counted on to give its own spin on events.

The press statements stopped as soon as the Combined Operations staff realized how badly things had gone. The main slant of their early releases had been to deny that the raid was an invasion; this was because they anticipated that the Germans would claim a major invasion had been turned back and a great victory won. With all of the speculation in the newspapers and on the radio about a second front, it would be natural for some people to think that the attack had been intended as a real invasion, and that the Allies—who hadn't had a real victory since the beginning of the war—had just suffered another major blow.

But now the problem was much more serious. Combined Operations had a true fiasco on its hands. Call the attack a raid or a reconnaissance or a garden party, there weren't many ways to put a positive spin on an operation that resulted in 60 percent casualties. Already the Germans were talking about a great victory; photos of the tanks and dead men on the beach were sure to follow.

The next statement from Combined Operations came a little after 8 p.m. Conceding that the Germans were claiming a great victory, the statement said that the withdrawal had been planned and had even begun six minutes after the scheduled time—a small fib meant to imply a much larger lie, namely that the complicated military operation had gone off as neatly as a train schedule. The statement did, however, mention that there had been fierce fighting and there were likely to be "heavy casualties" on both sides.

This was eventually followed by a communiqué that was highly defensive and contained a number of distortions, misdirections, and outright lies, and in retrospect seems to have been part of a move internally to, in modern military terms, CYA—cover your ass, or rather those belonging to the commanders involved.

The statement claimed that it was well known beforehand that the German defenses were very heavy, and said that an air battle had resulted that had been very favorable but had not been foreseen. It claimed that the main goal of the Air Forces engaged had been to support the landing and protect the force. These claims, of course, wouldn't have held up had the identity of the squadrons been identified—information that of course had to be withheld for military reasons.

The statement also claimed that the raid was a "reconnaissance in force"—a phrase that Churchill had suggested sometime before, but that Combined Operations had generally avoided. Now that it was clear that things had gone poorly, perhaps, any link to Churchill, even by implication, was probably welcome.

By this time, the statements Combined Operations issued were no longer the focus of the correspondents, as the invasion force was returning to port. The American press, and a good portion of the British, were focusing on the American Rangers, who had never been in battle before. They were a natural human-interest story for reporters starved for a "local" angle. Many of the U.S. newsmen and correspondents had been covering the war for some time, writing about things that they suspected few Americans truly cared for. Now they had a real human-interest story on their hands—and one that connected "our boys" to the bona fide Allied heroes of the war: the Commandos.

The reporters jumped all over the story. Over the next few days, Szima, Stempson, Koons, and Brady—the only Rangers who'd gotten to the beaches and returned unharmed—were in great demand. And unlike the Commandos and the other Rangers, the four were on their own, at least at first: they'd been given some flexibility in reporting first to London and then returning to the rest of the unit in Scotland.

The four men took a train to London, where they proceeded to give a series of interviews to radio and newspaper correspondents. They had a grand time in London, meeting generals and film star Douglas Fairbanks—or at least someone who looked, sounded, and talked liked him, since they were never formally introduced—in a bar in London.

According to a story Szima told writer Will Fowler for *The Commandos at Dieppe,* the four men showed up at the U.S. embassy in London the day after the raid and tried to convince the Marines to let them leave their bags and guns there for a while. A Marine officer replied with a stern lecture; Szima told him "Fuck you, sir," and left, half expecting to be arrested. But the Marines had actually called some news photographers, and Szima and friends managed to get a drink out of it.

Sometime later, Fowler wrote, Szima came face-to-face with a general whom he didn't know and whose name he never quite got. (Szima believes it may have been Major General Russell Hartle, who headed the 34th Division.)

The general asked Szima if he had shit in his pants during combat.

When Szima told him no, the general proclaimed that he had "carried a turd in my pants" for three days in Argonne.

They were treated to drinks and hailed as conquering heroes. Army headquarters eventually sent two cars to the bar and took them away, either to make sure they got to their press and radio engagements, or to avoid further raunchy conversations with generals. In any event, the four were media stars for about twenty-four hours, giving interviews and recounting what they had seen. Koons, photogenic, well-spoken, and with an understated account of his sniping during the battle, was especially in demand.

But along the way, Szima noticed a curious thing about the stories that were being printed and reported: if you read or listened closely, you'd never see or hear of an American killing anyone. The

stories were being heavily censored for the folks back home—
sanitized of anything that might turn people off.

It wasn't just the news stories either. Though it would take him
years to find out, the reports that Szima and the other Rangers gave
after the raid were heavily compressed and, according to Szima, contained significant errors, mistakes in details that left out much of the
horror and excitement of what they'd been through; a good deal of
what he called the "gung-ho" factor was stripped from the reports. It
would bother him for the rest of his life.

THE PRESS

Combined Operations tried its best to control the news stories about
the raid, blocking the correspondents who had been on the operation
from filing stories until they had been thoroughly "briefed"—which
meant no stories until a press conference the morning after the raid.
The press conference was then postponed. The correspondents—
whose stories were subject to military censorship in any event—
demanded to be allowed to file them by noon. Combined Operations
insisted on reading the stories first (a task ordinarily done by the
British Ministry of Information, but common for operations where
the Commandos were involved). The delay gave the German propaganda machine a running start, and they reported not only true
information—such as the fact that tanks had been on the beaches,
which the Allies had been loath to admit—but claimed loudly that
the plan had actually called for a much larger invasion.

The Allied stories that were eventually cleared told of a tough
fight but tried to put it in the best possible light. They were preoccu-
pied with the fact that it was a raid, not an invasion. And, possibly
because Combined Operations had been in charge, the first wave of
stories generally called the raid a "Commando" operation, even
when mentioning the Canadians.

Someone who didn't know anything about what really happened would be hard-pressed to read between the lines and interpret the first newspaper accounts as being anything but the story of a hard-fought victory or, at very worst, a stalemate. The stories were filled with misinformation. The *New York Times* declared, "It can now be revealed that British Commandos captured the Dieppe race course and converted it into a temporary landing ground for planes." The casualty numbers were extremely low. There was no hint that the battle represented the greatest loss of life for an Allied unit in the European theater since Dunkirk.

Given that context, Canadian readers were understandably baffled about the attention the American Rangers received. They had no idea what really happened, and the stories about a handful of Americans struck them as out of proportion. The fact that the accounts—laudatory and generally positive—focused on the Rangers was not surprising, since the only men the reporters had access to were the ones who had taken part in the raid's sole successful operation. But contrary to what some historians would later claim, most of the stories noted that the Rangers were a small part of the operation. They also made it clear that the battle had been brutal, without saying exactly how dismal the results really were. A UP story indicated that only five men in the twelve-man group Stempson was with lived.

Combined Operations released statements saying that it was "correcting" previous impressions that it had given, emphasizing that the Canadians had played a major role and that the raid really shouldn't be called a Commando operation and that the focus should not be on the Americans. A cynic might point out that a controversy about Americans getting too much press would divert at least some media attention from the real story—the Allies had just been hammered in one of the worst debacles of the war.

In America, the raid got a lot of play in the papers—but the Rangers were not the only story, and in some papers—the *New York*

Times, for example, weren't even the lead story. It then mostly dropped out of sight, as the war brought plenty of new developments.

In Canada, the government released a long report on the raid, which combined defensiveness—it went to some lengths to claim that the force had been highly trained—with spin and false information. The first reports of casualties were extremely light, compared to the actual tally: an August 22 story gave twenty-seven dead and twenty-one wounded, with eight missing, even though the government knew by then the total was far, far higher. At the same time, extremely close readers of newspapers may have spotted the first sign that things had not gone very well: the early battle reports were not followed up by human-interest stories focusing on the men in the units involved and their exploits.

At the same time, the Germans were reporting that over two thousand prisoners had been taken. Gradually, a fuller story of the debacle appeared, though mostly between the lines—there were leaks about the need for a new strategy of landings in a story that still called the raid a success. It wasn't until mid-September, nearly a month after the raid, that the Canadian government finally admitted that 67 percent of its force had been captured, killed, or wounded. Even then, the debacle was generally blamed on the "bad luck" of the convoy running into the boats, and heavier-than-expected defenses. Poor planning, insufficient training, and inadequate support—the real causes of the disaster—were not mentioned. The following May, a report by Canadian Army historian Colonel Charles Stacey gave the public a glimpse of some of the problems encountered during the operation and of the shortcomings in the planning; while the overall tone was still protective of Canadian figures such as Roberts, the report was far more candid than anything that had come before.

Feelings of resentment and questions would linger for decades, most especially among the many families whose loved ones had died or were in captivity.

POLITICS

Winston Churchill had left England to meet with Stalin at the beginning of August. At the meeting, which took place shortly before the Dieppe invasion, he told the Soviet dictator that there would be no invasion of France that year. He also strongly hinted that there would be none in 1943. The Soviet Union was still falling back under the weight of the German Army, and Stalin was hardly pleased. He complained that the other Allies were not willing to take risks to save Russia. After pointing out that England had been risking its very existence for several years, Churchill tried to placate the dictator by saying that the Allies were launching an intense air bombardment campaign against the German homeland. Britain would aim at devastating twenty German cities, and would continue obliterating cities until the war ended. He also told Stalin about the plan to invade northern Africa, presenting it as the necessary "second front."

Both men knew, however, that a campaign in Africa, no matter how successful, would never cause Germany to move enough troops from the Russian front to end the offensive. Stalin remained somewhat prickly as the discussions turned to other matters. On August 15, just before leaving for Cairo, Churchill told Stalin that a large raid was planned for northern France, exaggerating the size slightly but nonetheless calling it a reconnaissance in force, not an invasion.

By the time Churchill returned to England August 24, the raid was over and its failure obvious to those in the government. He had faced considerable political turmoil in the beginning of the year following major British losses in Asia, when his support was tested in a vote of confidence. While the Dieppe debacle encouraged another round of criticism, it did not cause a new crisis. He defended the raid in a speech to the House of Commons on September 8, again calling it a reconnaissance in force and saying that it was an important "preliminary" to a full-scale invasion. Churchill also picked up on the theme of the air battle, repeating RAF claims that a great victory had been won.

Behind the scenes, the Prime Minister was somewhat less than the enthusiastic supporter of Combined Operations that he appeared. He wanted to know who had come up with the attack plan, which he said appeared "out of accord with the accepted principles of war," not to mention good sense. He seemed especially anxious to know what role General Montgomery had had in the planning—not surprisingly, given that he had recently appointed Montgomery head of the 8th Army. Montgomery kept his job; so did Mountbatten and the rest of his staff at Combined Operations.

Combined Operations and the Canadians had started their own review of the Dieppe Raid on August 20, the day after the force returned. After-action reports were required from all who took part, and Mountbatten presided over a conference to hear the accounts of the officers who'd been involved in the operation. A conflict immediately broke out between Mountbatten and RAF commander Leigh-Mallory, who felt it was too soon to take statements—and who probably feared a great deal of criticism would be heaped on the RAF for a lack of full support. After the conference began, one of the Canadian officers present, Captain Denis Whitaker, charged that the Germans had known about the plans beforehand—a charge that he would make in greater detail many decades later in his book, *Dieppe—Tragedy to Triumph*. A naval officer said that the failure to take Puys was due to cowardice by troops afraid to leave their boats. The charge led to a formal, though secret, inquiry; though hampered by the fact that many of the men involved had died, it found that a significant number of soldiers had refused to or been slow to leave the landing craft.

General Roberts criticized the plan he had approved, in hindsight realizing that it should have been much more flexible, kept more reserves available, and most of all not provided for a frontal attack on the Dieppe beaches. He also said that the defenses had been underestimated.

Roberts's admissions did not help his career. Shortly after the battle, he was removed from his post and put in charge of training back in Canada.

Debates over the intelligence, over the decision to revive the attack, the military plan, the lack of bombardment, the use of raw troops—all would continue for years, hashed over first by the veterans and their commanders, then by historians and others interested in the battle. Mountbatten and Montgomery, whose military careers continued to soar after Dieppe, were both criticized for their roles in the raid after the war. They reacted in different ways: Montgomery minimized his role, said he thought the raid should have been called off, and never mentioned in his memoirs that he was the one who had advocated a frontal assault. Mountbatten said that Dieppe had taught the Allies a great deal, and that every life lost at Dieppe had saved a thousand at D-Day.

Probably not, but it was the sort of thing people wanted to hear.

A MEDAL FOR KOONS

In the first few days after the raid, Zip Koons must have told his story to reporters and radio announcers three or four dozen times. He had a self-deprecating, even humble tone when he spoke, and a matter-of-fact way of explaining what had happened. Whether because of his shooting or his overall demeanor, Koons became something of a public face for the Rangers, singled out for interviews and publicity shots. Intelligent, photogenic, full of vigor but not full of himself, Koons was the perfect representative of the battalion.

Koons's honors extended beyond a few press conferences. Cited by the Commandos for his role in the raid, he was eventually awarded the British Military Medal, an extremely rare honor for a foreigner. The award was presented in Casablanca, Morocco, in January 1943; among those in the audience were President Roosevelt and Prime Minister Winston Churchill, who were meeting there to discuss war strategy. For the ceremony, Koons—by then a sergeant—borrowed Colonel Darby's belt, wearing it over his Class-A uniform, a gesture of respect and appreciation to his commanding officer.

Mountbatten himself pinned the medal to Koons's chest.

RETURNING HEROES

Several days of practice assaults with a Royal Navy training ship came to an end August 19 for James Altieri and the company of Rangers he'd been training with. As a reward, they were granted forty-eight hours of leave. It was the first time off in two months that Altieri or any of the other men would have, and they aimed to make the best of it.

Or at least Altieri did until his sergeant called him and another corporal front and center and told them they had been volunteered for MP duty.

Altieri grudgingly complied, and he and the other corporal, along with a friend who took pity on them, began patrolling the town, watching sourly as their friends filled the bars. During their patrol, they befriended an amiable Scotsman, who wanted to have his picture taken with them. Finding a local photographer's shop, they began joking with the man, trading hats and posing, until one of the Rangers suggested that Altieri would look smashing in a kilt.

The Scotsman agreed, on the condition that he could dress up as an American. Altieri pulled on the kilt—which seemed a bit long at the knees.

Just then someone shouted for an MP. Still dressed in the kilt,

Altieri and the two other Rangers headed to a bar and discovered some of their friends in the middle of a fight with some British sailors and Royal Marines. The Rangers were outnumbered but ahead on points: three Rangers and five sailors were on the floor, all knocked out.

Altieri waded into the fight—and promptly got decked. When he came to, his company sergeant was standing over him, shaking his head. The kilt's owner soon entered, took one look at his ruined skirt—it had been ripped and trampled in the melee—and demanded restitution.

Fortunately, Altieri had won a considerable sum playing poker during the last training session, and he was able to settle the matter by paying the man for his clothes and then buying the locals a drink. The Ranger was still clearing his head when another man from the outfit ran in with a newspaper and threw it down on the bar. The men read the headline in silence:

**ALLIED FORCE INVADES FRANCE
CANADIANS, COMMANDOS AND AMERICAN RANGERS
MAKE DARING ASSAULT ON DIEPPE**

Altieri blew the rest of his money on drinks. They really were in the war now.

Captain Murray and the rest of the Rangers who'd survived the raid returned to their temporary training base at Van Crippsdale Island, Scotland, two days later. Szima, Sweazey, and the others were subdued at first, still sorting out everything that they had been through. Altieri thought his friends seemed older as well as quieter. It took several days before most were willing to open up and talk about the battle, even with their own comrades.

Captain Murray prepared a three-page after-action report that included a page worth of recommendations, ranging from the development of a smoke shell for the Rangers' 60mm mortar to a suggestion that men coming off a raid be given a seven-day furlough. Robert Flanagan, the lieutenant who'd been in charge of the men sprinkled among the Canadian units, wrote tersely that the Rangers should be better informed of what was going on before being dropped into units as observers.

By now it had become apparent how badly the overall raid had gone, and as the returning Rangers opened up, they were critical of the operation. Some blamed it on the loss of surprise because of the encounter with the German convoy, but for the most part they seem to have thought that the plan itself was at fault. If they said this to the intelligence officers and clerks helping prepare the after-action reports, however, those words never made it to the official records. More typical was the report by Lieutenant Charles Shunstrum, who'd been on the flak boat with Sweazey. After detailing the fact that they never got ashore and had come under heavy (and unexpected) fire at sea, the lieutenant—or whoever was helping him write it—finished with a single sentence: *The raid was a success.*

A BLOODY BAPTISM

Viewed from strictly the Rangers' perspective, the raid *was* a success. It introduced the unit to combat without subjecting the men to the sort of slaughter that decimated the Canadian Second Division, destroying it as an effective fighting unit. The Rangers who had worked with the Commandos had real tasks to do and were treated as full partners on the raid; they had been the perfect mentors for the Americans' willing apprenticeship.

The main effect of the mission on the 1st Ranger Battalion was to confirm the importance and value of training. The success of Number 4 Commando became an example, not just for the Rangers but for the Commandos as well. The conviction that training was critical hit home with the men as well as the officers; Altieri noted a renewed energy in the training as the Rangers continued to work with the Commandos in Scotland.

While it's difficult to measure how much or even if the publicity about the raid raised morale in the United States, there is one indication that it had a positive effect. Within days of Dieppe, many American soldiers were reported to have been telling women that they, too, were Rangers, apparently in an effort to pick them up. Darby used this as one of the reasons why the Rangers should get their own shoulder patch, similar to that worn by the Commandos. Truscott agreed, forwarding the request to Eisenhower for approval.

Though they didn't know it yet, the 1st Ranger Battalion was training for another, much larger operation than Dieppe—Torch, the invasion of North Africa, which would take place a few months later. The men who had survived the Dieppe Raid would play an important role in that battle, and those that followed. Darby looked to Szima, Koons, Sweazey, and the others as the "originals." Though the Rangers' slogan hadn't been coined yet, they were expected to "lead the way." And they did, taking on some of the toughest assaults in the European theater over the next two years. For the men who'd been on the Jubilee raid, it all began at Dieppe.

Pine Island, New York
Late November 2006

■ ■ ■

A day after I return from Dieppe, a friend calls with the news that his father-in-law died while I was away. He'd served in Europe during World War II, been at Normandy, and seen a good amount of action. Like a lot of veterans, my friend's father-in-law didn't talk much about his service, but when he did, he often scoffed at the image projected by Hollywood and books like The Greatest Generation. *It wasn't that the men who survived the Depression and fought in the war didn't do brave things or struggle through great adversity. As I understood it from our few brief conversations, his beef with the portrayals was that they erased everything that didn't fit with a perfect, loftier image: not just cowardice and pettiness and rage, but the hesitation and mistakes. These things were left out with all good intentions, whether in the name of morale or, much later, a fondness for parents and grandparents, or a need to find "pure" heroes. But they distorted the reality nonetheless, and took something from the men and women in the process.*

Did it matter that someone lay on his back in the middle of the battle for ten or fifteen minutes, too scared to face the enemy? If he recovered and got back up, were those fifteen minutes of paralysis important?

My friend's father-in-law, I think, would have said yes, of course; they were part of the record, his personal record, and they made what came before and what came afterward that much more important. And they were a link between that man and other men—not just in the war, but now. Taking those moments away, distilling the imperfections from the sepia images, removing the references to killing in after-action reports—each assault on the reality of what happened made it more difficult for others to understand fully what happened, and to use their understanding in a way that would benefit them, whether in taking a beach or contemplating war. Memory itself is a fragile thing, easily lost. Natural erosion is bad enough, but deliberate or sentimental distortion render it nearly useless.

Later that night, I'm reviewing some of my documents on afternoon concerning Dieppe when I come across this passage in Owen Sweazey's oral history:

Q: *What happened to you, were you able to get out of that unscathed?*

A: *Yes, I was lucky.*

Q: *Were you able to retreat back to your boats?*

A: *Well, after we had taken our guns it was found out that the coastal guns weren't anything but wood. They had been made of wood, camouflaged, so we thought they were coastal guns, and it wasn't anything but a bunch of wood. So we came down the cliff and back to the boats and got out. Of course we stayed in the harbor within range for most of the day, but we did come back to the boats.*

Sweazey was with 3 Commando, assigned to take out the Goebbels battery at Berneval. Major Peter Young's account of the raid mentions one fake, but otherwise Sweazey's account is at odds with every other account of the raid.

After reading Sweazey's personal diary as well as the oral history, and then reviewing Peter Young's account and the after-action reports as well as Jacques Mordal's Dieppe book with the German commander's notes, I realize that Sweazey must have been passing along a rumor based on a partial account of what the group with Young had actually seen. But what if the oral history was all we had of the battle? What if all the other sources were lost, or no one had survived to record them?

Would Loustalot's courage be any less significant if he had died leading a charge toward a harmless decoy? Would his bravery cease to exist if we didn't know about it?

Only our perceptions would change, not his reality. Dieppe clearly was a waste—a battle that shouldn't have been fought, for an objective that in the vast course of the war meant absolutely nothing. You can say that about many battles; the nature of war unavoidably leads to waste.

But that says nothing, absolutely nothing, about the acts of Lieutenant Loustalot, of Sweazey, of the Canadians, of anyone on that beach that day. We can't turn away from the facts, from the poor decisions that led to the attack, the politics, the mistaken assumptions and magical thinking that pushed so many men to their deaths. Those facts are important for us to understand and face, if only to remind us that we are capable of all those things ourselves. But to the men who took part in the raid at Dieppe, the assessment of the plan is secondary. Their actions at the point of the gun, their moment in the crucible of fire, was what was important. We can learn about what they did, try to understand it, appreciate it, and even celebrate it. But our understanding does not change what they experienced, and our judgments, good, bad, or indifferent, are irrelevant to what they did. If their example helps us, that is good for us; if not, it's our loss. They are already far beyond our ability to help or hurt.

TWELVE

WHY?

Fort William, Scotland
November 2006
...

After talking with one of the Commandos about Lieutenant Loustalot, we go on to other subjects—Commando training, World War II in general, the years after the war. Finally, some friends are waiting and he's ready to leave. As he gets up from the table where we've been sitting, something occurs to him and he stops.

"You know, I went back to Dieppe a few years back," he tells me, mentioning one of the anniversary ceremonies. "And I spoke to a French woman. She was glad for the raid. She said, 'It let us know we weren't forgotten.' I've never forgotten that. So it was worth it, in a way."

AN ASSESSMENT

In the sixty-some years since the raid on Dieppe took place, historians have asked why it failed so horribly. A number have blamed the lack of surprise and poor intelligence, just as the Canadian government did in the months following the raid. Neither claim stands up to scrutiny.

Many of the Rangers who were on the raid and didn't land believed that the loss of surprise because of the clash with the German convoy killed the chances of success. It was a natural reaction, and an opinion that many people still hold today, despite the fact that both documents and firsthand reports from the battlefield show the clash at sea did not actually alert the German defenders to the impending invasion.

The Germans were ready for an invasion, but not because of the clash with the convoy, or even because of the spies in southern England who heard talk of the plans. Everything the Allies had done during the several months leading up to Dieppe—from other Commando raids to propaganda concerning a second front to massing for the Rutter operation—warned the Nazis that they were up to something. That may have been one reason the planners weren't as concerned about reviving the raid against Dieppe after Rutter was canceled; they knew there was no way to achieve strategic surprise in any event. The Germans were ready for the landing forces just as the Canadian and English Armies would have been in Sussex two years before—because enemy actions had put them on a high state of alert.

A lack of proper intelligence has also been cited as the reason for the raid's failure. According to this argument, the Canadian planners didn't know what they were up against. They had the wrong German unit guarding the town, and weren't clear on the location of the reserves. They underestimated the number of soldiers in Dieppe.

The preraid intelligence was certainly not perfect. However, misidentifying the unit manning the defenses should not have had a serious effect on the plan. At that point in the war, any German division guarding Dieppe would have been rotated in from the Eastern front. All would have had inexperienced replacements, men who hadn't faced combat before, mixed in with seasoned troops. The misidentification of the unit is a red herring; the proper identification would have made no difference.

Some historians have claimed that the initial intelligence estimates underestimated the number of defenders in and around the city by half. It's hard at this point to sort the numbers and claims precisely, but this seems to be an exaggeration or, more likely, a misinterpretation. The original estimates put the force strength in the city at 1,400, with an additional 2,500 men available within four hours. The German documents show that city garrison had 1,500 men; there were more reserves available, perhaps twice the Allied estimate if the entire division is considered, but it's not clear how close to the battle they were or whether they were in fact deployed as reserves.

Troop numbers can be extremely deceiving, and looking at them without context or specifics is often misleading. For example, the force holding the Dieppe beachfront consisted of a single company. Only a portion of them would have been on manning positions at the time of the battle. In the abstract, it would appear a small, even insignificant force—a hundred and fifty men perhaps. But they not only manned strong defensive positions, they were buttressed by troops on both wings of the city, who had an unrestricted view of the beach and could fire in relative safety. They had effective artillery and mortar support; their enemy, for the most part, did not. An assessment of troop manpower in that situation is almost meaningless without a thorough understanding of the defensive situation, beginning with the physical defenses.

This the Allies had. Their photographic reconnaissance provided an extremely accurate view of the defenses—an assessment made by the Germans themselves.

The Allies' key intelligence error was not in underestimating the German division's identity or manpower, but their ability to man the defenses. And just as important, overestimating their own.

Truscott—whose résumé includes Anzio, another much-criticized operation—was in a unique position to reflect on amphibious operations after the war; few officers had his breadth of experience with them. In his memoirs, he noted that it was often the case that planners were far too optimistic when setting goals, thinking that troops could accomplish in one day what could only be done in three. He also felt that upper-echelon commanders in general were too far removed from the troops, and often had little idea of what their men were facing.

Truscott's assessments were about American generals, but they apply as well to the Canadians in charge of the 2nd Division and its plans. The detailed timetable worked out for the troops reads like something from a practice landing or maneuvers, where no enemy would be encountered. Indeed, it might have been ambitious even for that.

It's unlikely that any troops, no matter how well trained or "blooded," could have succeeded in a frontal assault on Dieppe without a heavy bombardment preceding them, and comprehensive air and sea support as the battle proceeded. But the performance by the troops on the two flanks, so critical to the mission, was admittedly less than optimal.

At Puys, confusion at sea helped stall the assault before it arrived; once there, the men were too paralyzed by the incoming fire to mount a coherent attack. The fact that a small force cleared the beach begs the question of what might have happened had either a larger force landed or the men who stayed on the beaches been somehow able to follow. There is no question that all of the objectives at Blue Beach could have been accomplished—the force was far too small and the time line too quick—but an advance party that could have secured the high ground, where most of the defenses apparently weren't occupied, might have led to more troops being available to attack the battery immediately behind the cliff.

At Pourville, problems were encountered at a later stage—the timetable was messed up by stiff resistance at the only bridge out of town (where it should have been expected), and the force that survived was too small to accomplish its goals.

It has to be admitted that men failed on these battlefields. It's not disrespectful to point out that for the bulk of the Canadians, this was their first introduction to combat; it's not surprising that many of them froze or didn't perform as well as they might have. It's also not disrespectful to point out that the Canadian training for the raid did not prepare them for what they faced. The deficiencies are obvious when compared to the Commandos, who had spent literally months training for the sort of assaults they undertook at Dieppe, and then spent several weeks on problems that duplicated the specific conditions they were to face there. Not only did their training routines include live-fire exercises, but they came on top of a rigorous physical-fitness routine. It paid off: Lovat's men *ran* a mile and a half with full combat gear after fighting their way up from the beach.

Few combat units in any Army can do that, nor is it the sort of task most would be called on to perform: that's why the Commandos and Rangers were considered elite fighters, and given the difficult jobs. But an examination of the Canadian objectives at Pourville and Puys finds them no less difficult than those the Commandos and Rangers undertook. On the contrary, they are much more ambitious, since the fighting forces were expected to move far inland after taking the guns. Granted, the attacking forces were larger than 4 Commando—but they weren't *that* much larger, nor did they have much more in the way of support than the Commandos and Rangers did. It was almost as if the commanders said, if the Commandos can do it, we can, too—without considering the difference in the forces.

That is a command mistake, not a lack of courage on the part of the men on the beaches. In many ways, the inexperience of the Canadian commanders was much more deadly than that of their soldiers.

The planners seem to have had no idea what they were up against, and had little idea of what their men were capable of. The same could have been said for an American commander at that point in the war, of course; fortunately, circumstances allowed the Americans to be eased into battle without overexposing them.

The plans worked out by the Canadian commanders were studies in wishful thinking. Commentators—beginning with the German commander—have noted that the elaborate timetable begged for disruption; it was like a house made of cards waiting for one to fall. The western high ground at Dieppe was to be neutralized by a single infantry company—a hundred and twenty men, give or take—arriving from Pourville roughly two miles away. The company was to land at 0450; the main assault would begin at Dieppe at 0520. Even if they had landed on the right beach without opposition, it would have taken more than a half hour for the company to get that far in the dark and mount a coordinated attack on the defensive positions.

The Canadian commanders weren't completely ignorant, of course; they had asked for bombardment of the headlands. But they were reluctant to use the lack of support there as an excuse to say the plan wouldn't work. Why not?

Partly because they felt they had compensated for it in their planning. And partly, I think, because their inexperience led them to be unsure of their own judgment.

They had pressed for a greater role in the fighting. Finally given a "job," they were loath to say it was too tough. Combined Operations, which to that point had a string of what seemed like long-shot successes, said it could be done. Montgomery, though not yet the godlike figure some took him to be by the end of the war, was still an imposing and impressive commander; he thought it could be done. The Canadians must have thought on some level that if these men thought so, surely it could be.

One key element of the plan—the number of troops that would

be needed for the assault—never changes from the initial outline to the end blueprint of the raid. The Combined Operations planners believed six battalions would be needed for its flanking assault, not counting the airborne raids on Berneval and Varengeville. The final plan called for essentially the same number of troops, even though the method of attacking Dieppe had changed from a flank assault to a head-on lunge from the sea. The thought process involved in considering the troop strength has not been recorded, so it's unfair to say that adjustments weren't considered fully as the plan shifted. But it is an interesting coincidence, especially in light of the fact that some of the assignments in the plan clearly overstretched the available personnel. How much of a role the shortage of assault ships and landing craft may have played in estimating the necessary amount of troops has never been addressed.

However wrong the Combined Operations skeleton plan had been, in the end it was up to the ground-force commanders—Ham Roberts and his planners, especially Churchill Mann—to map a suitable plan and task the appropriate manpower. And here was the Canadian leaders' greatest difficulty. For a general officer such as 2nd Division Commander Ham Roberts to call off the attack because his men were not up to it would have been tantamount to resigning in disgrace. Neither his boss, Lieutenant General Harry Crerar, nor his boss's boss, General McNaughton, was close enough to the situation to understand how formidable the task was. The men further down the chain of command—especially Churchill Mann, who was responsible for much of the planning—had even less stature and just as much to lose.

In the memo laying out his overall plan for the attack, Mann seems almost to argue himself into the idea that a frontal assault will work, noting that it may seem unconventional and unusual. Maybe he and the other men responsible for drawing up the plan had such an argument with themselves several times: *It doesn't seem like it will work, but it will, it will* . . . If so, however, they never admitted it, at least in a public way that has made it to the historical record.

Whatever their private reservations, the Canadians failed to appreciate how well the town could be defended, and gave little respect to the German Army. It's hard to understand exactly why, given that the Germans had chased the British from France two years before and were fielding the most experienced Army in the world. Mann's argument for the frontal assault says that an English town would fall under the same attack; it's hard to read that as anything but a criticism of his own forces.

After the raid, a story developed that Ham Roberts predicted the battle would be a piece of cake. The tale is probably apocryphal; historians haven't been able to find a witness and Roberts denies it. But the sentiment, if not the exact phrase, rings true, and not just for Roberts. Whether because they convinced themselves things would go easy in order to overcome their doubts, or because they were fooling themselves from the very beginning, the Canadian commanders did not understand how difficult their task was.

In the end, the burden for those mistakes fell on the thousands of dead, wounded, and captured. Roberts was held responsible for the disaster, shunted to a minor command, and hastened toward retirement. Historians have tended to say that this wasn't justified, claiming that he was a scapegoat. But Roberts was in the position of authority; the details of the raid were under his command and on the battlefield his actions contributed directly to the fiasco—if he's not held accountable, who can be? Crerar and McNaughton, on the other hand, might have been held more responsible as well, but that's a different argument.

On the British side, there were no direct repercussions in the command structure. Mountbatten remained in his command, and his upward career trajectory seems not to have been harmed at all. The man who instigated the frontal assault in the first place—Montgomery—was already in Africa at the head of the 8th Army. In later years, he attempted to cover himself from criticism by saying that he had said the entire operation should be canceled for all time. That doesn't quite cut it, especially given that he presided over the meeting that canceled any possibility of heavy air bombardment prior to the invasion. But Montgomery did not have any responsibility for the forces that took part in Jubilee; it was up to other men to cancel it.

The only person who probably could have done so was Mountbatten himself. He alone had the standing and reputation to make such a decision without looking weak or being undone by second-guessing. While he has been likened to a cork on an ocean, in fact Mountbatten did cancel operations, though never any as close to fruition as Jubilee. He had at least two chances when the plan was still Rutter—when the attack was changed from a pincer movement from the flanks to a direct assault on the city, and when the bombardment was denied. But he used neither one, apparently convinced that, despite the odds, the raid would achieve its objective. He might have done so again after Rutter was canceled, even if he was under pressure from Churchill to get something done; it would have been easy to predict a fiasco and blame it, privately, on the Canadians. But again, he seems to have been convinced the raid would succeed.

He also—as his speech to the Rangers with Number 4 Commando showed—thought there would be very heavy losses. Heavy losses were not unexpected in a Commando raid: there were heavy casualties at Saint-Nazaire. Indeed, if just the Commandos killed or captured are considered, the raiders had a 69 percent casualty rate—roughly what the Canadians experienced at Dieppe.

Perhaps if Mountbatten had given the same speech to the Canadian generals, they might have reevaluated the plan.

. . .

There are many situations where a frontal assault against tough defenses is necessary; given the objectives, Dieppe wasn't one of them.

The tactical goals can be easily stated: take over the city of Dieppe for several hours, capture the airport behind it, examine the radar station near it, blow up the train tunnel or tracks nearby, steal the small fleet of landing boats in its harbor. The difficulty comes when trying to put those objectives into a strategic framework—none of them, even if achieved, would have had much of an impact on the war. Dieppe had no military importance, and the Allies weren't going to be there long enough to take advantage of it if it did. Much was already known about the radar, and the operation to take it was always something of a sideshow. The airport was a secondary or even tertiary target, and the force assigned to strike it would have been too small to cause more than temporary damage—damage already being done just as effectively and with less risk by night fighters. The German landing "fleet" was so small that its complete destruction would not have had an impact on any German invasion plans, nor would possessing the relatively cheap-to-build craft help the Allies appreciably.

In order to make any sense of the attack from a strategic point of view, it has to be viewed in the context of other Commando raids, before and after, on the European coast. It differs from them in two respects—size, and the fact that the main attack force were not Commandos. Otherwise, Dieppe was not that much different from most of the others, where the stated strategic goals were to remind the Germans that the English were still in the war, and to gain some experience in amphibious assaults. Not coincidentally, those were the stated goals for Dieppe before the operation went off, and before statements by the participants attempting to justify themselves began to obscure the issue.

The Commando campaign had one other strategic objective, one that was implicit in the operations but generally isn't cited by military historians: public relations, or to use terms more familiar to the political leaders: morale building for the war effort.

The attacks on the continent, Norway as well as France, had captured the imagination of the public. The stories of the raids, at times exaggerated, were clearly morale boosters. *Everyone* wanted to be a Commando—that's the one thing all the men who joined the Rangers had in common. The idea that the Allies were fighting back was critical politically for both Churchill and Roosevelt; the raids were relatively inexpensive ways to spread that idea. The idea of massive bombing attacks against German cities—which had much greater impact on the war than the raids—never sold quite as well to the general public as the Commandos and the Rangers did. This wasn't because bombing caused civilian casualties; it was because the story of a small group of elite fighters battling against the odds was much more romantic than the story of a man dropping bombs from several thousand feet on an unseen enemy.

Today we tend to take a dim view of the role of public morale—or propaganda—in a war. For any American who grew up in the era of Vietnam or later, propaganda is associated not only with lies but with wrongdoing. But all of the Allied leaders—and the Axis ones, too, for that matter—realized that without public support or "morale," the war would be lost. The Rangers were American Commandos; as important as they were in later battles, at this stage in the war, their most important role was as a morale booster.

The strategic objectives of Combined Operations—harrying the enemy, gaining overall experience, morale—justify the overall Commando campaign, which was begun at a time when the British had *no* good news to tell their people. But do they justify Dieppe, where much larger forces were at risk in a much more dangerous situation?

You'd be hard-pressed to find anyone who said they did.

· · ·

The Royal Navy and Air Force gave their answer to that question when they refused to provide the support requested by the planners. From our vantage point today, it seems almost treasonable that bombers were not provided to level the defenses in front of the town as well as the strongpoints on either side. But in 1942, the idea of using heavy bombers for a ground-support mission had not yet been accepted. Even using fighter-bombers for close ground support was a new concept; there were no forward ground controllers who could direct air attacks from the ground at Dieppe, something that might have helped during the early stages at Puys and Pourville.

If heavy bombers had been used to "soften up" the defenses at Dieppe, there's no guarantee that the bombs would have been accurately dropped. The city itself would surely have suffered collateral damage, a fact recognized and, at least briefly, thought to be acceptable. Historians are split over whether Bomber Command ultimately decided that other targets had greater priority, or that the destruction to the town would be too high; in any event, the decision not to bomb the defenses beforehand was in the end a judgment of the raid's value.

Ships' guns were much more precise than bombers, with the notable advantage of being able to correct once a salvo was fired. A battleship or cruiser *might* have been able to silence the guns on the eastern and western headlands; certainly it would have had more impact that the four-inch guns carried by the small destroyers and gunboats in the invasion fleet.

Combined Operations generally did not rate highly on the Royal Navy's priority list; the Commandos had trouble getting the destroyers they needed for the attack at Saint-Nazaire, ending up with one rather than the two they requested. At the same time, the Navy believed that any large ship in the Channel would be an easy target for the Luftwaffe, and would be quickly sunk.

Most historians feel the Navy was being too cautious. It had been shocked by losses in the Pacific several months before, and may have overestimated the risks. In any event, the Navy's decision states clearly what its assessment of the raid's strategic value was: worth the risk of coastal ships, but nothing truly important.

THE D-DAY CONNECTION

Looking back on Dieppe after the war, Lucian Truscott—who had gone on to play important roles in the African and Italian campaigns and today is remembered as one of the great combat commanders of the war—decided that the raid had been an "essential lesson in modern warfare." Dieppe had shown the Allies how to plan for large-scale assaults, and what those assaults would need. He also thought that the attack had thrown the Germans off balance, as well as shown the Allies what their response would be to an attack.

At first glance, Truscott's assessment—which because of his résumé has to be respected—seems very much a minority opinion. But it's really just a sophisticated take on the argument most commonly made about Dieppe: it was a brutal but necessary rehearsal for D-Day.

It can be something of a dodge to say that important lessons were learned from a failure; lessons are or should always be drawn from all experience. So it's probably best to decide whether those lessons could have been learned in some other way.

On those grounds, Dieppe was a failure. The most important lesson supposedly learned at Dieppe was obvious beforehand: attacking into the teeth of a strong defense is foolhardy. The men who planned Dieppe clearly knew this; they repeatedly requested heavy bombardment, first by sea, then by air. The concept of bombarding defenses before assaulting them was developed long before the 1940s. Transferring that idea to a heavily defended seafront or city hardly required a great leap in logic—and if it did, the World War I assault on Gallipoli, another fiasco, should have supplied it.

The other lessons allegedly learned—how to land tanks on the beaches, how large landing craft would perform, the need for good communications during a landing, the desirability of a dedicated landing force—could have been learned elsewhere. And in fact they were. Even forgetting the American campaign in the Pacific, the Torch landings, Sicily, and the Italian campaign taught the D-Day planners considerably more than Dieppe did. No one has ever made a claim that the Torch landings, conducted about two months later, would have failed without Dieppe; indeed, no one has ever drawn much of a connection between the two, even though many of the same men were involved in planning both.

A more subtle descendant of that line of thinking has posited that Dieppe convinced the Germans that the Allies would invade Europe in a like manner, and that in its way Dieppe was an unintentional diversion that helped save lives at D-Day. Many historians analyzing the German response to Dieppe cite the last paragraph of Field Marshal von Rundstedt's report, which notes that "It would be a mistake to think that the enemy will organize his next operation in the same manner. He will learn lessons from the errors and lack of success this time, and will act differently next time." They then go on to claim that the Germans in fact did not learn the proper lessons, and were, if not ill-prepared for Normandy, at least less prepared than they might have been. The argument hinges on two points: the Germans' early belief that Normandy was a diversion, and their reliance on a strategy of defeating an invasion on the beaches rather than relying on a large, mobile defensive force to deliver a crushing blow sometime after the enemy had landed.

These arguments are difficult to settle, since they involve many factors and a number of questions that cannot be easily answered. Did the Germans believe that the landings at Normandy in 1944 were a diversion mostly because of Dieppe, or (among other reasons) because of the Allies' deception campaign? What did they learn (or fail to learn) from the numerous examples of amphibious landings in the roughly two years between Dieppe and D-Day? And most importantly—what would an alternative defense plan have looked like, and how would it have fared in the summer of 1944?

My opinion is that, while the shape of the battle might have been different, a radically different German defense was not possible and would not have resulted in a different result. Realizing earlier that the Normandy invasion was in fact the main event would have surely helped, but Dieppe played a very, very small role in that. Beach defenses were increased after Dieppe, but plans already called for extensive defenses. The German report following Dieppe argued *for* a mobile reaction force. And while the report concludes that the Allies would need a port in a major invasion, that's actually a commonsense conclusion—it was the invention of the Mulberry floating harbors that turned the German strategy upside down, not their reaction to Dieppe.

The key difference for the Germans in 1944 was the lack of air superiority they had enjoyed over the beaches and the English Channel in 1942. They could not harry the invasion fleet the way they had at Dieppe. More importantly, the Allied Air Force could be counted on to protect the ships bombarding the shore defenses. A head-on attack on a city would still have been extremely costly—but on the other hand, if the Germans had left important port cities lightly defended, the Allies might have struck there rather than Normandy.

WHAT IF?

An interesting what-if question: What would have happened if the original plan for an assault on Dieppe had remained in place? And what if that plan, besides calling for an attack to be made from the flanks, had provided for the use of *only* Commando units, with no involvement from the regular Army?

Jubilee evolved from the rudiments of such an idea; had it stayed closer to that, it's possible that instead of fifty men, the entire 1st Ranger Battalion might have seen action. It's a great what-if: Would they have had a victory similar to that of Number 4 Commando? Or would they have suffered the same fate as the Rangers with the Canadian units? Would Dieppe have launched the Rangers even quicker, or would it have ended the unit's career almost before it started?

Obviously, the answer depends on what you think would have happened, but it's likely that a massive defeat would have killed the battalion and the Ranger concept for the rest of the war. A victory could not have brought the unit much more publicity than Dieppe did. In retrospect, the American involvement at Dieppe was the perfect starting note for a unit that had only limited acceptance in the Army as a whole—albeit one that enjoyed the enthusiastic support of the President. The Rangers lost their "provisional" status following Dieppe; whether or not this was because of the publicity can't be definitely stated, but the positive press didn't hurt. Other Ranger battalions were soon started, each following the blueprint of the first, very much in the Commando mold, reinforced and encouraged by the experiences at Dieppe and then in northern Africa.

Questions remained about what sort of role the elite forces should take in battle. Were they solely for special operations, like Commando-style raids, or could they be inserted into regular battles as a "super infantry"? Should they even exist as separate units, rather than having Ranger-trained men inserted into regular units as spark plugs?

The debate was just starting in 1942. At times in Italy, the Rangers were used essentially as part of a "standard" infantry unit, and at other times as shock troops spearheading the attack. The Rangers' famous slogan, "Rangers lead the way," came about at

D-Day, when Rangers were being used essentially as a "regular" unit in a tactical situation not all that different from the main beach at Dieppe. Bogged down themselves, the Rangers rallied to the command, eventually helping secure Omaha Beach.

In the years immediately after the World War, being a Ranger meant that you were a specially trained soldier attached to a standard infantry unit as a kind of spark plug or specialist; coherent Ranger units weren't reestablished until the beginning of the Korean conflict, when companies were formed and attached to larger divisions. After another hiatus after Korea, the Rangers were reborn from long-range reconnaissance and patrol units in 1969 as the 75th Ranger Regiment (Airborne). Today, the philosophy has come full circle: Rangers are an important part of the U.S. Special Operations Command and, except for the fact that they often arrive via helicopter and parachute, are given objectives that Lord Lovat would have accepted for his Commandos. No doubt, further evolutions lie ahead.

Aside from specific tactical matters, Dieppe holds important lessons for us today. The first is that even the most obvious lessons must often be relearned, sometimes under the most bitter conditions, before they can really be grasped. The second is that a plan, any plan, once endorsed by a respected authority, gains weight that it may not deserve. A third is that mistakes are not easily admitted, even to ourselves. And finally, memory is a fragile thing; relying on it to discover the truth may not bring the results we hope for.

AFTERMATH

Dieppe had a profound effect on everyone in the 1st Ranger Battalion, not just the Rangers who participated in it. When his men returned to Scotland, Darby was still an untried commander. His insistence on following the Commandos' training regime, his high standards, and his willingness to endure what his men endured had won him great respect from the soldiers in the battalion, but he had not passed through the crucible of fire that truly makes or breaks a combat leader. In Africa, and then in Italy, he would not only pass through that fire but do so in a way that inspired his men to call him one of the greatest combat leaders of the war. They called him "El Darbo," and while many had occasion to curse him—he was never what might be called "easygoing"—to a man they held him in high esteem. He returned that affection, even at one point turning down a promotion to remain a Ranger.

Darby called the first group of Rangers to "graduate" Achnacarry "the originals," and made it clear that he expected them to lead the others because, well, they were the originals. They did so, as the unit's record of field promotions and commissions proves. According to Szima, one of Darby's favorite sayings was, "You will do this, or it will be your ass—and I mean your ass." The words conveyed something more than an order that had to be followed.

Darby could be self-deprecating—he told the students at his old high school when he came to speak during the war that the "class fool" had returned. But he also exuded a species of confidence in battle that was infectious and genuine. It seemed to rise, at least partly, from his belief that Ranger training was so tough and thorough that any man who made it through could in fact do what an ordinary infantryman saw as impossible.

Among other honors, Darby was awarded a Silver Star for action in Tunisia, where he led an attack on German machine-gun and cannon positions. But Rangers were not supermen, and Darby wasn't either. In 1945, having been rotated out of combat and assigned to staff work, then-Colonel Darby managed to get a post as assistant division commander for the 10th Mountain Division, fighting at the time in Italy. During a visit to a forward command post, he and the men he was with came under fire from a German 88. A small shell fragment hit him in the heart; he died almost immediately. Peace was declared in Europe two days later.

Ironically, Lucian Truscott was his commanding general, having taken over the 5th Army only a few weeks before. Truscott had served with Patton and Eisenhower, rising to the rank of major general and playing an important role in the African and Mediterranean campaigns. He led the 3rd Infantry Division during its assault on Sicily and in its campaign on the Italian mainland in 1943. Not surprisingly, one of the hallmarks of Truscott's command was his insistence on training and physical fitness; during the war, the 3rd Division was known for its "Truscott trot"—marching at a pace of four miles an hour. While not quite Ranger pace, it was twice as fast as most infantry units accomplished. Following the war, Truscott took command of the 3rd Army, succeeding George Patton. As commander, he oversaw the U.S. occupation of much of Germany.

Truscott did not achieve the fame of Eisenhower or Patton, but many students of World War II consider him one of the war's best generals. He earned the Distinguished Service Cross for his actions during the Sicilian campaign; he was also awarded the Distinguished Service Medal with Oak Leaf Cluster, the Navy Distinguished Service Medal, the Legion of Merit, and the Purple Heart. He retired as a lieutenant general. In addition to his memoirs, he wrote a history of the army covering World War I and the period up until World War II: *The Twilight of the U.S. Cavalry: Life in the Old Army, 1917–1942.* The general died in 1965.

Roy Murray was one of the most admired officers in the Ranger battalions. Even sixty-five years later, surviving "original" Rangers recalled the slim, athletic leader of F Company fondly, calling him the epitome of a fighting infantry officer. Promoted to major, Murray commanded the 4th Ranger Battalion, playing a key role in the battle for Gela on Sicily. After the war, Colonel Murray served as technical adviser to two movies, *The Story of G.I. Joe* (1945) and *Darby's Rangers* (1958).

Szima, Kness, Koons, Sweazey, Altieri, and most of the other "originals" went on to serve in Africa and then in Italy. Kness's battlefield achievements earned him a field promotion to second lieutenant in February 1943; when he left the Army in 1946 he went out as a captain. He attended business school and Drake University, owned a successful plumbing business for many years, and raised a large family with his wife. The Kness Ketch-All Mouse Trap, invented by his father and refined by Mr. Kness, is still sold today. Mr. Kness passed away in December 2006.

Sweazey earned a Purple Heart and Silver Star during the war. In Africa, he single-handedly captured a machine-gun nest and four Germans; in Italy, he carried a wounded comrade two miles down a mountain to safety, saving his life. After the war, he returned to Indiana and worked as a heavy-equipment operator for the city of Indianapolis. He died in 1991 at the age of seventy-one.

Szima, seriously wounded in the Battle of Monte Cassino in November 1943, spent three years and underwent numerous surgeries before recovering. After the war, he became an entrepreneur and businessman; he kept in touch with many of his former comrades, and eventually became a semiofficial historian and conscience for the Rangers. He died in 2006 at the age of eighty-six.

After the war, Franklin "Zip" Koons went back to Iowa and became a successful banker. In the summer of 2006, he was living in an assisted living facility in Florida. Though in poor health, Koons's mind was sharp and his memories of Dieppe remained vivid.

Sergeant Swank went on to become an officer and served during the Korean conflict, where he was a captain and training officer with the 1st Cavalry Division in Korea. In 1949, he met his old friend Lloyd Church, who had spent the war in a POW camp. Church, a good-looking man who'd listed his prewar occupation as an actor and motion picture director, had been decimated by his injuries and years in captivity. But he assured his friend that he didn't blame him for leaving him on the beach, and had always thought it was the right decision.

Church died the following year; all the Rangers who knew him attributed his death to the wounds he'd received at Dieppe, which had never properly healed.

Mauled on the stone beaches of France, the Canadian 2nd Division took many months to rebuild itself. General Roberts was reassigned the following spring. In the summer of 1944, the 2nd Division returned to Dieppe under much different conditions; this time there was no question of proper firepower. The defenders fled, and the Canadians marched through the streets, their bagpipes and bass drums setting a triumphant beat. The parade wound its way through the city to the outskirts of town, where the graves of their comrades, including three Rangers, had waited for two years. Most of the battle's dead rest there still; Loustalot, Randall, and Henry's bodies were disinterred and brought back to the United States after the war.

France
November 2006

■ ■ ■

Before I leave France, I stop at a small church to light a candle for the dead. The church sits above a cleft in the cliff to the west of Pourville, but it missed the fighting of August 19, 1942. It is a small, quiet place, though its cemetery hints that it, too, has seen its share of violence and war—Allied war dead, killed in 1940, are buried in simple graves in the yard that crowds its thick stone walls.

Unlike many churches, this one's pastor hews to the old ways and leaves the door open for the reverent and wayward. I'm more the latter, certainly, but the cool peace draws me in, an antidote to weeks of thinking and reliving war. Light filters through the stained glass, shading the interior red. I spend a few minutes simply standing in the side aisle not far from where I've come in, struck not by the art or statuary but by the atmosphere itself, so far removed from the war I've spent the past several days re-creating in my mind.

And then I remember why I've come. I head toward the back, where a small stand offers candles for those who wish to ask God or the saints for help or merely remembrance.

I light a candle. And then, as I kneel to add the prayer, I remember the question I asked myself after I got Mr. Kness's letter many months before: Is it fair to bother people in the name of history? Is it all right to make their past part of ours?

I realize I've already implicitly answered the question by continuing to work on the book—and in fact by writing back to him. I've tried not to bother Mr. Kness or the few other survivors of the battalion, tried to respect their privacy, but if I really wanted to respect personal boundaries, I supposed I wouldn't have written about Dieppe at all.

That's not what Mr. Kness suggested, not at all. There is a balance somewhere in between, some middle distance from personal to shared past. Finding that space is difficult, but not as hard as striving to understand the truth of what happened. And perhaps it's the truth itself that redeems the effort, however difficult it may be to perceive.

As I bend my head, another thought comes to me. I realize I'm not praying for the men who died at Dieppe; their souls were long ago redeemed by their own actions and sacrifices. My prayer is for their grandchildren and great-grandchildren—for all of us, that we may be inspired by their courage, and learn from the mistakes made here.

It is a short prayer, but I stay at the altar a long time.

SOURCES AND NOTES

GENERAL SOURCES

Two survivors of the raid corresponded with me and my wife, who assisted me in research: Les Kness and Franklin Koons. Two other "original" Rangers spoke with me by phone, Gerrit Rensink and Don Frederick. Several Commandos were also generous with their memories, most especially John Lowman and R. J. Cubitt.

In addition, my major primary and secondary sources included the following:

Documents, Papers, etc.

Swank, Marcel G., with Lieutenant Edward L. Smith. As told to article, "The 100 Pipers," an account of the Dieppe battle. *Infantry* magazine, 51:3 (May-June 1961).

Sweazey, Owen. Partial manuscript entitled "The Rangers Diary." Unpublished; left unfinished at the author's death.

Sweazey, Owen, with Douglas Clanin. Oral history transcript. Indiana Historical Society, Military History Section. Recorded December 14, 1983.

Szima, Alex. Unpublished letters to fellow Rangers, Lord Lovat, and Queen Elizabeth, 1975 to 1983. The letters include numerous copies of articles, photographs, and orders related to the Ranger 1st Battalion, and are included in the Harold Perlmutter Collection, USMA Library at West Point, N.Y.

Ranger after-action reports concerning action at Dieppe:

Captain Roy A. Murray

1st Lieutenant Leonard F. Dirks

1st Lieutenant Robert F. Flanagan

2nd Lieutenant Charles M. Shunstrom

Staff Sergeant Kenneth Stempson

Sergeant Alex Szima

Corporal William Brady

Corporal Franklin Koons

Orders relating to the formation and assignments of 1st Ranger Battalion, various dates, 1942.

Diary of 1st Ranger Battalion, 1942.

Orders relating to Dieppe assault plan, including signal plan, assorted administrative instructions, 1942.

Official Reports

Notes from Theatres of War No. 11, Destruction of a German Battery by No. 4 Commando During the Dieppe Raid. War Office. February 1943.

Br. 1736(26) Naval Staff History: Raid on Dieppe. Full report, including appendices and excerpts from German after-action assessment. Historical Section, Admiralty. April 1959.

Reports of the Historical Officer, Canadian Military Headquarters, relating to Dieppe, including appendices with interviews of the survivors, and subsequent revisions and additions. *Reports 89, 90, 98, 100, 101, 107, 108, 109, 113 (Sten gun) 116 (German report), 128, 130, and 142.* In addition, *Report 15* regarding Canadian activities prior to Dieppe and *Report 81* concerning Canadian participation in Abercrombie were useful for background. The reports were prepared under the direction of Colonel C. P. Stacey.

I also relied on captured German photos and newsreels in the Canadian military history archives.

Book-Length Memoirs

Altieri, James. *Darby's Rangers: An Illustrated Portrayal of the Original Rangers.* Durham, NC: The Seeman Printery, 1945.

Altieri, James. *The Spearheaders.* New York: The Popular Library, 1960.

Darby, William O., and William Baumer. *Darby's Rangers.* New York: Presidio Press, 1980.

Reynolds, Quentin. *Dress Rehearsal.* Garden City, NY: Blue Ribbon Books, 1943.

Truscott, Lieutenant General L. K. Jr. *Command Missions, a Personal Story.* New York: E. P. Dutton & Company, 1954.

Whitaker, Denis, and Shelagh Whitaker. *Dieppe—Tragedy to Triumph.* Whitby, Canada: McGraw-Hill Ryerson, 1992.

Young, Peter. *Storm from the Sea.* Annapolis, MD: Naval Institute Press, 1989.

Historical Works

Atkin, Ronald. *Dieppe 1942—The Jubilee Disaster.* Toronto: Gage Publishing, 1980.

Black, Robert W. *Rangers in World War II.* New York: Presidio Press, 1992.

Fowlcr, Will. *The Commandos at Dieppe: Rehearsal for D-Day*. London: Harper-Collins Publishers, 2002.

Henry, Hugh G. Jr., and Jean-Paul Pallud. *Dieppe Through the Lens of the German War Photographer*. London: Battle of Britain Prints International Limited, 1993.

Ladd, James. *Commandos and Rangers of World War II*. New York: St. Martin's Press, 1978.

Leasor, James. *Green Beach*. New York: William Morrow, 1975.

Mordal, Jacques; translated by Mervyn Savill. *Dieppe—The Dawn of Decision*. London: New English Library, 1963.

Neillands, Robin. *The Dieppe Raid*. Bloomington, IN, 2005.

O'Donnell, Patrick K. *Beyond Valor*. New York: Simon & Schuster, 2001.

Robertson, Terence. *The Shame and the Glory—Dieppe*. Toronto, Canada: McClelland & Stewart Limited, 1962.

Villa, Brian Loring. *Unauthorized Action*. Don Mills, Canada: Oxford University Press, 1989.

Ziegler, Philip. *Mountbatten*. New York: Alfred A. Knopf, 1985.

Anyone interested in the U.S. Rangers during World War II should start by reading Robert W. Black's *Rangers in World War II*. Black gives a brief but well-detailed account of the Rangers' action in Dieppe.

Patrick K. O'Donnell includes several firsthand accounts of Rangers at Dieppe in his outstanding oral history, *Beyond Valor*. He also maintains a Web site called the DropZone—www.thedropzone .org—which is a must visit for anyone interested in World War II.

There are several books on the Dieppe Raid. The most recent is Robin Neillands's *The Dieppe Raid*. The book is well written and intended for a general audience; some may find it a little breezy in detail and light on sourcing. While I don't agree with all of the author's assessments, the book gives a balanced study of the battle. Neillands gives the incorrect number of Rangers with 4 Commando and in the 3 Commando group that made it ashore, but mistakes regarding the Rangers' participation are the rule rather than the exception in accounts of the battle.

Number 4 Commando's mission is covered in exciting detail in Will Fowler's *The Commandos at Dieppe: Rehearsal for D-Day*. Alex Szima was among his many sources, and the Rangers receive full credit in the book for their exploits.

Though now out of print, James Altieri's *The Spearheaders* provides an unparalleled firsthand view of what it was like to be a Ranger with the 1st Ranger Battalion in World War II.

Library and Archives Canada offers a wide range of Dieppe-related documents and photos online. Most of the Canadian military reports are also available online through the Canada National Defense Directorate of History and Heritage.

SOURCES AND NOTES ON SPECIFIC SECTIONS

Prologue
I visited Scotland, London, Newhaven and Sussex, Dieppe, Berneval, Puys, Pourville, Varengeville and the surrounding areas in November 2006 while writing this book. This account, and those that follow, are based on that visit.

Some sources have given a different total for the number of Rangers involved in the Dieppe Raid. The unit records indicate, however, that it was fifty, and the Rangers accepted that number in the years after the war.

Chapter One
Alex Szima's experiences were culled from a letter sent to Armando E. "Eddie" Stewart Byrd in 1975. The letter and a number of others

are included in papers related to William Darby and the Rangers in the Harold Perlmutter Collection at West Point.

Hamilton Fish was quoted in the *New York Times* of June 23, 1941. Fish, a lifelong anti-Communist and a virulent opponent of FDR despite living in the same New York county, made similar statements throughout the war, and indeed throughout his life.

Estimates on how many men were trained at Camp Claiborne vary from five hundred thousand to nine hundred thousand. The five hundred thousand is used by the state in its historical documentation.

Bob Koloski's quote is taken from an account in *War Stories*, published by the Minnesota American Legion.

The Louisiana Digital Library includes a small number of photos of members of the 34th Division during their early stay at Camp Claiborne. Some can be viewed at the library's Web site, www .louisdl.louislibraries.org.

Owen E. Sweazey's comments were made to interviewer Doug Clanin as part of an oral history project conducted by the Indiana Historical Society, December 14, 1983. A transcript of Mr. Sweazey's talk was kindly provided to me by his son, Ron Sweazey.

The criticism of the training—common throughout the entire Army—was made by Private Frank B. Sargent in a pamphlet entitled "The Most Common Short-Comings in the Training of Battalion and Regimental S-2 Personnel, and Some Suggestions to Overcome Them," published by the Army in 1943. Widely circulated even though it received a "restricted" security rating, the pamphlet can today be found at the 34th Infantry Division Association Web site.

The 34th Division played an important part in World War II after the Rangers were selected out. The division included the 133rd, 135th, and 168th Infantry Battalions, an artillery unit, a combat engineer battalion, and an assortment of special units. Its 100th Infantry Battalion was a Nisei or Japanese-American unit that won honors during the war in Europe; another Nisei unit, the 442nd Infantry Regiment, was attached to the division during the summer of 1944. It took part in campaigns in Africa and Italy, including the invasion at Anzio, one of the most vicious of the war. Army records show it served five hundred days in combat, the third highest in Europe and the sixth highest overall.

In a side note, just before the Dieppe invasion, the 34th Division's 168th Regimental Combat Team began training with British Commandos in Scotland and was part of the spearhead that landed near Algiers at the start of Operation Torch, the Allied invasion of northern Africa.

The 34th Infantry Division Association maintains a Web site at www.34infdiv.org, where several documents pertaining to the group's history are readily available. Among the items found there is a history compiled by members of the division during World War II.

The 1st Armored Division—known as "Old Ironsides"—also took part in Operation Torch and engaged in heavy fighting in northern Africa in late 1942 and 1943. Battered by Rommel at Kaserine Pass, the unit survived to join the Italian campaign later that year, landing in Salerno and spearheading the drive on Naples. The 1st Armored helped take Rome in the summer of 1944, and continued to operate in the Italian campaign until the end of the war.

The current 1st Armored Division includes historical information on its Web site, at www.lad.army.mil. The site includes some photos from the division museum.

Chapter Two

Much of the information on then Colonel Truscott and his assignment comes from *Command Missions—A Personal Story,* by Lieutenant General L. K. Truscott Jr.

Truscott's orders from Eisenhower, quoted in full in his book, explicitly call for the creation of a separate American unit based on the Commandos, as opposed to an American Commando composed of Americans but operating under British Special Services, the parent military organization. Mountbatten, however, felt that the Rangers should be under the direction of the Combined Operations Headquarters; Truscott alludes to the debate in his memoirs.

Truscott says that a compromise was reached, with the unit as a whole under American control but responsibility to be taken by Combined Operations for specific raids. This was the pattern during training, and at Dieppe, where the Rangers were actually integrated into Commando units. But once the 1st Ranger Battalion completed training, they operated independently of the British Commandos and Combined Operations, so it's hard to see this as a real compromise. If Dieppe played a role in any decision to make the Rangers a separate *American* unit—which some Rangers believe was the case—Truscott doesn't say. He left to work with General Patton shortly after the raid, so it's conceivable that he didn't know. But the overwhelming evidence indicates that Eisenhower and Marshall always saw the Rangers as an American unit, and would have been loath to put it under Mountbatten or anyone else's control.

The sketch of Mountbatten is based on several sources, most importantly Philip Ziegler, *Mountbatten,* published by Alfred A. Knopf, New York, 1985.

Darby mentions his appointment in *Darby's Rangers: We Led the Way,* written with William H. Baumer. The bulk of the book was written by Baumer, based on a series of audiotapes he recorded with Darby during the war. Additional sources for Darby's life include transcripts from *The Army Hour,* a radio show prepared May 21, 1944, at Fort Benning, Georgia, declassified comments made by Darby to Army Navy Staff College during the war, and memories of his sister and childhood acquaintances.

The Commando brigades' parent organization was Special Services and the command's proper title was used in some official papers when referring to Commando brigades or the command. In 1944, Special Services Group was redesignated as the Commando Group. To avoid confusion, I've used Commando, even when the official papers use the proper terminology.

The dialogue involving Altieri sprinkled through this chapter is drawn from *The Spearheaders* by James Altieri, Bobbs-Merrill, 1960. Vaughn's remarks and some of those by Darby are also taken from his book. Altieri was working from memory in recounting the conversations and speeches.

The infantry "song" was a common one, with its origins dating perhaps to the First World War. Altieri used pseudonyms for some of the men in the book, including Szima.

The impressions of Loustalot come from Commandos and Rangers who knew him and shared those memories with me, especially Rangers Don Frederick and Gerrit Rensink, and Commando R. J. Cubitt.

Szima's story comes from his letters, especially his March 21, 1975, letter to E. Stewart-Byrd. The first sergeant of a battalion was called sergeant major, even if (like Szima) he did not hold the rank of sergeant major.

The incident involving Sweazey and the grenade—which appears in other accounts as well—is drawn from Sweazey's oral history, cited above.

The appearance of the royal family, and Szima's thoughts about women, are from a long letter Szima wrote to Queen Elizabeth and a number of British dignitaries in the 1970s. The date of the royal visit is not recorded, though Szima's letter indicates it was toward the end of his stay at Carrickfergus. Other Rangers did not remember the visit.

The selection statistics come from the 1st Ranger Battalion's diary.

Some sources have indicated that the Rangers were issued their

M1 rifles *after* Achnacarry. However, a training schedule for July 1941 lists the M1, beginning with the most basic lesson a rifleman would receive: "Mechanical training, care, cleaning, functioning."

Szima's story about the sergeant major is told in an undated letter to Lord Lovat, and repeated in at least one other.

Additional information on training was obtained from interviews with Commandos who trained with the Rangers, the Rangers themselves, and declassified orders and related reports covering the Rangers' formation.

The tale of the lieutenant who dressed as a nurse is in *We Led the Way.*

Chapter Three

Quentin Reynolds uses the phrase "poor man's Monte Carlo" in his book, *Dress Rehearsal: The Story of Dieppe.*

Roberts's speech and Eisenhower's comments are quoted from Terence Robertson, *The Shame and the Glory—Dieppe.*

The names of the Rangers who joined Rutter is drawn from the list in the battalion diary. The men returned to Achnacarry and continued their training. None were included in the plans for Jubilee. By that time, other Rangers had completed the first phases of Commando training, and it would have made more sense for them to go on the raid.

Besides the Rangers, Truscott in *Command Missions* says that "most" of the American officers involved at Combined Operations Headquarters went to the Isle of Wight to observe the sailing of the troops.

The information on Sergeant Rensink and his meeting with General Eisenhower comes from my discussions with Ranger Rensink.

British historian Robin Neillands, the author of *The Dieppe Raid* (Indiana Press, 2005), believes that Ultra information *should* have alerted the British to the fact that 302nd Division and 10th Panzer were in the area. Brigadier General Denis Whitaker, who wrote *Dieppe: Tragedy to Triumph* with his wife, Shelagh Whitaker, makes a similar point regarding the use of Ultra, and criticizes the intelligence gathering in general.

Historians writing on Dieppe after the existence of Ultra became widely known have tended to conclude, like Neillands, that Ultra intelligence relating to the battle wasn't passed on, at least not in a meaningful way. Because of the way Ultra information was used during the war, it's difficult to know for certain whether the information was ever made available to the Dieppe planners on any level; it would not have been recorded in the minutes of the planning meetings.

But Ultra information was largely beside the point; the specific identity of the units in the area would not have made that much a difference to the planners. Neillands points out that there's an "optimism" in the notes of the meetings that seems to border on carelessness. Whatever forces were in the area, their potential for defense was not being deeply considered.

I address the intelligence issue in more detail in Chapter 12.

Besides the official British and Canadian reports of the raid, my description of the planning relies on Robertson's book and the memoirs by Mountbatten and Truscott. Because the raid was such a disaster, it is difficult to know exactly how much to trust of what anyone said later about the planning. Montgomery and Mountbatten have been fiercely criticized on the one hand and strongly defended on the other for their roles in the debacle.

My summary by necessity simplifies the complex decisions made by the planners and commanders.

The comment by Fleet Admiral Pound is recorded in *Mountbatten* by Philip Ziegler.

Abercrombie, the April Commando raid, involved Number 4 Commando under Lord Lovat. The failure of the Canadians to land was blamed by the Canadians on the incompetence of the Royal Navy sailors in charge of their boats. The raid was a major embarrassment to the Canadians at the time, and may have added to the determination of the Canadians to get into battle. For a report on the Canadian involvement in the raid, see Report No. 81 of the Historical Officer, Canadian Military Headquarters, dated August 26, 1942.

While I've given the capacities of the fighters and attack aircraft, mission constraints would have meant most of the fighters carried smaller payloads; eyewitness accounts talk of a single bomb falling from planes.

Roosevelt's orders to Hopkins, Marshall, and King are quoted in Robert E. Sherwood, *Roosevelt and Hopkins—An Intimate History*.

The remarks by Roberts saying he wanted to get cracking are from Robertson. The actual extent of opposition to the plans by Roberts's underlings is hard to determine now. Robertson, who besides relying on documented sources spoke to a wide range of the Canadian commanders including Roberts as he researched his book, believes the three generals directly under Roberts and responsible for carrying out the attack "protested forcibly." This might explain why Roberts felt it necessary to have his bosses at the next briefing for his commanders, where it appears that considerably less opposition was voiced.

Mountbatten devotes roughly a page and a half of his five-hundred-page *Memoir* to the operation. He also says that the Commandos should have been *added* to the assaults on the guns at the flanks, rather than completely replacing the airborne troops. Had that happened, it's possible that the airborne troops could have prevented 3 Commando's force from being cut off as it returned to the beach. But it is also possible that the airborne unit would have run into problems moving overland as well. In any event, the failure of the Commando flank assault to the east was not a major factor in the debacle.

I think the argument that Mountbatten did an end run around

the Chiefs of Staff and mounted the operation on his own is unsustainable. On the other hand, Villa presents an insightful probing of the interservice and Allied politics in his book.

Chapter Four

The sources for the Rangers' experiences are unpublished letters from Alex Szima, an oral history by Owen Sweazey, and after-action reports by Captain Murray and Lieutenant Dirks.

Szima talks about being a substitute for another man in his letter to Stewart-Byrd, March 21, 1975. Who the other Ranger was is never mentioned anywhere. The orders pertaining to the group Szima was with indicate that they are a corrected copy, presumably because of the change in personnel.

Szima's quote about Lord Lovat comes from his letter to Lovat. Szima shared his admiration of Lovat with many interviewers.

Interestingly, Szima says in his letter that Darby's instructions included introducing the unit as the "American Commandos." This was one reason that he believed the Ranger unit remained provisional until after the Dieppe battle, which contradicts the records.

Szima also seems to have been in charge of the small delegation, even though on paper Stempson would have outranked him.

Lovat's comments on Mountbatten and other members of Combined Operations are recorded in Will Fowler's *The Commandos at Dieppe: Rehearsal for D-Day.*

Sketches of the battle area made after the raid slightly underestimated the actual height near the ravines, putting it at a hundred feet. News stories, on the other hand, said the cliffs were about 250 feet.

The landing craft used by the Number 4 Commandos and the Rangers who were with them have been identified alternatively as LCAs—landing craft assault—and ALCs—assault landing craft—and even on occasion LCP(R)s. The descriptions make it clear that the same class of small landing vessels are being described. The confusion probably comes from the fact that the British in 1942 called the vessels ALCs; by the end of the war, LCA had been adopted. The Rangers at the time followed the British term. The dimensions I've given are those listed in *Notes from Theatres of War, No. 11,* the Commando training manual based on Operation Cauldron. There were several varieties of LCAs; some were a few feet longer and a foot or so wider.

The (L) in LCP(L)s has been identified variously as "large" and "light." These were different craft from the LCAs, more boatlike (though not necessarily more comfortable) as I describe later on in the text.

Speaking of landing craft, the version of LCTs—or TLCs, as they were designated at the time—comes from *British Vessels Lost at Sea, 1935–1947.*

The Commando memories may have been a little harsh toward the Canadians. It appears that most of the landing force didn't know what their target was for sure until after they were on the boats, and no one has ever found any link between "loose lips" in southern England and the fiasco that followed. The training did make it obvious that something was in the wind, and a few Canadians seem to have guessed that Dieppe would once again be the target. A very small number of men were detained or disciplined for saying something publicly about the raid before the force left for the beaches.

Szima's comment about his marksmanship and the British bayonets was made in a letter dated March 21, 1984, to James Altieri and another friend. Szima told essentially the same story to Patrick K. O'Donnell, who records it in his oral history of World War II Rangers and Airborne troops, *Beyond Valor.*

Some questions remain about how many guns and what types were actually located at the Goebbels battery. The official histories and most sources generally describe the weapons as four guns of 5.9 or 6 inches, similar to the 155mm captured French cannon used by the Hess battery. Jacques Mordal in *Dieppe, Dawn of Decision,* says the battery had three 170mm and four 105mm weapons. Mordal used German sources when preparing his book, including the report of the battery commander at Berneval, though he does not specifically cite his source for the size of the guns.

According to Major Young in *Storm from the Sea,* at least one of the weapons at the battery was a fake, and he believes that only one weapon may have been firing when Number 3 Commando arrived.

The information about the rest of the attack plans comes primarily from the Canadian reports.

It's impossible now to say precisely how many men from the Black Watch were to accompany the Royal Regiment; figures for the units' strength at Dieppe included mortar squads that were to land at the main beach. It would have been well under the total of the 111 men reported to have disembarked for the beaches in the Canadian report. Fifteen men were injured during the crossing because of a grenade attack and were not counted in the total.

Fourteen LCTs never landed at Dieppe; the official histories do not indicate how many tanks were aboard these craft. The plans call for "up to sixteen tanks" to make up the final waves. The German report, presumably based on prisoner interrogations, said that twenty-eight were available but did not land. At least one of the LCTs held in reserve carried armored vehicles but not tanks.

The plan for the tanks to enter the city has never been discussed in detail, but is clearly another of the deficiencies in the overall attack plan. It called for engineers accompanying the tanks to destroy the thick concrete barriers; nearly all the engineers who landed were killed or wounded—152 out of 169. Whether they would have succeeded in getting past the well-protected tangle of obstructions at rue de Sygogne or removing any of the other heavy tank barriers—eight feet high and four feet thick, and protected by snipers and machine guns—is a question that has to remain unanswered.

Chapter Five

Lieutenant Flanagan's after-action report tells of the Rangers' arrival at East Bridge Home. Swank provided details of the contingent's arrival in an article he wrote entitled "100 Pipers." The accounts do not precisely match.

Nissenthall's exploits are covered in James Leasor's *Green Beach,* and also mentioned in R. V. Jones's *The Wizard War: British Scientific Intelligence 1939–1945.* Jones says that the order to shoot Nissenthall was actually a mistake, since the young radar expert couldn't have told the Germans anything that they didn't already know.

Reynolds told his story in *Dress Rehearsal,* published by Random House in 1943, still under wartime censorship.

The order of battle is based on the after-action reports and annotations made by the Rangers found in Szima's papers. However, some of the Rangers came to believe that Lieutenant Randall had actually landed on Green Beach—Pourville—with the South Saskatchewan Regiment. I discuss this in Chapter 9.

Several of the Rangers' names are spelled in different ways in different records; the spellings here are from the available personnel and enlistment records, with these exceptions: Charles Shunstrom's name is spelled "Shundstrom" in all of his records, but his obituary records it without the *d.* Marcel Swank's name appears in many records and places with two *l*'s, but his signed letters have one. Albert Jacobson's name is generally spelled with two *o*'s, but it appears as Jacobsen in a report following the battle, and in a handwritten note by Szima years later. I was unable to locate his personnel records.

Mountbatten's quote about "reconnaissance in depth" appears in Fowler's *Commandos at Dieppe* and several sources. The term itself originated with Churchill and was used after the raid, so it's possible that elements of the speech reflect postbattle thinking, when the commanders were trying to justify sending the men. Mountbatten's "60 percent" is mentioned in a letter by Szima to a friend, "Eddie"

Stewart-Byrd. While the letter is dated March 21, 1975, the date appears to be a mistake; it refers to a campaign in 1976 that Szima and others carried on to win military death honors for fellow Ranger Charles Shunstrum. Shunstrum died in December 1975, and my guess is that the letter was written in 1976.

The number of aircraft involved in the raid is given differently in several sources and often ignored completely. Part of the problem for historians is the fact that aircraft were added to the raid after it began, in answer to requests from the military commanders. These numbers are from Neillands, *The Dieppe Raid*.

Reynolds's story about the downed pilot and his thoughts about his time aboard the *Calpe* and the press conference are recorded in *Dress Rehearsal*. It's hard to know now if some of what was said at the press briefing was inaccurate or whether the reporter, who had to rely on his memory months later to write the book, simply made the same sorts of mistakes others made later when talking about the operation. For example, in his book, the batteries the Commandos and Rangers target have two guns, not six. Reynolds credits the time line to Mountbatten's staff, but most of it would have been prepared by the division planners. There's no apparent irony in his account about the thoroughness of the plan; the reporter simply wasn't informed enough to realize that trying to run a battle like a train schedule was foolish. Then again, the men who prepared the schedule didn't seem to know any better either.

Truscott's descriptions of the invasion fleet are among the most eloquent and vivid in his memoir; like many men, his introduction to combat left an indelible impression on his soul.

Szima told his story about the uniforms several times; my version is drawn from a letter March 21, 1984. The rum story is from Fowler's book.

Peter Young's description of the crossing in *Storm from the Sea* gives a listing of boats that is slightly different from the original

"Composition of the Force" sheet included in the operational plans; the sheet shows three more LCPs than he says were on the mission.

I'm unsure of the number of Rangers, if any, who were in the first four boats that dropped out. This doesn't seem to have been recorded anywhere, and last-minute boat shuffling and the interspersion of the Americans with the Commandos makes it hard to determine.

The description of Lovat's clothing is based on a photo of him after the raid, with an assist on the monogram from Fowler.

Owen Sweazey recorded his impressions in an unpublished memoir entitled "The Rangers Diary." Sweazey's comment about the flak boat carrying more firepower than the destroyer appears at first glance to be far off the mark; the destroyers had four-inch guns, much larger than the flak boat's weapons. But take away the four-inchers, and the destroyer carried only four pom-poms and a pair of Oerlikons, so Sweazey wasn't far off.

SGB 5 was later named *Grey Owl*.

Chapter Six

Few sources agree on the size and components of the German convoy.

The Royal Admiralty report on Dieppe, based partly on captured German documents and prepared in 1959, says there were three E boats in the initial encounter, with another three coming to their support from the harbor area. Survivors of the vessel sunk during the encounter and subsequently captured and taken back to England identified their ship as *UJ 1404* and said there were a total of four escorts with eight smaller ships. An Italian translation of the German report on the incident states there were five small merchant ships accompanied by three submarines. The word *submarines* is clearly an error; the Royal Navy historians believe the translator missed either an initial or part of a word, and the vessels were submarine hunters, *Unterseeboots-Jägers,* which were designated as "UJ" boats. There was a wide variety of ships with this designation; most were armed trawlers converted for use as a submarine hunter.

French historian Jacques Mordal, whose review of German sources and interviews with local residents gave his *Dieppe—The Dawn of Decision* by far the best view of the defenses among Allied histories— believes there were two *Unterseeboots-Jägers* and two R boats, along with a fifth escort, a minesweeper. An R boat—*Räumboot*—was a light patrol boat often used for escort and minesweeping.

To add to the confusion, what the British called an "E boat" was referred to by the Germans as an S boat—*Schnellboot*. These were small, fast torpedo boats that prowled the Channel in small packs. Encounters between S boats and small English patrol boats were very common.

So who's right?

One would suspect that the German sailors had the best idea of the small fleet's composition, and their description comes close to matching that of the German documents. The British Admiralty report on Dieppe also notes that the landing convoy was fired on by three- and four-inch weapons—much too large for an S boat, whose biggest weapon at this time of the war would have been a 4.0-cm Bofers (about one and a half inches). An *Unterseeboots-Jäger* could have carried a larger gun. It also seems significant that there are no reports of torpedoes fired in the battle, which would be an S boat's most potent weapon in an attack.

Eyewitnesses reported seeing trawlers firing during the battle. Confusing a UJ boat with a trawler is easy; S boats are much sleeker and unlikely to remind anyone of anything but a speedboat with guns.

British long-range radar on the coast had apparently picked up the German escorts before the encounter. A message was sent at 0244 indicating that small craft were patrolling in the area of Le Tré-port; their speed—thirteen knots—and bearing—190 degrees—was recorded. Tréport is about fifteen miles east of Dieppe, and the heading would put the ships on a collision course with Group 5, the landing craft carrying 3 Commando. The message reached the *Fernie* but apparently not the *Calpe* or the two destroyers on the task force's flank; in any event, word was never sent to SGB 5.

It's not clear why the message about the German patrol wouldn't have been relayed. The explanation seems to be that the lone ship to receive it, the *Fernie,* assumed that *Calpe* had gotten the message. It's also possible that if the radar contacts were interpreted as E boats, they might not have been seen as a threat to the invasion force, since they would have passed out of the area relatively quickly.

There is one additional mystery related to the convoy, though it is seldom discussed. The encounter took place while the convoy was en route to Berneval. Afterwards, the Germans retreated to Le Tréport, which is about ten miles back along the coast to the east; it would seem they sought safety in a port nearly twice as far from them as Dieppe. This detour meant that they never knew the extent of the convoy they had encountered; it also meant that the authorities at Dieppe did not have firsthand knowledge of the clash.

The German report has the encounter occurring twenty kilometers from Dieppe—not eight (or roughly four and a half nautical miles), which is the actual distance between Berneval and Dieppe. Even allowing for the fact that the encounter took place as much as seven miles out to sea, the Germans probably had calculated their position incorrectly—one explanation for the decision to head back east. If that had been the case, then any information about the encounter reported to shore would have misled the German defenders rather than alerting them to the fact that an invasion was under way.

Sweazey's thoughts come from his unpublished memoir. In his memoir, he says that he saw two E boats sink and "an armed trawler" go up in flames. The armed trawler sounds like *UJ 1404,* which most sources agree was sunk by the LCF's gunfire. Sweazey thought at the time that the ships were hit by the Allied destroyers, which were never involved in the engagement.

Kness's details in this chapter and later come from a 2006 letter to my wife, who helped me with my research. They parallel and add some details to the oral history included in *Beyond Valor,* Patrick K. O'Donnell's compilation of Ranger and Airborne soldiers' experience during World War II.

The account of Yellow Beach 1, which is where the group Loustalot and Furru were in landed, is based on descriptions by Furru's first-person account in O'Donnell's *Beyond Valor* and Neillands's re-creation in *The Dieppe Raid,* as well the German report, Owen Sweazey's unpublished diary, and handwritten notations of the battle by Marcel Swank on a Canadian map of the battle that were included in the West Point papers. The accounts understandably differ in some of the details, such as how much gunfire the party took on landing. Furru's account seems to indicate that he was in one of the first, if not the first, boats to reach the shore.

The exact number of Commandos and Rangers who made Yellow Beach 1 has never been precisely determined. Robertson believes there were 96 Commandos and 6 Rangers; Neillands gives estimates that there were a total of 120, counting the sixth boat that wasn't with the first group. Both state that there were 6 Rangers ashore. However, only 4 Rangers—Loustalot, Furru, Jacobson, and Bresnahan—actually made it to the beach.

The LCPs carried from nineteen to twenty-one men.

The account of Young's raid on the Goebbels battery, both here and in the following chapter, is based on Peter Young, *Storm Before the Sea,* the Commando's memoir, with additional information from Neillands, *The Dieppe Raid,* sources of which included a personal interview with Young.

It's possible that Private Bresnahan was actually with the group

Loustalot led in the charge on the machine gun or just behind it. See Black's account in *Rangers in World War II*.

My version of Loustalot's death is based largely on what Edwin Furru told Patrick K. O'Donnell for O'Donnell's oral history, *Beyond Valor*. Not counting variations of the Furru account that appear in different sources, there are at least two other versions of how Loustalot died: In Altieri's *The Spearheaders*, Edwin Thompson says that he died after taking over the leadership of the company when Commando Captain Richard Wills died. In the Thompson version, Loustalot was killed while climbing *up* the ravine. Thompson, though he was with 3 Commando, never made it to shore; possibly he heard the story from a returning survivor. Ronald Atkin, in *Dieppe 1942*, quotes a Commando who says *two* Rangers died as they came *down* the path, saying he heard their screams. Jacques Mordal, who used Peter Young's book as one of his sources but augmented it with some accounts from local residents, has Loustalot dying on the beach.

I've chosen the Furru story as the most likely because he was an eyewitness, and because it seems to fit best with the flow of the battle.

Loustalot is often called the first American soldier to die on European soil during the war. Two other Rangers died during the Dieppe battles, Lieutenant Randall and T-4 Henry. The truth is, it's impossible to know for certain when any of the men died, let alone who died "first."

Most historians have said that Young's action prevented the Berneval battery from attacking the invasion force. This, however, is an exaggeration. The battery commander reported after the battle that it had fired 558 105mm shells and 47 170mm—not an impressive rate of fire over seven and a half hours for seven guns, but far more than nothing. Young's attack is clearly reflected in his report, where he lists a dozen shots in the roughly two hours he was under attack. All were in support of the battery—in other words, at the Commandos.

The battery seems to have directed most of its shots at the water directly in front of it, possibly at troop ships out of range. Its shells are not seen as having played a decisive role in the fight.

Chapter Seven

The account of Number 4 Commando here and in the pages that follow is based on the Rangers' after-action reports, Alex Szima's unpublished letters, especially a letter to Jim Altieri dated March 21, 1984, a copy of a hand-drawn map probably by Swank found in the West Point papers, *Notes from Theatres of War No. 11* (the official account of the attack, published by the British War Office in 1943 and used as a training manual by the Commandos), and Fowler's *The Commandos at Dieppe*.

The map sketches the points of each Ranger attached to 4 Commando, along with the major defenses they encountered. While clearly not to scale, the hand-drawn map agrees far better with the actual geographical features than any of the official maps rendered after the battle, and also correctly shows that the sections landing on Orange Beach 1 were west of their objective, not directly in front of it as the original plan called for.

The hand-drawn map as well as *Notes from Theatres of War* switch the beach designations used in the Royal Navy history and most historical works and the official maps, naming the beach to the far west, where Lovat's group landed, Orange 1. As far as possible, I've avoided using the numbers, but where pressed, I stuck with the beach designations that have been used in the official maps for clarity's sake.

There are some questions about whether the assault crafts approaching Orange Beaches 1 and 2 were spotted from shore. *Notes from Theatres of War* indicates that they were, and says that starburst shells were fired. Other accounts say they arrived on the beach without alarms being sounded. Fowler quotes several men in 4

Commando who believe they saw the starbursts and gunfire from the clash between 3 Commando's landing craft and the German convoy. Szima also says this in a letter. But this is extremely unlikely, given the timing. Szima says there was enough light for him to read by; this could only mean that the starburst came from nearby, such as from near the lighthouse.

Szima's manure story comes in several different versions— sometimes it happens before he began firing and involves a *considerable* amount of manure. My version here follows the brief description he gives in his letters, which may leave out some of the smellier details.

Fowler's description of the thirty-five German soldiers taken on by Lovat's F Troop gives some doubt to the report in *Theatres of War* that the men were to make a counterattack, as opposed to simply reinforcing the battery. *Theatres of War* has them as assault troops; Fowler points out that a number were unarmed and had probably just come from the houses where they slept. He thinks they were artillerymen who were being collected and were on their way to the battery.

The cordite charges that were struck at Varengeville should not have been exposed as they were to enemy fire, and a number of commentators have theorized on why they were out in the open. Fowler, who, besides doing extensive research on the 4 Commando attack, was a mortarman, has several complementary theories, most notably that the battery was undermanned and undertrained.

It has been alleged in some accounts of the Dieppe battle that members of 4 Commando killed German prisoners on the beach. That seems highly unlikely, given that Lovat had decided to leave his own men on the beach. It is certainly possible that men at the battery who were trying to surrender were killed. Fowler discusses the charges in detail in his book.

Chapter Eight

My description of the Puys beach and nearby defenses is based on a German photograph taken immediately after the battle, as well as personal observation. My description of the battle is based on the Canadian Military Headquarters historical reports. Among those accounts is the story of Captain G. A. Browne; an artillery officer who was supposed to command the guns at the headlands when they were captured, Browne couldn't help commenting on how well those guns were being fired, even though the shells were aimed at him. Browne surrendered with Lieutenant Colonel Catto; after his capture, he discussed the operation in some detail with other captured officers and Germans. He then escaped from the Germans, was recaptured by police in Vichy, France, escaped from them, was caught and imprisoned by the Italians, and finally escaped them for good.

Sergeant Swank's story is drawn from his first-person account, "100 Pipers," published in *Infantry* magazine. Swank mistakenly believed that the gunfire that woke him up was from the clash between the 3 Commando boats and the German convoy; given the time and place that it occurred, it was clearly from the beach ahead, where the South Saskatchewan Regiment had already landed. Swank also gives the planned time for his unit's landing (0520), when it's agreed that the landing was about a half hour late.

Additional information on the battle at Pourville comes from Neillands, *The Dieppe Raid*.

The information on how the Canadians adjusted the Stens comes from Robertson. The gun's magazine was a particular source of trouble; handling it roughly, gripping it while firing, and even filling the box with its full complement of bullets could cause the gun to jam.

Chapter Nine

Truscott's experiences are from his memoir, *Command Missions*. Reynolds gives his account (which has several errors regarding the battle itself) in *Dress Rehearsal*.

The accounts of what happened at Red and White Beaches are based primarily on the Canadian Military History Reports. The times of the radio transmissions marking progress are somewhat confusing and were made from sparse records. Additional information on the movement of the tanks onto the beach at Dieppe comes from Hugh G. Henry Jr.'s *Dieppe Through the Lens of the German War Photographer*. Henry re-created the tank landings and subsequent movements using captured German photographs, military records, and interviews with surviving Calgary tankers. Further information came from Neillands's *The Dieppe Raid* and Robertson's *Shame and Glory*.

The tank that drowned was nicknamed Bull. There are different versions of how the "drowned" tank's commander died; the eyewitness account quoted in Henry's book has him drowning. Others say he was shot as he came ashore.

The information on Henry and Randall comes primarily from a four-page letter from Alex Szima to Marcel Swank. On the copy of the letter available in the West Point papers, the date is obscured. As I said in the text, Swank did a great deal of detective work trying to figure out who died where.

I'd missed the fact that the captured war photos showed a dead Ranger until I saw the photo on the Canadiansoldiers.com Web site, maintained by Michael A. Dorosh, CD. (Dorosh follows information in Black, which presumably comes from the after-action reports, and identifies the dead Ranger as Lieutenant Randall.)

Chapter Ten

The account of the Marine Commando is drawn from the Canadian Military History and *The Dieppe Raid*, whose author, Robin Neillands, spoke with Marine Commandos who survived the battle. The Canadian report notes that it was impossible to verify the story of the white gloves; its description of the battle leaves some doubt that Lieutenant Colonel Phillips was actually signaling for the other boats to retreat.

The accounts of the units that made it into town come from the Canadian Historical Reports, which were revised as additional information became available. Additional information on Hickson's foray comes from Robertson, who interviewed him for *Shame and Glory*.

No tanks made it up past the barriers and into the city streets, despite numerous rumors that they had.

Truscott's exchange with General Mann is recounted in *Command Missions*.

Szima's experiences are drawn from his letters, especially the four-page letter to Marcel Swank.

Chapter Eleven

Swank's story is drawn from "The 100 Pipers," where he also mentions that he met Quentin Reynolds aboard the *Calpe*. Reynolds's perspective is taken from his *Dress Rehearsal*. Reynolds also writes about meeting the four Rangers who were with Number 4 Commando aboard the *Calpe,* but he seems to have actually met them later in England. He also confuses a story that either Szima or Koons must have told, attributing it to Sergeant Kenneth Kenyon. Kenyon had been with the Canadians going to Blue Beach—Puys—but his landing craft turned away; he never landed. Additional information is from the four-page letter by Alex Szima to Swank.

The estimates of the number of men picked up from the beach are included in the Royal Naval History.

The account of Szima's homecoming is from Fowler's *The Commandos at Dieppe*. The story is also told in bits and pieces in several of Szima's unpublished letters.

Truscott's return is described in *Command Missions*.

The casualty numbers are from the Canadian reports, with the exception of the final death tally for Number 4 Commando, which comes from a listing of names in Fowler.

Szima's stories about the Marines at the embassy and the general are from Fowler, *The Commandos at Dieppe*. Szima told a far less detailed and much less colorful version in an undated letter to Lord Lovat, included in the West Point papers. His reaction to the news stories is from his unpublished letters, including the Lovat letter, and is also mentioned in Fowler.

The reaction of the American press to the Rangers has been a source of annoyance for several historians. But the American press response has been overstated; while some tabloids blasted the story on page one, others—such as the *New York Times*—carried pieces inside some days after the raid was first reported. The news stories about the Rangers tend not to talk much about the Canadian role—but then that's not the intention of the stories. And while it has been claimed that the headlines were the biggest on the war since Pearl Harbor, that's simply not true. Just one example: the Doolittle raid had drawn considerable press some months before. (The claim seems to have been made first by Ronald Atkin in his book, *Dieppe 1942—The Jubilee Disaster;* he cites three New York City newspapers as his proof. Atkin actually seems to have been taking a bit of poetic license to make a point that the American press was trumpeting the Rangers above the Canadians, but the words have taken on a life of their own and been reprinted elsewhere, without credit, as literal truth.)

The UP story, which would have been subject to censorship and military approval, seems to have been based on an interview on the docks after the Rangers landed—Stempson mentions that he still has his camouflage paint on his face—and contains a number of errors.

Canadian audiences were said to be incensed when American

newsreels portrayed the Rangers as heroes after the battle and barely mentioned the Canadians at all. While such a reaction is understandable, it says more about the dominance of American media in Canada than it does about anything else.

It should be noted that the news reports of many Commando actions, not just those concerning Dieppe, contained numerous mistakes. Sometimes this was due to errors originating with the officers at Combined Operations, who of course were speaking second- and thirdhand; other times the news media chose poor sources to begin with. The *New York Times* printed a story in May citing a source in Stockholm that claimed the British Commandos had taken over Saint-Nazaire for two days. The story also claimed the commanding British officer was giving the Germans a tour of the ship when it blew up.

Altieri tells the kilt story in *Spearheaders*. While he identifies the Rangers' temporary base as Van Crippsdale Island, I was unable to independently identify it.

Chapter Twelve

The original Combined Operations outline plan called for six battalions to seize Dieppe; the Canadians sent six regiments into battle. To an American—used to the World War II allotment of three battalions to a regiment—that looks like an increase. However, though they were being called regiments, the Canadian units at Dieppe fielded the equivalent of four companies of infantry (ignoring the support and other associated units like artillery, which were not involved in the battle). This is the same number that a British battalion would have fielded at the time Combined Operations drew up the plan.

Szima's comment about Darby's "your ass" line comes from an unpublished letter dated April 8, 1979, sent to Len and Carl, fellow Rangers.

The deeds and honors mentioned here are merely representative of those given to members of the unit during the war. A full list of the medals awarded individual Rangers and the 1st Ranger Battalion would stretch several pages; the battalion had fourteen Silver Star and over fifty Purple Heart honorees after its February 1943 engagement in Tunisia alone.

ACKNOWLEDGMENTS AND THANKS

I was helped by many people, directly and indirectly, as I worked on this book.

Two Rangers on the Dieppe Raid corresponded with me and my wife: Franklin Koons and Lester Kness. I appreciate the memories they shared, but most especially their graciousness in responding to our inquiries at a time when both were in ill health. Two other "original" Rangers were equally generous, Don Frederick and Gerrit "Ted" Rensink. These men patiently tried to answer my many questions, which I'm sure were very tedious at times. All four contributed greatly to my understanding not only of the battle and the unit, but of the war and its era.

Members of the British Commando Veterans Association were also very kind and generous with their time, inviting me to join them when they gathered in Fort William, Scotland, for Remembrance Day. I would especially like to thank Commando and poet John Lowman for introducing me to various members, as well as providing me with important perspectives on the war. R. J. Cubitt was unselfish with his time and thoughts.

Ron Sweazey was extremely generous with information about his father, Owen Sweazey. The Sweazey family provided additional materials and personal remembrances, for which I am greatly indebted. The records that Mr. Sweazey and his wife, Paula, preserved gave me an important perspective not only on the battle but on the men involved.

Colonel Don Patton, the driving force behind the World War II Round-table in Minnesota, was an invaluable resource and a great and unexpected help. His contacts in the area that many of the 1st Ranger Battalion came from led me to some of the last surviving members.

The Special Collections and Archives Division at the U.S. Military Academy at West Point, New York, proved an invaluable resource. The Harold Perlmutter Collection includes ten boxes of microfilmed material on the formation and history of the Ranger battalions, and two boxes of material on its commander, William O. Darby. The archivists and librarians at West Point were a tremendous help, first in alerting my wife to this material, and then in helping her sort through it. Their assistance was invaluable. We would especially like to thank Associate Director for Special Collections and Archives Suzanne M. Christoff, manuscripts curator Susan M. Lintelmann, rare-book curator Elaine B. McConnell, and library technician Deborah A. McKeon-Pogue. We also greatly appreciate the assistance of their boss, Librarian Joseph M. Barth, in making the collection available.

A number of people assisted me while I was traveling in Europe, visiting the Ranger training grounds and Dieppe itself. In Scotland, Donald Young was a stalwart and knowledgeable companion. Stéphane Garreu, a congenial and thoughtful young Frenchman whom I met completely by chance—and whose English is light-years ahead of my French—gave me a midnight tour of Dieppe. Jenny Johnson literally saved the day for me in France and England, helping me stay on schedule despite difficult circumstances.

It would not have been possible to write this book without the work of many historians and others who first recorded interviews, dug through records, and wrote what they found. Our understanding of the battle relies on the work of a large number of people, from the intelligence officers and military historians, in most cases uncredited, who first attempted to record the Dieppe experience, to the modern historians who have assessed its significance. While I have occasionally cited the errors of fact that crept into some of their works concerning the Rangers and the raid itself, those errors in no way invalidate the bulk of their work. Such mistakes are inevitable in any human endeavor, and most especially in a history, which depends largely on fragile memories and the whims of time and chance.

My editor at Berkley Caliber, Natalee Rosenstein, encouraged me to pursue the story with rigor and vigor. Assistant editor Michelle Vega saw to many details that might have otherwise fallen through the cracks. I am also grateful for the efforts of the entire publishing team on my behalf in getting the manuscript to press and into bookstores.

My interest in Dieppe began when I was in high school and read a short account of the battle. That seed lay dormant until a conversation with my agent, Jake Elwell, many years later; Jake had heard of the Ranger involvement in Dieppe and thought it would be a good subject for a book. Without his interest and encouragement, I would never have undertaken this project.

My wife, Debra, assisted me on this project by doing a great deal of research and offering comments on the manuscript. It may sound like a cliché, but it's true: I couldn't have done it without her.

Finally, a large number of friends and acquaintances gave me advice and suggestions as I worked on this book. While I didn't always take their advice, their feedback was important.

And after saying all that, let me add that all of the mistakes are my own.

INDEX

Best known as a novelist, Jim DeFelice's most recent book is *Leopards Kill*. Contact him at jdchester@aol.com or visit his website, www.jimdefelice.com.